Economic & Social Affairs

The World Ageing Situation

Exploring a Society for All Ages

United Nations

New York, 2001

NOTE

The designations employed and the presentation of the material in this publication do not imply the expression of any opinion on the part of the Secretariat of the United Nations concerning the legal status of any country or territory or of its authorities, or concerning the delimitation of its frontiers. The term "country" as used in the text of this report also refers, as appropriate, to territories or areas.

The views expressed in the signed papers are those of the individual authors and do not necessarily reflect those of the organization with which they are associated or those of the United Nations.

Papers have been edited and consolidated in accordance with United Nations practice and requirements.

ST/ESA/271

UNITED NATIONS PUBLICATION
Sales No. E.00.IV.4
ISBN 92-1-130205-6

CONTENTS

PREFACE

As we enter the twenty-first century, the International Year of Older Persons serves as an introduction to ageing in the new millennium. *The World Ageing Situation: Exploring a Society for All Ages*, is intended to broaden our understanding of the many challenges and opportunities that will lay claim to the millennium's changing demographic vista.

The International Year has been virtually unique among such celebrations and observances. It has sought to highlight the lives of ordinary citizens. It has aimed to see older people not just in the light of the extraordinary exploits of a few, such as the astronaut John Glenn who orbited the earth at age 77, but rather to view elders as possessing the very basic, but unremarkable rights and obligations of all members of society, leading productive, but unremarkable lives, taking their place in the ranks of humanity as valued human beings.

We entered the International Year obsessing about increased life expectancy, but too often overlooking the questions of what we might expect from later life. The image of ageing populations draining our resources permeated the media, while older people as vital, contributing members of their communities were almost invisible.

But our collective efforts are bringing about a new day. A corner has been turned and, thanks to countless educational initiatives and media ventures, this picture is fading into obsolescence. People are beginning to grasp a future where all ages will be represented in all spheres of society —in a society for all ages.

With older people looming larger in the statistical profiles of most countries, what might be the nature of intergenerational ties in the future? What is the significance of the feminization of ageing? How can we formulate political and social strategies to deal with ageing that may be adapted to developing countries and to economies in transition? Perception precedes policy, and the International Year has successfully laid the foundation upon which we can begin to engage these issues productively.

Older persons are a potential national resource of great importance. They are the repositories of a lifetime of vigor, accumulated knowledge, skills and experience that we should tap. But we can only do this with their participation.

Our Year has been special, not only because it has proclaimed the normality of older persons, but also because it will not let them drop from sight as the ball drops from the tower to signal a new century. The second World Assembly on Ageing, to be held in Spain in 2002, will ensure that, for older people, this time will be their time.

Ambassador Julia T. **Alvarez**

FOREWORD

We have reached a significant crossroads, the closing of one millennium and the beginning of another. This is a momentous occasion by all accounts. Yet what is remarkable is what awaits the world in this new era as it undergoes a demographic revolution. The world is changing as it ages, and just as older persons are agents of that change, they must also be its beneficiaries.

At the same time, we must rethink rigid distinctions that define age and give it boundaries. Everyone, individually and collectively, is joined in this single human venture, and everyone will respond, each in their own way, to the opportunities as well as the challenges. Ageing is not a separate issue from social integration, gender advancement, economic stability or issues of poverty. It has developed a connection with many global agendas and will play an increasingly prominent role in the way society interacts with economic and social welfare institutions, family and community life and the roles of women.

The complex infrastructure of society as well as the unique life course of individuals can be dramatically altered by a progressive upward shift in the global population. The total effect cannot be easily absorbed. The present imperative is that societies must respond to the extraordinary potential and range of variability in individual ageing, seize the opportunity to rethink our notion of limits and recognize the far-reaching benefits societies stand to gain from the contributions of their older citizens.

We have all heard of the remarkable demographic change that is under way. But our task is not to dwell on what we already know. It is rather to equip ourselves and future generations with the tools to meet its challenge and imagine what can be. Let us see this new century as an opportunity to reinforce the belief in the possibilities of non-violence and peaceful cooperation in order to promote progress for all ages in all areas.

We are all constituents of an ageing society, rural and city dwellers, public and private sector identities, families and individuals, old and young alike. It is crucial that societies adjust to this human paradigm as record numbers of people live into very old age, if we are to move towards a society for all ages.

This publication, *The World Ageing Situation: Exploring a Society for All Ages* presents an overview of the many issues we face and beckons us to continue the dialogue and build on partnerships that can bring us closer to a society that weaves all ages into the larger human community in which we thrive.

Nitin **Desai**
Under-Secretary-General
Department of Economic and Social Affairs
United Nations

Explanatory notes

Symbols of United Nations documents are composed of capital letters combined with figures.

Use of a hyphen (-) between dates representing years, for example, 1986-1990, signifies the full period involved, including the beginning and end years. A slash (/) between years indicates a school year, crop year or financial year, for example 1989/90.

A full stop (.) is used to indicate decimals.

Reference to "tons" indicates metric tons and to "dollars" ($) United States dollars, unless otherwise stated.

The term "billion" signifies a thousand million.

Annual rates of growth or change, unless otherwise stated, refer to annual compound rates.

Details and percentages in tables do not necessarily add up to totals because of rounding.

The following symbols have been used in the tables throughout the report:

Two dotes (..) indicate that data are not available or are not reported separately.

A dash (—) indicates that the amount is nil or negligible.

A hypen(-) indicates that the item is not applicable.

A minus sign (-) indicates a deficit or decrease, except as indicated.

I. A SOCIETY FOR ALL AGES: EVOLUTION AND EXPLORATION

United Nations programme on ageing*

We live in an ageing world. While this has been recognized for some time in developed countries, it is only recently that this phenomenon has been fully acknowledged. Global communication is "shrinking" the world, and global ageing is "maturing" it. The increasing presence of older persons in the world is making people of all ages more aware that we live in a diverse and multigenerational society.

At the same time, the study of ageing has broadened its landscape, shifting away from a widespread view of older persons as patients or pensioners. The content and approach to ageing is more reflective than ever of the vast diversity of the world's expanding older population. The experts, many of whom are older persons themselves, including academics, scientists, planners, economists, technicians, teachers, writers and artists, use a variety of approaches to view age, borrowing from demography, medicine, psychology, economics, anthropology, sociology, history, religion and philosophy.

The 1999 International Year of Older Persons played a key role in placing ageing foremost in the public's mind and on the global map. The strengths of the programme for the year were manifest in the prodigious amount of activity and the rich texture of partnerships formed in the international community of Member States, United Nations bodies, intergovernmental organizations and international non-governmental organizations.

This publication, *The World Ageing Situation: Exploring a Society for All Ages*, coincides with the beginning of the follow-up to the International Year of Older Persons and, with its theme, "A society for all ages", takes its first step into the next century. As befits such a passage, a regeneration of thought is underway as information from the Year plays out in new language, formulation and integration of policy.

The World Ageing Situation seeks to take the reader through various experiences of ageing throughout the world and the wide range of challenges, opportunities, responses and suggestions profiled by its authors. This is the third in a series; the first edition was published in 1985 and by the second in 1991.

This edition of *The World Ageing Situation* expresses, as did the previous publications, the ideas of the authors, and does not necessarily reflect the views of the United Nations. The United Nations programme on ageing hopes, however, that readers will find in it a launching point to continue the debate.

THE DEMOGRAPHIC REVOLUTION

The ageing of the world's population is now a twenty-first century phenomenon, a testament to the broad demographic forces sweeping the earth. The trend towards population ageing that began in the developed countries in the middle of the twentieth century is now manifest in the developing regions of the world.

There are 600 million older persons in the world today. They will grow in number to nearly 2 billion by 2050, at which time they will outnumber the population of children (0-14 years) for the first time in human history. The majority of the world's older population today resides in developing countries—Asia has the largest share, with 53 per cent; Europe the next at 25 per cent.

Worldwide, countries, organizations and individuals are beginning to comprehend that the world is undergoing demographic change, the likes of which will, sooner or later, affect every institution and individual in society. Demographers note that, if current trends in ageing continue as predicted, a demographic revolution wherein the proportions of the young and the old will undergo a historic crossover, will be felt in just three generations. The Population Division of the United Nations Secretariat provides a global demographic profile that presents the following outlook which can be viewed in the figures and tables in the present chapter.

- One out of every 10 persons is now over 60; by 2050 one out of every 5 will be; and by 2150 this number will shrink to one out of every three.

- Striking differences exist between regions. One out of five Europeans, as compared to one out of 20 Africans, is 60 years of age or older. In some developed countries today, the proportion of older

*The UN programme on ageing is part of the Division for Social Policy and Development, of the Department of Economic and Social Affairs of the United Nations Secretariat.

persons is close to one in five. During the first half of the twenty-first century, that proportion will reach one in four and in some countries one in two.

- The increase in older persons will be much more dramatic in the developing countries, where the population aged 60 and over will be multiplied more than nine times between 1998 and 2050. Already, approximately one million people cross the threshold of age 60 every month, 80 per cent of them in developing countries.

- The oldest old (80 years or older) currently make up 11 per cent of the population 60 and older; they are the fastest growing segment of the older population and, by 2050, they will reach 19 per cent. Those over 100 are expected to increase 15-fold in the next 50 years.

- The majority of older persons, 55 per cent, are women. Among the oldest old, 65 per cent are women. These proportions will remain relatively unchanged over the next 50 years.

- The older population is increasingly urban. The majority of the world's older persons (51 per cent) live in urban areas. By 2025 this figure is expected to climb to 62 per cent of older persons, although large differences exist between more and less developed regions. In developed regions, 74 per cent of older persons are urban dwellers, while in less developed regions, which remain predominantly rural, only 37 per cent of older persons reside in urban areas.

This portrait of change in the world's population parallels the magnitude of the industrial revolution—traditionally considered the most significant social and economic breakthrough in the history of humankind since the Neolithic period. It marked the beginning of a sustained movement towards modern economic growth in much the same way that globalization is today marking an unprecedented and sustained movement toward a "global culture". The demographic revolution, it is envisaged, will be at least as powerful.

While the future effects are not known, a likely scenario is one where both the challenges as well as the opportunities will emerge from exploration and research, dialogue and debate. Challenges arise as social and economic structures try to adjust to the simultaneous phenomenon of diminishing young cohorts with rising older ones, and opportunities present themselves in the sheer number of older individuals and the vast resources societies stand to gain from their contribution. A change of significant magnitude is already unfolding, as noted by the Secretary-General of the United Nations, Kofi Annan, at the launching of the International Year of Older Persons on 1 October 1998,

"...We are in the midst of a silent revolution that extends well beyond demographics, with major economic, social, cultural, psychological and spiritual implications."

This revolution has two interrelated, overlapping phenomena, individual ageing and the ageing of the population as a whole, which have distinct "revolutionary" patterns of their own.

Individual ageing

The last 50 years of the twentieth century will go down in history as having witnessed a significant lengthening of the human life span. Life expectancy at birth has climbed globally by about 20 years since 1950, to its current level of 66 years. Whether genetic, environmental or medical, determinants of longevity are the focus of continuous research. But the fact remains that individuals are living longer lives, including in the developing world. During the period from 1970 to 1997, Honduras, increased its general life expectancy by 17 years, from 52 to 69; Nepal by 15 years, from 42 to 57; and Oman by a staggering 24 years, from 46 to 70 (*Human Development Report, 1999*) .

This advance is a remarkable achievement of the twentieth century, and one that is now gathering momentum into the twenty-first. While welcomed by society at large and by its individual members, the topic of increased longevity generates much discourse on quality of life and healthy ageing issues, age and social integration and the fostering of support and collective security over the long course of life. At the same time, the plumes of longevity seem to fascinate; when people reach very high ages, they are met with attention of a curious nature. Even many of the present "oldest old" never expected to reach their current age, as noted by Dr. Gunhild Hagestad in her keynote address on the 1998 International Day of Older Persons:

"...because when they started life's journey early in this century, interrupted lives and broken ties were common, due to infectious disease, famine, and life's dangers. The changes in survival patterns have been so rapid that they have created 'surprised survivors'...[including] families groping for solutions...and overwhelmed planners and politicians who often are not even able to express their lack of readiness."

This "surprised survivor" phenomenon, while more characteristic of economically developed countries, is a dramatic triumph of survival for the developing world. At the same time, life expectancy at birth has experienced alarming declines in some developing countries and countries in transition due to the devastating

Figure 1.

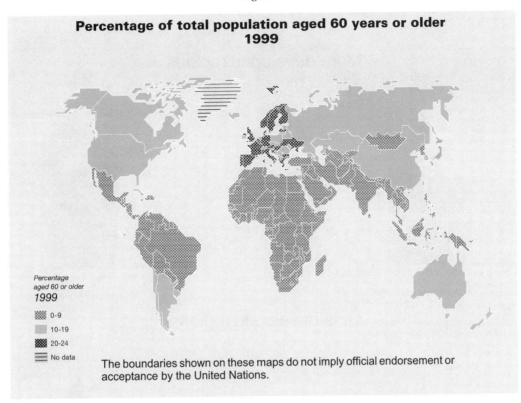

**Percentage of total population aged 60 years or older
1999**

Percentage
aged 60 or older
1999

- 0-9
- 10-19
- 20-24
- No data

The boundaries shown on these maps do not imply official endorsement or acceptance by the United Nations.

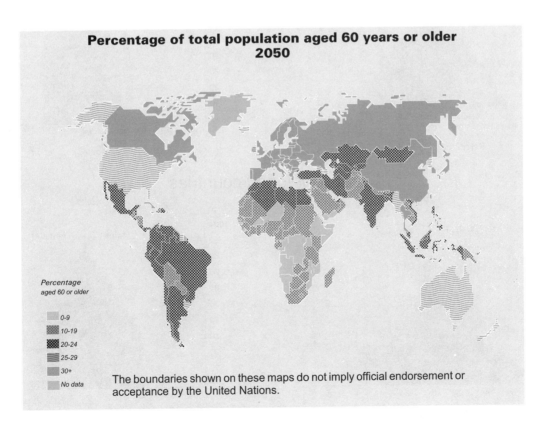

**Percentage of total population aged 60 years or older
2050**

Percentage
aged 60 or older

- 0-9
- 10-19
- 20-24
- 25-29
- 30+
- No data

The boundaries shown on these maps do not imply official endorsement or acceptance by the United Nations.

Figure 2. Global Population by Age and Sex in More and Less Developed Regions and Least Developed Countries: 1999 and 2050

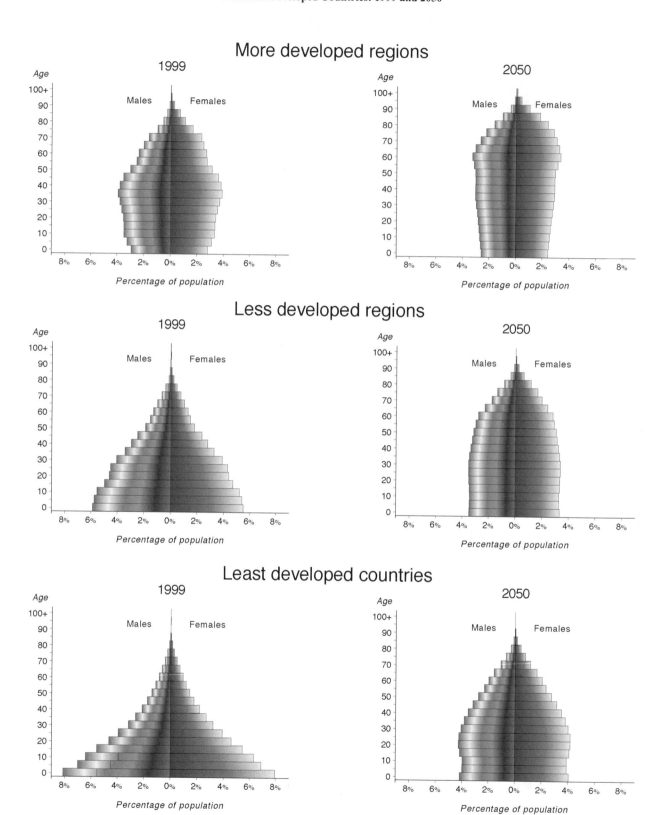

effects of warfare, economic and psycho-social hardship, and the AIDS epidemic.

TABLE I.   MEDIAN AGE BY MAJOR AREA, 1950, 1999, 2050
(*medium variant projection*)

	Median age (years)		
	1950	1999	2050
World total	23.5	26.4	37.8
More developed regions . . .	28.6	37.2	45.6
Less developed regions	21.3	24.2	36.7
Africa	18.7	18.3	30.7
Asia	21.9	26.0	39.3
Europe	29.2	37.4	47.4
Latin America and the Caribbean	20.1	24.2	37.8
North America	29.8	35.6	42.1
Oceania	27.9	30.9	39.3

Population ageing

If longevity has increased, population ageing has been accelerating. The world is becoming older, with a diminishing proportion of children under age 15 and an increase in persons over age 60. Currently, 10 per cent of the world's population is over 60; this is expected to rise to 13 per cent in 2020, and jump to 22 per cent in 2050.

In developing countries, the proportion of older persons is expected to increase to 21 per cent in 2050 from its present 8 per cent, while that of children to decrease from 33 to 20 per cent. But what is perhaps most compelling and urgent about the ageing of the population in the developing world is the rapid pace at which it is proceeding, and the sheer proportion—70 per cent—of the world's older population that will constitute the population of the developing countries in 30 years time. In Sweden, for example, it has taken 84 years for the proportion of the older population to double from 7 per cent of the population to 14 per cent. In developing countries the same change may occur in 25 years or less.

The developed regions have already reached historical levels in their age structures: in 1998, the number of older persons exceeded that of children for the first time. It is particularly noticeable in Western Europe, where the oldest population resides in Italy, with 60 per cent more older persons than children; followed by Greece, Japan, Spain and Germany. In these more developed countries, projections indicate that, by the year 2050, the number of older persons will be more than twice that of children.

This ageing of the population permeates all social, economic and cultural spheres. Revolutionary change calls for new, revolutionary thinking, which can position policy formulation and implementation on sounder footing. In our ageing world, new thinking requires that we view ageing as a lifelong and society-wide phenomenon, not a phenomenon exclusively pertaining to older persons. This requires investing in the phases of life, fostering enabling societies and creating flexible but vibrant collaborations in the process, through which the future building of a society for all ages can take hold in the present.

TABLE II.   POPULATION AGEING IN DIFFERENT WORLD REGIONS: SELECTED INDICATORS

Area/Region	Percentage of older persons in the population		Potential support ratio [*]	
	1999	2050	1999	2050
World total	10	22	9	4
More developed regions	19	33	5	2
Less developed regions	8	21	12	4
Least developed countries	5	12	18	8
Africa	5	12	17	8
Asia	9	24	11	4
Europe	20	35	5	2
Latin America and the Caribbean	8	22	12	4
North America	16	28	5	3
Oceania	13	24	7	3

Source: Population Ageing 1999 (Population Division, Department of Economic and Social Affairs).
[*]Potential support ratio: number of persons aged 15-64 years per older person aged 65 or older.

Figure 3.   Proportion of Total Population aged 0-14 and 60 and over, more and less developed regions, 1950-2050
(Medium variant projections)

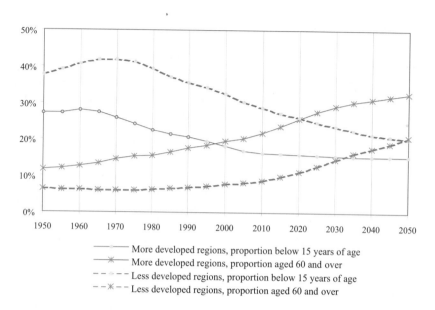

——◆—— More developed regions, proportion below 15 years of age
——✳—— More developed regions, proportion aged 60 and over
– – ◆ – – Less developed regions, proportion below 15 years of age
– – ✳ – – Less developed regions, proportion aged 60 and over

Source: United Nations Population Division, World Population Prospects: the 1998 Revision

A SOCIETY FOR ALL AGES

The concept *of a Society for all ages* is rooted in the Programme of Action adopted at the World Summit for Social Development in Copenhagen in 1995. At the Summit, Member States explored the meaning of "a society for all". Viewed as the fundamental aim of social integration, it is a society where "…every individual, each with rights and responsibilities, has an active role to play". By integrating 'age' into a society for all, the approach becomes multigenerational and holistic, whereby "…the generations invest in one another and share in the fruits of that investment, guided by the twin principles of reciprocity and equity" (A/50/114, para 38).

Creating a new "architecture" for ageing and transmitting it to the worldstage and into policy has been the focus of the United Nations programme on ageing since 1982 with the adoption of the International Plan of Action on Ageing at the World Assembly on Ageing in Vienna (also known as the Vienna Plan). The Plan of Action was the first international instrument of its kind to guide global thinking and policy formulation on ageing and, while a revision is underway to bring some of its language and policy approaches up-to-date, its essence remains intact. There are 62 recommendations in the Plan of Action, addressing numerous issues, including research, data collection and analysis, training and education, as well as health, housing, environment, income security, the family and social welfare.

In 1991, nine years after its endorsement of the Plan of Action, the General Assembly adopted the United Nations Principles for Older Persons. The Principles bestow particular recognition to the status of older persons and fall into five sectors: independence, participation, care, self-fulfillment and dignity.

The decision to observe 1999 as the International Year of Older Persons and to promote its theme, "A society for all ages" came in 1992 with the adoption by the General Assembly of the proclamation on ageing, " in recognition of humanity's demographic coming of age and the promise it holds for maturing attitudes and capabilities in social, economic, cultural and spiritual undertakings, not least for global peace and development in the next century". Thus began an extensive undertaking by the programme on ageing to build a framework that would create a flourishing environment for "a society for all ages", define its parameters and give it substance. The conceptual framework was conceived in 1995 (A/50/114). To this day it has facilitated global thinking, exploration, and policy orientation on a society for all ages that is expected to continue well beyond 1999.

Four dimensions make up the conceptual framework and provide a solid foundation from which to explore and engage the prolific meaning of "a society for all ages". The Framework's vision lays bare an understanding of what is both fundamental and sustainable for family and community life in the twenty-first century. Charged with an awareness of the profound changes in the global age structure, it fosters reflection on how to adapt to these changes, confront disillusionment and seize opportunities. Its four dimensions are the situation of older persons, lifelong individual development, multigenerational relationships and the interplay between population ageing and development.

Situation of older persons

The situation of older persons looks at the day-to-day lives of older persons and how they fare and flourish vis-à-vis income security, multi-sectored healthcare, housing, and social service provision, and their participation, integration and developmental potential within society. This is an area that has enormous diversity among older persons within and between cultures. Policies that shape the provision of care systems and material well-being also help to shape the major contours of change in society, as they extend well beyond the boundaries of the older population, impacting *inter alia*, political and social institutions, relationships and the world. These issues are addressed, along with human rights for older persons, in the 18 United Nations Principles for Older Persons and in the International Plan of Action on Ageing.

The potential of added years is bringing to the fore a dynamic that views ageing with a resourceful, active and engaging pulse. The mounting involvement of older persons in all areas of life, be it cultural, political, economic, social, spiritual, is seen as essential to the progression of any society. These seeds of "mainstreaming" ageing were planted nearly 20 years ago in the Vienna Plan of Action, which stated that "The slowly expanding lifespan of the population even in developing areas constitutes a hidden resource for national economies which, if properly stimulated and utilized, might help to…ensure the status of [older persons] as active participants in national life and production, rather than as passive and vulnerable victims of development".

But while society embraces "active" ageing and all its obvious benefits, care must be taken to recognize the diversity of interests and abilities that can characterize "active", and not to disregard those older individuals who are unable physically to join in the same activities as their peers. Reflections, wisdom and experience cannot always be portrayed in physical terms or even in words, and no matter the situation, older persons must not be left out of the creative and participatory process.

Overall, the growing universal opportunity of living to old age is a humanitarian windfall. It can expand, firstly, the vantage point from which Governments view, explore and make use of the capabilities of their older citizens, and secondly, the opportunities for older persons to increase their involvement in society, owing not the least to the growth their numbers.

Lifelong individual development

Lifelong individual development promotes the vital link between early-in-life experiences and choices, with later in life overall health and well-being. Individuals go through the life course experiencing a range of influences and interactions that may positively or negatively impact their capabilities in later years. Age-adjusted policies and programmes that promote lifelong learning, healthy lifestyles and workplace flexibility during transitional periods, that is, youth to midlife and midlife to the later years, can influence choices with accumulative effects. A clear priority target for old age policies is the younger generations, the individuals who may have to reinvent themselves again and again in fast-changing societies. They will need to cultivate healthy lifestyles, flexibility and foresight, continually upgrade work skills and maintain social networks if they are to experience security and well-being in late life.

In a "genuine" *society for all ages*, environments for growth, learning and moving toward creative fulfillment are within the reach of all. What we are learning today about the extraordinary range of abilities and interests of older persons can help us in the task of creating such environments and remove obstacles for new generations. Preparation of the entire population for the later stages of life as stated in the Vienna Plan of Action, "…should be an integral part of social policies and encompass physical, psychological, cultural, religious, spiritual, economic, health and other factors".

Multigenerational relationships

Multigenerational relationships have sustained family and community life for centuries, being our evolutionary blueprint for transmitting lessons of the past. They symbolize a shared enterprise of citizenship. Older persons have the advantage of experience and a knowledge of their generation's history, while younger individuals look to the future, not least to discern those objectives which will mark their own existence. The varied skills and expectations of all ages can be brought together in mutually benefiting ways that can be approached from multiple directions, including lifelong education, community planning for people of all ages, social and economic development, as well as socially-active efforts to end poverty, exclusion, human rights abuses and war.

While various factors and responsibilities moderate the needs and interests of all ages, old, young, and in between, everyone is joined in the common historical task of shaping the public world and understanding themselves as participants in that world, one that existed before their birth and will remain after their departure. Vibrant collaboration and understanding are needed to create harmony between the generations in the context of fast-changing societies.

Population ageing and development

Population ageing and development is a complex interaction of global patterns in labour and capital markets, governmental pensions, services and traditional support systems, such as intergenerational transfers, which are further shaped by technological change and cultural transformations.

Social and economic support systems come in numerous forms that range from the formal to the informal. Some are based upon local community membership and solidarity, some are cooperative ventures, some private, company-based schemes and some are provided by the State and through welfare programmes. The sustainability of these systems in managing risk and cushioning support in both the developed and developing world is undergoing tremendous change. The ageing of populations is affecting the potential support ratio (the number of persons aged 15-64 years per older persons aged 65 years or older), which is falling in both more and less developed regions, having important implications for social and economic support systems (see table II).

If the ageing of populations is revolutionizing our social and economic infrastructure, globalization and technological advancement are revolutionizing our "tool" system, that is, management and workplace skills, creative synthesis and political and social development. One element of this system is information technology, which, in the last five years alone, has revolutionized the speed and manner in which access to information is rendered and received. Older individuals are increasingly tapping into this culture in varying degrees, often in multigenerational settings, meeting the educational demands to stay informed concerning new technologies and systems. The majority of older persons, however, mostly in developing countries, do not have access. When whole communities and individuals are sidelined in this information tidal wave, existing gaps and imbalances become all the more apparent.

While a course seems charted for the globalization of information and technology, this is not the case regarding how the world will respond to gaps in the communications infrastructure, nor in its most durable underpinning: human relationships. As global ageing converges with technology and globalization, a new culture has emerged, with its own production and consumption patterns and its own facilities and services.

But a new culture can also contribute to and activate policy dialogue, research and training, and the building of the crucial elements of a global ageing society.

MEANINGS AND IMAGES IN AN AGEING SOCIETY

Images of ageing are rooted in culture and cut right to the marrow of the society in which we live. However, the understanding of one's language and culture can very often contrast with the meanings and images given it by others. This paradox also mimics ageing in advanced societies, where, with the accumulation of years and experience, roles diminish, and images play a part.

Mass media, the machine of image-making, is also a link in the globalization chain and can have profound effects on the developing world, and particularly on the older women who live there. For its part, the flow and interchange of ideas and information through new technologies is as much an extraordinary achievement as it is an ordinary fact of life. The positive impact that is gained from other ideas, learning about other populations, areas of expertise and alternative ways of life is boundless. But knowledge and images are often mutual passengers in the information voyage and the image landscape conveyed by the western media weighs heavily on the side of glorifying youth, while either omitting older persons or depicting them in stereotypes. This has a particular impact on the lives of older women, as they tend to suffer greater political, social, and economic exclusions than do older men.

As society ages however, it also changes in ways that relate to age. Perceptions of the transitions that mark the boundaries of age are being altered as family, kinship and community structures change. In many parts of the world it is not uncommon today to be part of a four-generation family, where the chronological rules for assuming the roles of grandparents or grandchildren are increasingly blurred. At the same time, more individuals are growing older outside of traditional family networks and are simulating family life through communities or primary groups. The rhythm of the life cycle continues to develop through these different dynamics and, consequently, is not as tightly bound by chronological age or stages as it once may have been.

The same can be said for images that surround the idea of change. While change often arouses anxiety, challenges that stem from new orders of complexity should be met with inquiry rather than reproach. Situations or choices that once seemed incompatible, work or retirement, strength or vulnerability, can be approached and accommodated within the same creative mix that occupies the vastness and diversity of life in the human community.

The new architecture of ageing requires policies that remove obstacles and facilitate contributions. It also requires seminal thinking and images that reflect reality and potential, not stereotypes and myths. So relative are the experiences of ageing in different parts of the world, and so complex and multiple their roles, that the world can no longer accept images of ageing as a panorama of near homogeneity.

FUTURE STRATEGIES FOR A SOCIETY FOR ALL AGES

The 1999 International Year of Older Persons concluded with significant advances in the understanding of issues of global ageing, brought about by a great deal of international exposure and the interest that followed. The Year enriched the dialogue, raised awareness, energized debate and substantive exploration and generated a vast array of innovative initiatives. The Year's impact at the individual, community, national and international level is evident in the partnerships and collaborations that were formed and in the inspired commitment of all parties to build a future society for all ages.

The Year's impact on the United Nations programme on ageing is evident in its commitment to explore the roles, opportunities, entitlements and contributions of older persons in fast-changing societies.

The following projects are part of the mandate and activities of the United Nations programme on ageing for the future:

- The continued formulation of a policy framework for a society for all ages, with a key research component. The still evolving framework, which is annexed for review, grew out of the conceptual framework for the International Year of Older Persons, encompassing, as noted previously, the situation of older persons, lifelong development, multigenerational relationships and the macro-societal implications of population ageing. This undertaking has been supported by the Government of Korea and Swiss Re Life and Health.

- The development of a research agenda on ageing for the twenty-first century and its movement onto the world stage for use in policy formulation and implementation. The convening of three expert group meetings will contribute to this comprehensive research agenda on ageing, which will serve as a background for policy responses to population and individual ageing, with particular emphasis on the developing countries. This project has been undertaken in cooperation with the International Association of Gerontology, supported by the Government of Germany and the Novartis Foundation for Gerontology.

- The development of a database of policy approaches and innovative projects, supported by the Government of the Netherlands. This Internet-accessible database will be the first of its kind on a global scale and is a significant contribution to the international ageing community. It can be accessed on the programme on ageing's website, at www.un.org/esa/socdev/ageing.

Meetings are planned for the near future with leadership or close collaboration of the United Nations programme on ageing: an expert examination of the interaction of social technologies and multigenerational ties in Addis Ababa, supported by the Government of the United Kingdom of Great Britain and Northern Ireland and in collaboration with HelpAge International; and an international conference on rural ageing, being organized by the University of West Virginia.

The Second World Assembly on Ageing is to take place in Spain in 2002 in response to General Assembly resolution A/54/262, entitled "Follow-up to the International Year of Older Persons: The Second World Assembly on Ageing". The Assembly will be devoted to the overall review of the outcome of the first World Assembly, as well as to the adoption of a revised plan of action and a long-term strategy on ageing in the context of A Society for All Ages. Preparations are underway in the programme on ageing to elicit input from Member States, intergovernmental organizations, the United Nations system and Non-governmental Organizations on the revision of the plan of action and elaboration of a long-term strategy.

CONCLUSION

For most of the twentieth century, old age policies were designed with a youthful society in mind. From this point onwards, policies for older persons, younger persons and in those between must be designed with an ageing society in mind, a society where soon every third individual will be over the age of 60. International, national and local communities must begin now to adjust and align their infrastructures, policies, plans and resources.

Policy interventions that include social and human as well as economic investments can prevent unnecessary dependencies from arising whether in late life for individuals or downstream in ageing societies. Furthermore, when judicious investments are made in advance, experts suggest that ageing can be changed from a drain on resources to a build-up of human, social, economic and environmental capital.

Finally, recognition of the uniqueness that unfolds throughout one's life is core to igniting society's embrace of the contributions of its older citizens. The "package" of knowledge, wisdom and experience that so often comes with age is part of an inner awareness that cannot be traded, sold or stolen. It should, however, be activated, amplified and utilized in all the crossroads, fields and storefronts of society, and in the windows of our creative imaginations.

Annex
Highlights of an expert consultation on developing a policy framework for a society for all ages

1.   This annex outlines a possible new 'architecture' of ageing combining strategic thinking with pragmatic measures. It aims to be preventative, holistic, interactive, sustainable and even 'wealth-creating'. It is suggestive, not prescriptive. And it represents the latest stage in a continuing process intended to facilitate movement 'towards a society for all ages', the theme of the International Year of Older Persons, 1999. It was elaborated throughout the Year, notably at a United Nations Inter-regional Expert Consultation in Seoul, Republic of Korea from 11 to 16 June 1999, hosted by the Government of Korea and supported by Swiss Re Life and Health.

Evolution

2.   Policy responses to ageing until now have tended to focus on provision of care and income security for older persons, which remain important but inadequate to the scale and rate of ageing now occurring and projected to intensify in coming decades. The World Bank Report 'Averting the Old Age Crisis' (1994) and other commentaries have attested to the unsustainability of many conventional policies in developed, developing and transitional economies.

3.   Governments have recently begun to expand their approaches to individual ageing, complementing care and security measures for older persons with ones promoting 'active ageing'. For example, in 1997 at its Denver Summit, the Group of 8 industrial countries recognized the need to abandon stereotypes of older persons as dependent. They discussed how to promote active ageing including, with due regard to older person's choices and circumstances, the removal of disincentives to labour force participation and lowering of barriers to flexible and part-time work.

4.   Active or resourceful ageing requires an enabling environment, principally: (a) opportunities over the entire lifecourse for building up capabilities or 'capitals' and (b) adjustment of family, community and country environments in keeping with the new demographic trends such as the inversion of the family pyramid already evident in China and other countries, and the astonishing continuing rise in the proportion of older persons throughout the world from one in 10 today to one in five by 2050, one in four by 2100 and one in three by 2150 (though several developed economies will reach the latter proportion within the next 30 years).

5.   Thus, adjustments must be made by individuals, families, communities and countries—in the micro, meso and macro levels of societies. These adjustments are rendered more complex, and potentially more fruitful, by the convergence of the demographic transition with a development transition, the latter holding promise of new economic as well as socio-cultural enrichment.

6.   The build up of human, social, economic and environmental capital is important in all countries. The age-advanced and economically-developed countries need a contributing 'young- old' population as their 'oldest old' rise in numbers and the working-age population declines. The developing economies—where 60 per cent of the world's elderly now live, projected to rise to 70 percent in twenty years—are challenged to develop human and economic capital while strengthening the social capital of family and community security systems. Economies in transition, which lack both the economic capital of developed and the social capital of developing countries, need to devise creative uses of their human capital to address immediate emergency needs of an age-advanced population.

Strategic approach

7.   The four fundamental elements of the society for all ages framework are: efforts by older persons themselves; capabilities or 'capital' accumulated over the lifecourse; mutually enriching multi-generational relationships in families and communities; and adjustment of national infrastructures in line with demographic and other changes. These were first outlined in the conceptual framework for the Year

8.   The four elements can be rendered dynamic by blending them with the idea of generating capital in four areas—human, socio-cultural, economic and environmental—in order to produce a proactive and wealth-creating approach to ageing, going beyond a mere reactive, or maintenance, stance. The following matrix illustrates the idea of capital-generation. It lists some primary investors for each type of capital, their assets, some operating principles, and some possible outcomes.

9   The diagram on the following page illustrates the flow between the four elements and the four kinds of capital.

Measures

10.   The strategic approach requires pragmatic measures which creatively avails of national resources, aspirations and the capabilities of actors including government as well as non-governmental and for-profit sectors: Measures for consideration include, among others:

(a)   Lifelong education—leading to a skilled population, enlightened elders and a learning society;

(b)   Promotion of healthy lifestyles— resulting in delay or defeat of disease;

(c)   Multi-generational community development initiatives including micro-enterprises and micro-credit—generating all four capitals to strengthen communities;

(d)   Flexible labor policies including phased retirement, the better integration of women in the workforce and men in the lives of families—which would allow for more gender equity, inter-generational care and opportunities for resourceful ageing;

(e)   A barrier-free and age-integrated built environment supporting all-age access and multi-generational encounters—which could foster better intergenerational dialogue;

(f)   Investment in civil society including in intergenerational organizations and organizations of older persons—towards enrichment of civil society;

(g)   Creative approaches to ensuring material well-being and provision of appropriate social services and welfare coverage—for sustainable national welfare policies;

Capital	Human	Social-cultural	Economic	Environmental
Primary investors	Individuals Families Schools etc.	Families Local communities Communities of interest Media etc.	Individuals Families Communities Private sector Governments	Local Government Planners Developers (urban and rural) etc.
Principles	Independence Resilience	Interdependence Reciprocity	Growth Sustenance	Enablement Connectivity
Assets	Health Knowledge, skills Understanding Capabilities, will	Networks Trust Communication Mutual supports	Formal/informal Work skills, assets, security systems etc.	Barrier-free All-age compatible
Capital outcomes	**Long-lived individuals who are:** Skilled Resilient Reflective Adapted Flourishing throughout life	**Societies that are:** Caring, supportive Tolerant, pluralist Integrated Learning and capable of blending innovation and tradition in appropriate balance	**An economy that is:** Secure Open Equitable Responsive Competitive Adapted to an ageing Society	**An environment that is:** Livable Flexible Accessible Adaptable Age-integrated

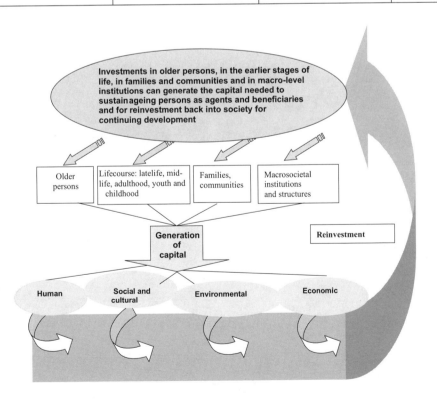

(h) Income security measures that generate national capital through savings and pension schemes and foster human solidarity as in the case of savings cooperatives and informal community solidarity systems—towards poverty elimination;

Questions

11. Some guiding questions on devising a society for all ages policy might be:

(a) Is the policy sustainable in the light of anticipated demographic and societal change?

(b) Is the policy able to contribute to the development of any or all of the capitals and the essential balance between them?

(c) Does the policy enable accumulation of capital across the life course?

(d) Does the policy enhance the continuing evolution of gender equity in family caring and nurturing?

(e) Does the policy enhance individual choice and autonomy and, simultaneously, community solidarity?

(f) Does the policy promote the interdependence of generations?

Conclusion

12. In light of rapid population ageing and the projected demographic shifts extending into the coming century, action is necessary in the short, medium and long term. Such actions will vary according to a country's rate and extent of ageing as well as its socio-economic development.

13. Governments are faced with the responsibility, in partnership with others, of ensuring the wellbeing and health of all citizens. This responsibility transcends any considerations of gender, social class, and age group, ethnicity or any other individual or group characteristic.

14. Many of the conventional approaches to ageing in different societies have tended to remain intact in spite of extraordinary changes in demography, individual life expectancy, family structure, technology, economy and culture.

15. Fresh, imaginative and more positive responses to the prospects of further increases in life expectancy and the ageing of populations need to be instituted. To be effective, such approaches need to be based on fundamental shifts in orientation. It is necessary to move from an emphasis on reacting to the negative characteristics of older persons to seeing also their contributions; and from responding to ageing as a problem to seeing it as a potential for wealth creation and catalyst of flourishing lives.

16. Each society according to its own priorities and resources must follow its own course towards the realization of a true society for all ages and determine its first crucial steps to be taken in that direction at this time. There is no question that now is the time to begin the process in all societies.

II. DEVELOPMENT AND THE AGEING OF POPULATIONS: A GLOBAL OVERVIEW BY EXPERTS ON AGEING IN AFRICA

Margaret Grieco and Nana Apt*

"The twenty-first century will be the century of the ageing of mankind"
—Alfred Sauvy, 1989

1. MEETING THE CHALLENGE, EMBRACING THE FUTURE

Despite the consensus that the ageing of populations in the developing world will happen on larger population bases and on lower levels of per capita income than in the developed world (World Bank, 1994), there has been little attention to what this means for social policy in the developing context (Apt and Grieco, 1994). Comprehensive planning for the ageing of populations in the developing world, including research on the circumstances and social support systems of older persons, needs to be undertaken. Attempts have been made to integrate the existing literature on ageing and development into global and regional overviews but the materials are somewhat limited. The data on ageing populations is still largely of a raw demographic character, and raw demographic data are not sufficient for the development of appropriate ageing policies for the low and middle income world.

If the challenge of an ageing world is to be met, it is imperative that:

- Comprehensive data on the social processes which currently accompany ageing be collected;
- Systematic research be undertaken into policy actions which can be taken to better support the older person.

Although policy concerns about the graying of populations has greatly increased in the high income countries of the world (McCallum, 1989; United Nations, 1991) - the societies in which the ageing of populations is already most pronounced - the integration of ageing into the development plans and policies of low and middle income societies has received inadequate attention.

For many low and some middle income countries, the continuing high fertility rate combined with higher infant survival holds down the relative significance of the upper age bulge. Nonetheless, the numbers of older persons are increasing rapidly. With the ageing of these societies and the growth in the absolute numbers of older persons, both Governments and international development agencies are facing policy development challenges in respect to the growing numbers of aged in the developing world.

The increase in the numbers of older people in the developing world is taking place in a context where the traditional social arrangements of household organizations and kinship obligations are undergoing change (Azer and Afifi, 1992; Tout, 1989). The domestic arrangements of the intergenerational family that traditionally supported the older person are themselves under threat.

Family structure is changing and the traditional attitude of respect and veneration for elders cannot always be expected to prevail.
(Andrews, 1992: 22)

Yet where low and middle income countries have paid policy attention to the growing numbers of older persons within their societies, the assumption is made that social provision for older persons will be provided by and take place largely within the context of the intergenerational family (Phillips,1992). Whereas the industrial countries of the world, with the exception of Japan (Hashimoto, 1992; OECD: Organization for Economic Cooperation and Development, 1994), made extensive formal provision for the increasing ranks of older persons through publicly and privately financed pension funds and social services, the developing world will depend largely upon the informal services provided by kin in accommodating the needs of its growing numbers of older people.

This brief overview of social policy orientations in the region (east and south east Asia) highlights one major feature which is common to virtually all coun-

* Margaret Grieco is with the Centre for the Study of African Economies, University of Oxford. Nana Apt is with the Centre for Social Policy Studies, University of Ghana.

13

tries in this book: the family is being regarded almost universally as the principal supporter, carer and home provider for elderly people and particularly those unable to look after themselves. This imbues the region with a characteristic that is not common in many developed countries where it has become increasingly recognized (if not always fully implemented) that the public sector should provide, or at least underwrite financially, the majority of social care for elderly people. However, it is important to recognise that stress can potentially be placed on families who are expected and called on to provide support for their elderly relatives but who may find this difficult to do.
(Phillips, 1992:15)

The ageing of populations and the growing numbers of older persons are impacting kinship structures. Longevity creates the possibility of four and five generational household and kinship structures where previously three generations was the predominant form; thus requiring the working generation to take care of its parents, grandparents and great grandparents. If the developing world is to depend on kinship as the key mechanism for the care and participation of older persons when family size is declining, policy concern must focus on supporting intergenerational families of four or five and not simply three generations (Phillips, 1992). Clearly, building social policies anchored in the family will require strong public and community complementary measures if the four and five generation family becomes the norm.

In industrial societies, the existence of sufficient support for the autonomous living and financial arrangements of older persons has simplified the structure of obligations and exchanges between the generations. The emergence of the new phenomenon of four and five generation kinship structures has been largely unremarked (OECD, 1994) apart from the recognition that it is primarily the old-old who find themselves living on their own. In the OECD countries living alone is more common in the very old age groups—66 per cent of those aged 80 or more live alone in Denmark (Sandstrom, 1994) and the fastest growing segment of the population in many of the OECD countries is now the over 80 age group. One marked feature of the increase in the proportion of older persons living alone is that it affects particularly older women.

Translated into the developing world, the increasing numbers of the old-old will have major consequences for the patterns of exchange and reciprocity between the generations. Great grandparents in the developing world are unlikely to enjoy the financial and residential autonomy of their counterparts in the industrial world and unlikely to displace the young-old in the performance of the key household functions such as child care, food preparation and ensuring household security that have been at the heart of intergenerational exchange within the three generation household structure (Sushama,1992; Hashimoto, 1992). If low and middle income countries depend upon the family as the key structure in providing for the social participation and care of the old-old, then much of the responsibility for this provision will fall upon the shoulders of the young-old. Although care for and participation of the old-old is still likely to be provided within the framework of kinship, it is, in the absence of major social policy interventions, increasingly likely to be provided outside the household. In Malaysia, Fiji and the Philippines, the older elderly are already less likely to be living with children than the younger elderly (Phillips, 1992:16).

Although there is a general consensus that developing countries do not have the resources for catering for large increases in the numbers of older persons through public sector provision (World Bank, 1994; Tout, 1989), and although the policy focus has largely been on the family as the key agency in meeting the ageing challenge in the developing world (Phillips, 1992), this simple opposition between public sector or informal sector provision conceals a wealth of policy options that must be explored. The tendency to view the old simply as recipients of care and services has served to conceal the prospects of and opportunities for mutual support (Ping Kwong Kam,1996).

In societies where older persons represented a small component of the population, social expectations of ageing either promoted a learned helplessness or accentuated reverence for the old by their separation from normal social functioning. Older persons were to be taken care of either as helpless or as gods rather than viewed as full participants in social and economic life. Population ageing is producing a movement away from the gerontological approach of learned helplessness and towards an approach based in mutual support and empowerment (Ping Kwong Kam, 1996). The political importance of the growing numbers of older persons in electoral terms also plays a part in creating a new paradigm of empowerment and mutual support in gerontological discussion. In the industrial world, namely Australia, Canada and the United States of America, the lobbying power of older persons is already beginning to make it felt—older persons have begun to participate in the political process as older persons. Already a change in the traditional gerontological paradigm has begun with discussion moving from elderly to older person. But the increase in the numbers of older persons provides not only the strong membership base for the new political influence of the older generations, but also a basis for new sociability, companionship and mutual support activities within these generations.

The new demography will move older persons from a position where their interests were weakly represented within society to a position where they are a major constituency for all polities in the foreseeable future. The ageing of society will produce the political base that can bring about a fundamental shift in the traditional erotological policy paradigm. Policy focus has fallen largely upon the pressures that an ageing of society will bring to bear on public resources (World Bank, 1994; Tout, 1989). The policy makers' focus on the economic burden of ageing has served to conceal the increased political capacity of the older world—a capacity which is bound to bring with it changes in social as well as political relationships between the generations. Many societies have ministries and government departments devoted to youth; few have yet dedicated ministries or departments to the specific needs of older persons. As the demographic balance alters, the political balance between youth and age and changes in the appointment and work of ministries and departments is to be expected. In the industrial world these changes are already evident; in the developing world, the process is likely to take longer.

The development of generational politics in the industrial world has its consequences for the development of the political capacity of older persons in the developing world. Advocacy by the lobbying institutions of older persons in the industrial world is raising the profile of older persons in the developing world. Institutions such as the American Association of Retired Persons have sought to extend their activities to the developing world through seminars and meetings on the relationship between age, poverty and development (Grieco, 1996). And through lobbying efforts at the United Nations, older persons groups have effectively facilitated, since 1982, the placing of ageing on the global agenda. This, in turn, set in motion a formal attempt by many countries to develop national structures to focus on meeting the needs and challenges of an ageing world. For the most part, these structures provide a marked increase in awareness of the issue. At present, the institutional links between the highly developed older person pressure groups of the industrial world and their social counterparts in the old age clubs or community groups of the developing world are relatively weak. Indeed, even the governmental agencies concerned with the interests of older persons in the industrial world make little contact and share little information with their counterparts in the developing world, although frequently they share information amongst themselves (United Nations, 1991). Consequently, those agencies in the developing world do not have adequate access to the information and resources they need to improve the quality of life of older persons in low and middle income countries. Historically, the

costs of sharing information between agencies were high; with new technology, these costs can now be greatly reduced. Web sites on social policy and ageing can provide a very useful means of information exchange between the industrial and developing world. Web sites that give information on the success and difficulties encountered in trying out various policy options or web sites that link grassroot older persons' ageing in the developing world with sponsors in the industrial world can make a major contribution to better the policies and prospects for older persons in the developed world.

The majority of lobbying by older persons within a national framework is clearly an opportunity for global lobbying, which is much strengthened by the new information technologies. Historically, the conduct and dissemination of research were largely matters for specialists and experts; lobbying groups very often were confined simply to the commissioning of research. New information technologies place powerful tools for designing and participating in research in the hands of the layperson, whereas historically, the overview of the literature lay predominately in the hands of the expert. New technology provides older persons' interest groups with an active tool for redesigning the gerontological paradigm into a more positive and less isolating social description. It provides older persons with an ability not only to link up and network within a society but across societies as well.

In the industrial world, the rapid decrease in the costs of home-based information technology provides older persons with an infrastructure for sociability and social functioning that does not rely on arduous travel. With donor assistance and some innovative organizational design, grass roots ageing in developing countries can be connected to new world information technologies. It is not necessary to purchase a technology; simple access is all that is required. The potential for highly effective twinning between older persons' organizations in the developed and developing world through new technology is clear.

Through global lobbying and the use of new technology, the opportunity exists for more participatory research into ageing. Existing research in developing countries is highly fragmented; the knowledge of policy options and progress on ageing is divided amongst many experts who are not necessarily in contact with one another. Well-organized web sites on ageing can do much to mend these existing fractures. The gaps in research would become readily apparent; good policy initiatives or best practices would be more quickly disseminated; knowledge of what works and exists elsewhere would help older persons gain resources; and, most importantly, the balance would shift away from the difficulties of maintaining the traditional formal insurance schemes and focus on practical measures to improve the lot of the older person in the developing world.

The consequence of this current fragmentation of knowledge on ageing, most particularly in respect of the developing world, is that many key policy topics are left largely undiscussed.

- In the major donors' discussions of poverty and within the literature in general (Strietland, 1996), the position of older persons is left largely unmentioned. Within the large development agencies such as the World Bank, techniques of poverty monitoring and discussions of poverty alleviation rarely incorporate the old, a fact which is easily established by reviewing the listing of publications or contents of project operations. Ageing has not yet taken its necessary place on the development policy radar. In discussions of older persons and development, the older person is simply regarded as a constraint and not a resource.

- Gender, itself a new item on the majority of policy agendas, is of particular importance in defining social relations within an ageing world. Women live longer than men and over their lifetime have less opportunity to accumulate financial and other resources than men. In many societies in the developing world, women have constrained economic and social rights. Where States rely on families to support the older person and where only men have strong financial bases, parents who only have daughters can experience very real hardship. As family size falls, the number of households which only contain daughters will increase, generating very real financial divisions between "only son" and "only daughter" households; gender divisions within society will have real consequences for the old. Yet the major donors and development agencies still have not focused on the gender dynamics of an ageing world.

- Development agencies have given little concern to an intergenerational approach to development, including the development of intergenerational housing, ensuring intergenerational employment opportunities, designing intergenerational roles into the education system or developing intergenerational credit union and micro- banking structures. The focus of development activities has been unambiguously on youth and, very often, male youth.

Given the scale of such gaps, a more holistic approach to ageing and development is clearly needed. Where such gaps are identified, web sites provide a mechanism through which pressure can be exerted on donor agencies, experts and Governments for their inclusion on the policy agenda. Interested parties can refine and strengthen policy options through a web site before harnessing the same technology in advocacy with the big gun institutions. Ensuring ready access to key information on ageing and development through new global technologies precludes the possibility of the giants of development, the major donors, claiming ignorance of the issues and enables the minnows of development, the grass root organizations, to actively and visibly participate in the shaping of the ageing and development agenda.

To summarize, the ageing of the world is happening at precisely the same time at which there has been a rolling back of the public sector globally and when the developing world is seeing the breakdown of its informal system of family care. The emergence of a new demography of a four and five generational world will necessarily result in altered social roles and identities; the old patterns of exchange between the generations being based on a three generational form. The ageing of society will, unless the existing gender inequities are addressed, result in the accentuation of gender disparities in respect of wealth and quality of life. Given these considerations, there is an immediate policy requirement to consider the development of new bases of sociability and social esteem for the older generations. The increase in numbers of older persons will provide a first base for new patterns of social esteem: the old will increasingly have political might. The rolling back of the public sector will increasingly necessitate the development of mutual support amongst older persons for the performance of services and assistance. This will produce a new base of sociability. New technology can be harnessed in increasing the political capacity and enhancing sociability of older persons. New technology provides a technical bridge for the linking of older persons globally and enables the old of the developing world to gain direct assistance from their counterparts in the developed world. It also provides new opportunities for the older person to participate in shaping the research and policy agenda appropriate to a graying world.

Within the framework of the changed constraints and capacities of an ageing world, the rest of this article will identify and discuss policy concerns and options relevant to the integration of ageing issues into development practice. Its objective is to shift the reigning policy paradigm on ageing away from a simplistic discussion of the economics of a graying world and towards the development of sustainable social relationships for a new and enduring demography.

2. OVERCOMING THE PRESENT POLICY LIMITATIONS: ADOPTING THE EMPOWERMENT PARADIGM, DEMYSTIFYING THE FAMILY

Development agencies and national Governments of low and middle income countries are still largely focused on the relative rather than the absolute numbers of older persons in their societies. Whilst for these societies the number of older persons is substantially larger than ever before, and growing, it is still the case for many countries that the percentage of youthful members is substantially greater than the percentage of old. Despite the absolute numbers of older persons, the policy attention they receive is drowned out by the predominant focus on the young—investment in development programmes unambiguously focuses on youth. Yet the literature clearly indicates that the social processes which accompany development, most particularly urbanization, migration and changes in household composition, have adverse and unsettling consequences for the older person (Sushama, 1992; Chow, 1992).

A world now accustomed to planning in terms of baby bulges may find it difficult to adjust to the new phenomenon of a 'graying population'.
(Tout, 1989)

In 1992, in discussing the imbalance of policy attention between older persons and other interests in Malaysia, P.C. Sushama stressed the deficiencies of the present approach. He talked of the meager acknowledgements of the needs of older persons when compared with other sectors of the population (1992: 170). Development thinking is still clearly locked into the old paradigm: social investment is for the young- educating the young- is the path to the development. But this paradigm emerged out of a world which was largely three generational: and increasingly our new world is four and five generational.

It is estimated that between 1950 and 2000 the number of persons over 60 years of age in the world will have risen from about 200 million to 590 million. The elderly will then constitute 13.7 per cent the world's population. While the effect is already being felt in many developing countries, the full impact in those countries is yet to come. Whether this is considered good news or bad, the world is now faced with what one writer has called the demographic imperative of an ageing population, that is a population in which proportionately more people live longer.
(Tout, 1989:17)

And the older generations are living in a world which has undergone the fastest and greatest social and technical changes in history. Not only are there increasingly larger numbers of older persons in our world but they have great educational needs which have to be met if major human resources are not to be wasted. These educational needs range from literacy and technical training, through civic and political education to banking and enterprise skills.

Researchers have discovered in the new urban zones a negative image of the elderly based on the older person's lack of preparation for functioning in the urban setting. In the family unit itself there is an increase of distancing. The normal process of cultural educational and economic distances between the generations is exacerbated and expedited by the exceptional circumstances of migration. The stress and confusion of the shanty town existence often means that, whereas the extended family system is beneficial to the older person in rural areas, the close proximity in the slum shanty, wedged among many similar dwellings, turns the older person into an unwelcome and unproductive extra burden on space and basic services, especially where, for example, water for every purpose has to be purchased instead of fetched by the elder from copious mountain streams. This leads to the dual disadvantage that the normal spatial family unit of the city becomes nuclear in capacity, while the old are seen as objects to be cared for by official services rather than being the prime concern of the family. The old become marginalized in respect of work opportunities, education, leisure, specialist health care and basic services.
(Tout, 1989:52)

Lack of education represents as large a problem, if not larger, than physiological constraints to the social and economic participation of older persons. An increase in the number of generations in a fast changing world accentuates the educational distance between the younger and older generations when education is viewed purely as the preserve of youth. A lifetime approach to education that equips older generations with new skills minimizes this distance. Evidence shows that age barriers to acquiring new skills are minimal (Ping Kwong Kam, 1996). In regard to training, gerontologists have pointed out that older people have considerable potential to learn. Indeed, seniors are now a major force within home computer technology users in the United States (Open Management Software Incorporated, 1996).

Longevity has now become a cause for concern because of its consequences on the durability of the social security system, medical and social services and family support, as well as the structure of the future labour market. The reality of limited resources in the face of growing demands is becoming more and more apparent against the background of rising expenditures, greater geographical and occupational mobility and the growing trend toward smaller nu-

clear families. There is alarm that current forms of State, community and family support cannot endure, as the number of Japanese elderly increases by millions, and their needs become more complex in nature.
(Hashimoto, 1992:36-37)

The imperative is not the financial costs of a growing ageing population, as much as the literature would have us believe. Rather it is how to develop patterns of social and economic participation for a four to five generational as opposed to a three generational demographic structure. The focus must be on how to develop appropriate patterns of exchange and reciprocity between the generations as well as on how to develop mutual support structures within generations. The expansion of the world's generational structure is likely to result in very different sociability needs as between generations. Whereas most of the focus has been on the economics of an ageing world, the sociology of an ageing world has been largely neglected. And this neglect is highly pernicious, for the economists' solution to an ageing world has largely been a social one (World Bank, 1994)—care of and responsibility for mankind's new generations, the old-old, should lie with the family. This social solution of returning the responsibility for care to kin side steps the issue of the degree of stress and breakdown this will generate within society if there are no accompanying social policy measures. The evidence is that support systems do not emerge spontaneously but require intervention and encouragement for their growth.

It should also be noted that greater demands to provide care are often made on families which are under stress such as those in low income groups. On the other hand, there are no signs at the present moment that neighbours and service networks are emerging as viable alternatives to provide care for elderly people.
(Chow, 1992: 70 on Hong Kong)

Social investment in the older person is not an option, it is a necessity for development. The lag in the paradigm requires correcting. Economizing on caring will not do the job; investment in participation is what is needed. And there are, indeed, some small signs that the paradigm is beginning to shift. A literature has begun to emerge which challenges the traditional stereotypes of ageing and focuses on the need for changed social policies in respect of ageing in the industrial world.

The population of the OECD countries is an ageing one. The long term trends of rising standards of living including improvements in health status and of lower birth rates are leading to a steady growth in the proportion of older people defined as anyone aged 65 and over in our populations. The development can be seen as a successful outcome of earlier economic and social policies leading to longer and healthier lives and greater scope for individual choice and lifetime fulfillment. It does however also raise questions whether the traditional social policy prescriptions for the elderly—many of which have their intellectual origins around the beginning of the 20th century—will continue to be both relevant and sufficient....Demographic changes require new services and greater provision of existing services.
(OECD, 1994)

A clear marker of such a change in the United States was the abolition of the compulsory retirement age. Chronological age no longer provides such a ready measuring guide to occupational and employment performance, most particularly amongst the young-old.

In line with our way of thinking, a recent conference recommended that all countries should move towards increased flexibility with regard to retirement with a view towards the eventual abolition of the mandatory retirement age. The older worker should participate in decision-making and have certain flexibility as to when to withdraw completely from active employment.
(Azer and Afifi, 1993:112)

Similarly, commentators on the developing world have identified mandatory retirement as a factor that contributes towards a negative shaping of the social and economic opportunities of older persons. Mandatory retirement is an imported logic. The concept of retirement at a certain age is alien to traditional life. In Vilcabamba, Ecuador, 20 percent of the population is aged over 60, compared with 4.5 per cent for Ecuador as a whole. Tout (1989) focuses on the temperate environment, unpressured rural culture, and the full social and economic participation of older persons as explanations of this island of immunity where persons living to 100 and upwards are a normal feature of existence. Also in Soviet Georgia and certain areas of Pakistan, longevity and traditional life are exceptions to the rule. In China, there is considerable pressure on elders to leave the job market (Tout, 1989:103) in order to provide employment opportunities for their offspring.

Japan: *A relatively large proportion of Japanese elderly people continue to work beyond official retirement age (55 years of age) to supplement their pension incomes. In fact, 36 per cent of Japanese men over the age of 65 are engaged in full or part time employment. Comparable figures for other industrial countries are France, 5 per cent, West Germany 7 per cent and the United States of America 18 per cent. However, earnings available from the kind of employment available in old age are usually low, except for senior ranking people who work in large enterprises.*
(Hashimoto, 1992:41)

Malaysia: *A proportion of those being withdrawn from the workforce remain capable of making a sound contribution and they do often strive to find parallel or alternative employment in the private sector, not for remuneration alone, but because they wish to remain active.*
(Sushama, 1992:167)

The Nigerian research team also found older people generally at work or wanting to work.
(Tout, 1989:8)

In Singapore, however, retirees do not want to return to the work force (Cheung and Vasoo, 1992: 83). This may reflect the security older Singaporeans feel in respect of their social entitlement to family care, an entitlement which the Singapore government is ready to enforce through law if the social erosion of family care begins. The Singapore Government put forward the controversial suggestion of a law of filial responsibility. Due to public resistance, the suggestion was not implemented but the Government is prepared to implement it if the pattern of family care for elderly continues to erode (Cheng and Vasoo, 1992:98). In a national survey on senior citizens in 1983, 84 per cent reported receiving financial and material support from family (Cheung and Vasoo, 1992). However, Singapore has taken substantial measures to enhance the employability of older persons by introducing a change in provident fund contribution rates for older persons—lowering them in order to increase employment opportunities for older persons. Currently, only 22 per cent of elderly people are in the work force and, with Singapore's older population set to constitute 25 per cent of the population by 2030 as compared with 4 per cent in 1957, the Government already sees the need to induce employers to employ and retain older workers.

Well-established State pensions schemes, social security provision and private pension arrangements are routine features of the social and institutional infrastructure of the developed world. This is not the case, however, for the developing world.

Given the prevalence of modern pension, social security and general insurance provision in developed countries, it is perhaps briefly necessary to mention the inadequacy, and often complete absence, of retirement or old age pensions and social security in most developing countries. One United Nations report States that at present retirement benefits are not generally high enough in developing countries to have widespread retirement effects.
(Tout, 1989:45)

Malaysia: *When discussing welfare, the issue of adequacy of services is pertinent, as neither the Government nor voluntary organizations have yet been able to meet requirements in a wholly satisfactory manner.*

The person in need cannot turn to either source with confidence for an immediate response. Furthermore, welfare needs have, until recently, been seen in limited terms . In the absence of a universal old age allowance scheme, public assistance is not only inadequate, but varies and is not readily available.
(Sushama, 1992:82)

Nor is the developing world likely to follow along the same path of public sector pension provision. The industrial world has itself run into difficulties, with the ageing of its populations, in the financing of its present arrangements for State pension provision, social security and medical care. Pension systems and related forms of social insurance are under redesign; adjustments to the new demographics are working their way through these systems and the advice to developing countries from the first world experts is not to tread the same path (World Bank, 1994). Developing countries are advised to avoid dependence on State pension schemes and to make greater use of the informal social structures of kinship and community in designing social provision for old age.

Few developing countries have public pension schemes, and where they do, they are typically restricted to a very small percentage of the older population - those who have enjoyed formal sector employment and have been public officials. Some developing countries, including Egypt, have substantial schemes and entitlements on the statute books which receive little translation into social reality. Provision on paper and provision on the ground are substantially different realities. Egypt put its first scheme for social security into place in 1950 and enshrined the entitlement to social security in law, yet the evidence is that many do not know how to access the provisions and few benefit from them. Similarly, the levels at which pensions are set provide little financial autonomy for the older person, and there is a widespread dependence on children for support.

The percentage of those who are entitled to a pension and who receive support from their children is 38.5 per cent; this indicates that pensions fall short of meeting the needs of these pensioners. Second, the percentage of those who are not entitled to a pension and rely on support from their children is 52.2 per cent. This finding reveals that the welfare system is in need of serious rethinking .
(Azer and Afifi, 1992:69)

Weak pension provisions result in the substantial involvement of the family in providing for older persons. The family is a default system in a context where other provision is either weak or not made at all.

Some factors that sustain family care for the aged can be identified. This is important in order to appreciate its continuity and change, and the future vi-

ability of such a support system. The first factor relates to the relatively low level of public resources made available to elderly individuals in Japan, which makes the attainment of self sufficiency and independence from the family difficult. Financial dependence on children is particularly notable for those receiving the Old age welfare pension and national pension at a low level.
(Hashimoto, 1992: 41 on Japan)

Plans to intensify the responsibilities of the family is part of policy thinking in the developing world as new older generations become part of the developing world's demographic structure.

Korean Government policy is one of regarding ageing as a personal or family matter.
(Phillips, 1992:14)

The resort to the family as a policy instrument has two main prongs: firstly, it reduces the public sector costs of an ageing world, and secondly, it harnesses an existing institution to deal with the new economic and sociability requirements of an ageing world rather than having to invest in and develop new institutions. It is argued by many policy makers that the traditions of filial piety in developing societies are largely unbroken. Paradoxically, where societies are seen as having undergone fundamental change, family structures are perceived as the epitome of continuity and their enduring as unproblematic.

Belief in the family as the prime source of care can stem from, for example, Chinese, especially Confucian traditions of filial piety and respect, or from similar Malay attitudes, or from the religious emphases of Islam, which in the Koran and elsewhere stress the need for children to accept responsibility for the care of their elderly relatives.
(Phillips, 1992:15)

Some societies have longstanding filial piety laws while other societies have recently established or strengthened such laws. However, it is far from clear if traditions of filial piety are indeed unbroken. The social and material bases upon which these traditions operated have disappeared in many societies. Modern legal systems have eroded the traditional rights of older generations to honour or withhold familial property and land from their offspring.

In principle the Old age welfare pension and most formal social services presuppose the family as primary providers by determining the level of eligibility by household composition. This arrangement is also supported by Japanese family law which stipulates legal responsibility for a child to support an elderly parent.
(Hashimoto, 1992:38)

Another factor which traditionally affected the older man's status (in the United Republic of Tanzania) was his ability to control land tenure and thereby the (mainly agricultural) commerce of yesteryear. The development of land sales and industrial commerce has transferred much of that power to the young person who has the training to understand real estate finance and the physical strength to operate within industry and the commercial activities that are its by-product.
(Tout, 1989: 12)

The emerging national policy on ageing unequivocally emphasizes both humanitarian and developmental concerns. In considering humanitarian concerns, the needs of elderly people are to be met largely by the family with support from the State. The family however is expected to remain as the cornerstone of the support network for elderly people.
(Cheung and Vasoo, 1992: 102 on Singapore)

Even where traditional schemes are honoured, the nature of provision may be traditionally restricted to a sufficiency or minimal base as opposed to equity. Such is the case in Sharia law as interpreted in Egypt.

A person in poverty is responsible for his wife, his parents and his offspring only. ...A son alone is legally obliged to support his parents and grandparents....Support is on the basis of sufficiency.
(Azer and Afifi, 1992:79-80)

While policy makers continue to stress the family as the cornerstone of ageing policy, researchers are indicating the growing weakness of the family. There are many misconceptions about the robustness of intergenerational family relations given social, economic and demographic changes. Furthermore, where families are intergenerational, this arrangement is often predicated upon the older generation making substantial contributions to household organization and upkeep.

The assumption of extended families was overturned in mid 1970s when sociologists discovered that the unextended family had become the norm.
(Chow, 1992:70 on Hong Kong)

Another noteworthy point is that, in spite of much rhetoric about filial piety in a Chinese society, it does not seem that this tradition has been particularly influential in fostering a harmonious relationship between elderly people and their children and thereby increasing the likelihood that the former are receiving support from the latter. Admittedly it is difficult to verify the relevance of certain traditional concepts such as respect for the old. But as far as the provision of family care for elderly people is concerned, evidence clearly indicates that certain factors, such as the extent of support that the elderly members manage to provide for their families, are as

important, if not more so, than the simple rhetoric of filial piety.
(Chow, 1992:72 on Hong Kong)

The Malaysian who is 60 years or older can claim and usually is accorded a position of respect within the family and community. Traditionally the family is expected to care for the older members of its unit but with many changes in the country this expectation can no longer be taken for granted.
(Sushama, 1992:170)

Many elderly people are givers rather than receivers of economic and other support.
(Sundstrom, 1994:22 on the OECD)

In 1984 a series of studies funded by the Australian Government, under the general title "Socio-economic consequences of the ageing of the population", was initiated as a component project of phase III of the Asian Population Programme in five countries of the Association of South-East Asian Nations (ASEAN), countries Indonesia, Malaysia, the Philippines, Singapore and Thailand. In these studies a core questionnaire was developed to gather information on household structure, housing, economic resources, living support, health and social activities. Some secondary data analysis was undertaken and existing policies and programmes on ageing in the countries were examined and evaluated. The project which was coordinated from Singapore; gave its main objective as the raising of awareness of policy makers and planners to the issues of ageing throughout the ASEAN countries. A key finding of this study noted in its cross national report was the potential stress which could be placed on family members by continued reliance on family support by the elderly population (Chen and Jones, 1989) The authors argued that increased urbanization and social mobility, smaller families and the tendency for married women to enter the paid workforce all suggest the possibility that parents will not be able to assume that their children will care for them in their old age.
(Andrews, 1992:25)

Even in the societies where filial piety and intergenerational arrangements are the strongest, changes from these traditional arrangements are in progress:

Proportion of elderly people living with their children in Japan: In 1960, 82 per cent; in 1985, 65 per cent. ....polls of elderly show limited and decreasing interest in co-residence by aged including Japan
(OECD, 1994: 26)

60 per cent of elderly people have no close relatives or friends living close to them.
(Ping Kwong Kam, 1996)

During the past three decades a strong trend towards the independence of children after marriage has prevailed in the country. Migration from rural areas and numerous opportunities for work in Arab countries has increased mobility. These factors have contributed to the realization that elderly persons are starting to become vulnerable and that the intervention of social policy is needed .....The joint household hardly exists at all in the sample because of the impracticality of housing several families in small flats. The average size of the dwellings among the sample was 3.5 rooms.
(Azer and Afifi, 1992: 48-49 on Egypt)

Smaller family size changes the family's ability to meet the demands on its human and financial resources. The greater the number of siblings the more potential links an individual has to social and economic support, especially in societies that deem the sibling link to be a major basis for mutual bonds of obligation and reciprocity. Family size provides the foundation for the degree and extent of mutual support. Research into the pattern of exchange and responsibility and how changing demography affects these patterns of exchanges has been neglected, but is clearly critical if the family is to be the cornerstone of the developing world's social policy on ageing.

The Philippines has had a traditionally laissez faire approach to many aspects of welfare and housing policy. Whilst earlier regimes have focused considerably on primary health care, extending a range of services to rural and urban areas, this has, to an extent come down to an abrogation of public responsibility to the barangay (parish) level. However, family size in the Philippines is larger than in many other countries of the region and therefore family support may remain more realistic than elsewhere for some time to come.
(Phillips, 1992:14)

Some researchers talk of an emerging contradiction between the expectations of policy-makers regarding the availability of family resources and the pressures placed on the family when this expectation falls short. The default status of the family in the absence of other provisions has been elevated by policy makers to a fully functioning institution capable of handling the social policy requirements of the new demography. Because the family has central responsibility, and because it is not an institution of the public sector, the requirement for counterpart and corresponding supports from the public sector can go largely unrecorded and unrecognized until a crisis point is reached.

This means that there is an emerging contradiction through which elderly people might suffer from an expectation of family support (and housing) and a concomitant lack of publicly funded alternatives.
(Phillips, 1992:15)

What is the scale of increased support that the smaller family will have to provide in the first half of the twenty-first century?

Low or reducing levels of fertility in the past few decades have meant that there are proportionately larger numbers of people in the older age group (65 and over) than in the late middle age group (55 and over) in certain of the countries in this region, notably in Hong Kong, Singapore and China. However, there is set to be a greater percentage increase in population aged 55 and over during the decades to 2020 in many of the countries with large populations, such as Indonesia, the Philippines and Thailand, which means that the numerical importance of older people is bound to increase inexorably during this time.
(Phillips, 1992:9)

Japan faces a huge urban elderly population early next century and it is highly likely that this trend will be witnessed in other countries in the region.
(Phillips, 1992: 10)

Both numerically and proportionally, therefore, the incidence of old age is becoming increasingly important. Longevity is also increasing and the proportion of the very old is growing. For example, in 1961 only 3.8 per cent of the elderly population was aged 75 years or more, but by 1981 this had increased to 19.2 per cent, and by 1986 to 21.9 per cent.
(Phillips, 1992: 47)

The staggering fact that there will be an increase in Singapore's elderly population from 4 per cent in 1957 to 25 per cent in 2030 implies that there will be a shift in the pattern of consumption of goods and services among the population.
(Cheung and Vasoo, 1992:102)

Ironically, it is precisely those societies which are about to encounter the greatest change in their demography—and which therefore have experienced the greatest changes in family structure—that are advocating kinship as the solution. In the face of such numbers, and accepting that the family will indeed be the cornerstone of ageing policy in developing countries, the issue arises of how best to develop supporting and counterpart institutions within the peer group, neighbourhood, community and State. A first step is to be found in the development of a more transparent contract between the State and the family as to responsibilities. Chow (1992) raises an alarm on the issue, pointing out that the description of informal social policy provision for older persons is largely in terms of community, while the structures utilized are mainly those of the nuclear family.

It is not surprising that a community care approach has been adopted in countries with a growing ageing population in which elderly people are encouraged as long as possible to live in the community and with their families. The attraction of this approach is not difficult to see as most countries with an ageing population are finding it increasingly difficult to finance programmes and services to meet the needs of elderly people; and families and communities present themselves as the most viable alternatives to share part of the burden. While acknowledging the desirability of the community care approach, recent research on caring for aged people shows that it is not without its limitations. First, as with many other countries adopting this approach, the meaning of community is only vaguely perceived in Hong Kong and very often people are unclear about the networks of social relationships constituting it. Secondly the exact definition of care and where the burden actually falls is another area about which questions are often asked but which seldom receive an answer.
(Chow, 1992: 65-66 on Hong Kong)

In the developed world, similar concerns have arisen:

It would appear that few Governments have taken an explicit policy stance about the relationship between public and private sphere in the provision of informal care.
(Sundstrom, 1994)

Home care services can be integrated with family care, but tend in all countries to concentrate on those without family care. Programmes aimed specifically at caring families are relatively few. Types of programmes include payment for carers, paid time off work, respite care and mutual support groups. Gerdt Sundstrom proposes that the range of home help service should be extended to take in more elderly people, if necessary by spreading the existing services more thinly, in order to give some support to family carers. He suggests there may be a need for a new form of contract between family and State, based on the availability of alternative sources of care to increase the choice for family members, both young and old.
(OECD, 1994: 9)

There are consequences resulting from the lack of an explicit contract between the older person, the family and the State; where State services are available for older persons, they are often restricted to those persons without family support. Older persons have the benefit of either family services or State services, but rarely enjoy a mix of the two. Developing a better integration between State and community and family services could do much to improve the older person's position within the household.

While both family support and community support are needed, they seem to be serving two different groups of elderly people: one with families and the other without, and there are only rare occasions when the two types of support interact.
(Chow, 1992:73 on Hong Kong)

Social service administration for the aged in Japan tends to take a targeted approach rather than a blanket approach. Vital services such as home health care, bathing services, meal services or telephone reassurance are available mostly for a target population, namely those living alone or those bedridden at home. These services often require that the recipients satisfy some eligibility criteria determined by age, income, disability and household composition. This kind of targeting is made possible by the extensive use of local municipal agents who locate and monitor the needs population
(Hashimoto, 1992:38)

The scale of the numbers involved means that, despite the preferences of Governments for informal sector solutions, an increase in State involvement and provision is inevitable.

Given the rising numbers of elderly people in Malaysia, as elsewhere in the region, it is clear that services for them will have to be planned.
(Sushama, 1992:181)

Care for elderly people has emerged in Japan as a critical element of public and private concern and this is a precursor for many other countries in the region....the unit of self sufficiency and of self help for the aged does not rest with the individual, but with the family. Targetted State interventions of the kind described earlier are designed to provide for persons whose families fail to support their members in one way or another. It is ironic that, at the time when other developed nations were experiencing huge cost explosions in the provision of a range of care and support for elderly people, Japan did not seriously have to contend with cost containment, as the country's age structure appeared to work in its favour. During the decade of the 1990s and early next century, this will be adjusted quite radically.
(Phillips, 1992:5)

The policy question is how best to design a sustainable mix of State and informal sector provisions. A key element in any such design must be the incorporation of the local State and voluntary organization. Social planning is not simply about the allocation of State resources but also about ways of supporting and amplifying the contribution of the informal sector through instruments such as tax breaks, preferential loans for social purposes, providing low cost access to public buildings and facilities for community purposes

and the establishment of cooperative and community alternatives to public sector or market services. Similarly, action can be taken to change the scheduling requirements around older persons' social and economic participation. Just as flexible retirement provisions enable society to retain the able older person in the work force, flexible working arrangements would permit more older persons to remain within the workforce longer.

There are considerable differences between the living patterns of older women and the mainstream institutional patterns of school and work.
(Setterlund and Abbott, 1996)

Government assistance could also be made available for the development of market services to enable greater participation and contact among younger and older persons, e.g., the promotion of commercial housing designs that accommodate inter-generational living. To date, Government focus has been on the regulation of market services that respond to growing numbers of older persons rather than on research and development investments required within a new demographic order.

Malaysia: *today there is also a growing demand for services from people of different social situations as is evidenced by the establishment of commercially run homes for elderly people, catering to a range of middle class clients.*
(Sushama, 1992:172)

A framework for outlining the relationships in the context of demographic change can be viewed through three areas: gender; peer group empowerment and mutual support; and intergenerational design of social institutions. The exact formulation of the productive social relationships that are connected to ageing will vary from society to society and culture to culture. These themes are fundamental to all but have yet to make a significant entrance on the global policy agenda.

Gender

Gender has received little attention in mainstream development operations, although change is now on the way due to the awareness created by the Fourth World Conference on Women in Beijing in 1995. Ageing has had less than its share of attention in development operations and policy. Consequently, the gender and ageing issue has barely been addressed. Yet good gender design is a key element of good ageing policy and operations. Women live longer than men and experience greater financial and cultural constraints, which affect their quality of life as older persons. Women are the principal care and health providers within the family and have fewer material resources to care for their dependants, be they young or old. Programmes for cultural arrangements concerning gender vary greatly from one society to another. In some societies, women are very likely to live close to their mothers and other female kin who can provide them with support, in other societies, women are cut off from their female kin by physical distances, resulting from marriages which have led them far from their original family homes, or by rules which preclude them from leaving their marital homes. Good gender practice on ageing requires considerable knowledge of local circumstances, local opportunities and local constraints.

In many societies, there is a clear gender split concerning the provision of finance and care for older persons. Men are responsible for providing the financial support for older persons while women are responsible for providing care and health services. Men meet their responsibilities by being engaged in the public world; the caring responsibilities of women often confine them to the home.

This shows that sons and daughters are by far the strongest supporters of the elderly; however, the son's support (whether alone or with others) is much greater than the daughters (whether alone or with others): sons provide 67.7 per cent and daughters 15.6 per cent of the total financial support given to the elderly.
(Azer and Afifi, 1992: 80 on Egypt)

The tendency to live with children, particularly the eldest son, is prevalent regardless of age, sex and marital status of the aged, and is a legacy of the primogeniture inheritance practice that operated before the Second World War. There has been a decline in the overall proportion living with children, but the custom persists, and elderly parents today continue to live with their sons, daughters in law and grandchildren. Typically the financial responsibility rests with the sons and the caretaker responsibility of the frail elderly at home rests with the daughters in law.
(Hashimoto, 1992: 38 on Japan)

Longevity of society clearly has consequences for female work loads and opportunities if care for the old-old is to take place primarily within the family. The general assumption is that the child rearing age groups will bear the responsibility for the provision of this care. But there is indeed the substantial prospect that the young old will perform a good part of this function as an extension of the household services they already provide in many developing societies. Whichever cohort of females performs the care and health service tasks within the household, the stresses and strains of their performance are likely to take their toll on these care givers.

The system of social support based on private initiatives and principles of mutual obligation seems effi-cient and even convenient from the viewpoint of society, as it provides greater security at low economic and social cost. However, the psychological price exacted from individuals of different generations is high because of the conflicts, tensions and compromises that have to be managed within the three generation households. The price is becoming higher, particularly for the daughter in laws, as increasing longevity and prolonged illness become more prevalent, and care for frail aged family members becomes more than a full time job. In the long run, diversification of support services and increased options of care will become essential, as the intangible and tangible costs of family care become higher for a greater number of Japanese, both young and old.
(Hashimoto, 1992: 43 on Japan)

Because women provide these valuable household and care services, they are often viewed, while they are active, as more valuable members of a household.

One researcher concluded that the breakdown of the extended family affects the male more than the female. She found that housewives were able to continue living with, and rendering service to, the younger generations, even when widowed, because of the continued usefulness of this service. But the widowed male was generally seen as unproductive, of little service to the younger generation, and indeed an increasingly heavy and unwelcome burden upon family resources and loyalties.
(Tout, 1989: 15)

Older women, more often than older men, find themselves living on their own. In many societies, customary rules around widowhood preclude women from remarriage, while men may readily take another partner and from a much younger cohort. Indeed, in some societies, the marriage of old men to young brides is seen as a means of ensuring health. As a result of women living longer than men, and the fact that many societies frown on the marriage of older women and younger men, the pool of partners from which men can draw in their older years is greater than that of women.

A Nigerian study found that some people equated old in a female with the menopause. Yet in the same areas men were not regarded as old until 80.
(Tout, 1989)

Jamaica: *Caring grand mothers, great grandmothers and great great grandmothers... In 1982, there were twice as many women of 85 years and over than men.*
(Tout, 1989:107)

The increase in life expectancy underlying this trend has indeed been rapidly rising from 59.7 years for men and 63.0 for women, in 1950, to 75.6 years for men and 81.4 for women in 1988.
(Hashimoto, 1992: 37 on Japan)

The gender divisions in society that provide men with greater employment access mean that the loss of a woman's partner often constitutes a major change in financial circumstances—husbands are the mechanism through which many women connect with material resources, including pension rights, property and land ownership and salaried or waged income. Loss of a husband is often the loss of a way of life.

The Gambia: *In younger years, relatively few women work. The rate drops even lower for the child bearing years. Then it rises to a peak as husbands die or go to live with another woman and the children move away. Older women therefore often have more need to procure their own incomes than those in younger years.*
(Tout, 1989: 79)

It is also clear that females receive a much higher percentage of financial support than males. This points to the fact that females are more vulnerable and rely to a large extent on the support of their children. Only a few manage to work for a salary.
(Azer and Afifi, 1992: 56)

Consequently, widows who have no male children have very restricted material opportunities. While the social, economic and employment opportunities for women are substantially weaker over a lifetime than for those of men, there is a need for ageing policy in the developing world to address the poverty problems of widowhood. Consideration needs to be given to creating income opportunities for older women in order to tackle their poverty. Assuming that the needs of widows and older women will be met within families is a mistaken social policy. Thought must instead be given to developing appropriate enterprise, banking and employment arrangements. The ageing of society necessitates a change in the traditional gender arrangements where women's financial position was mediated through their male partners. Life time partnerships for women will increasingly become exceptional rather than a demographic norm. The ageing of society may be a major contributor to the pressure for change in existing gender divisions.

Developing programmes and policies that endow women with social and economic resources at the point of widowhood provides opportunities for women to negotiate for better services within their own kinship structures. Having external resources creates a virtuous spiral where older women are able to negotiate for a better share of domestic resources and more adequate incorporation into families. The current situation of gender-linked economic dependency can best be tackled by generating schemes that provide older women with the resources for leverage inside the family and the community.

Nigeria: *The problem of support appears to be more acute for women than for men in old age.*
(Tout, 1989: 81)

Social changes that enable women to enter employment and take financial control of their own lives mean that they are less dependent in their older years. However, these same changes deplete the domestic workforce, which has traditionally cared for the old.

Malaysia: *Industrialization has opened the door to paid work for large numbers of young women and they are recruited from villages....The trend is towards nuclear families and neither the extended family system nor the traditional role of the woman in the household can be taken granted for granted any longer.... It is now the norm rather than the exception for women to go out to work..*
(Sushama, 1992:171)

Similarly, reductions in family size have positive consequences for women's health status and lifetime earning capabilities. Such reductions also have the consequence, however, of spreading care amongst a smaller number of persons. Smaller family size also decreases the prospect of sons, and, in many societies, possession of a son is critical to a viable life. Reductions in family size also take away the key role of caring for grandchildren from women. These effects have already been observed in China where the one child per family policy coupled with a patrilocal system of marriage means that parents have often lost support from their daughters.

Children have a constitutional duty to support parents. Patrilocal system of marriage means a girl parents lose support when she moves away. Dearth of children takes child care functions away from grandparents.
(Tout, 1989: 102)

Finally, women's longevity raises the issue of developing appropriate forms of mutual support based on gender. Policy research and consideration needs to move towards new housing forms, which can enable older women to take an active part in public life. The domestic character of women's life frequently leaves them unprepared for entering the public sphere on the death of a spouse. Orientation and self-esteem courses should be a routine feature of older women's education. In designing policies and programmes for enhancing the social and economic participation of older women, attention needs to focus on the conflict between the demands of motherhood and kinship and the maintenance of women's own interests. Older women frequently place themselves on standby in response to the needs of their offspring for child care. Truly participatory schemes for older women must be flexible enough to accommodate such role conflicts (Setterlund and Abbott, 1996).

Gender and ageing is clearly an area that needs immediate attention from policy researchers and development agencies in poverty alleviation strategies for the developing world.

Peer group empowerment and mutual support

The grounds for approaching ageing through peer group empowerment and mutual support have already been discussed in respect of gender. But peer group empowerment and mutual support is important for all older persons, enabling them to take a proactive role in determining what the new models and institutions should be. Furthermore, the new longevity will produce same age companions for older persons in the mass. Historically, older persons were the exception, the survivors, and were without such supplies of same age companionship. Developing locations and forums in which same age companionship can occur is critical. Such companionship already exists in the most advanced technological location of cyberspace. Peer group empowerment and mutual support, however, should not develop to the exclusion of other forms of social, economic and inter-generational participation. Peer group empowerment and mutual support is simply one, albeit necessary, item in the social relations portfolio of older persons. In order for good social policy on ageing to develop, older persons have to be able to articulate their needs and concerns as older persons.

Developing an empowerment perspective, a movement away from the progressive deterioration medical paradigm of ageing, enables older persons to define an active life for themselves and to access the resources that enable that participation. Mutual support structures provide older persons with more control over their lives; being linked with others can help with routine tasks and can support an older person in times of crisis. Associating with persons who have the same time endowment to spend on tasks produces greater sociability; a fact testified to by the phenomenal growth in gateball clubs amongst older Japanese. It is also imperative for older persons to cooperate in providing services for themselves, which the State is increasingly unable to provide.

Discussions of the development of older persons' volunteer services to meet the imminent crisis of caring have begun to emerge in the literature. One of the most interesting of these is that provided by Ping Kwong Kam (1996) on Hong Kong. The discussion is not simply in terms of the rights of individuals to participate in the solving of their own problems but also stresses the obligation of the elderly to participate in finding solutions. The inevitability of a paradigm shift from passive clients to active and empowered individuals is clear within this account of developments in Hong Kong. Both the veneration of elders and the medical paradigm of ageing can be seen to have created an environment of learned helplessness; policy action against learned helplessness is a critical step.

There are many services that older persons themselves can provide, for their own generation as well as for others. Empowerment is not simply about rights; it is also about obligations. However, the empowerment of older persons and their development of mutual support structures is not an issue for older persons alone. Enabling conditions have to be present in order for older persons to have maximum autonomy. Providing leverage funding for mutual support schemes is frequently the more sustainable alternative to blanket or even targeted social security provision. Tout (1989) discussed precisely these issues in his proposed approach to the situation of older people in developing countries:

> Rather than advocating mere 'do-gooding' or alleviation of the immediate sufferings of a relative few of the most needy, the intention is to build structures for the future, when there will be so many more elderly people in every country. This means stimulating awareness of this incipient but rapidly developing problem and providing local communities with the resources to take their own action; and mobilizing and maximizing the many talents and the wealth of experience of the elderly themselves into productive programmes. Most important, it means supplying skills in matters such as management, fund raising, financial control, training information and similar day to day activities, without which the spontaneous flame of enthusiasm and volunteer response may so quickly dim and die out.

Mutual support should be viewed in terms of the active participation benefits it brings, not simply as the cheaper option. It offers the opportunity for enhanced sociability, greater bargaining power across the generations and greater security in the context of shrinking kinship structures—the development of retirement communities in the United States attests to this. One area that clearly needs considerable policy thought is the linking of older persons mutual support associations to those of other generations. In terms of developing societies, mutual support associations should seek to twin with external agencies such as older persons clubs and associations, banks and development agencies. With the advent of new banking technologies, mainstream banks could be approached to take on mutual savings associations in the developing world as part of their portfolio. While local banks in developing countries may not be ready to undertake the risk of financing older persons' savings and investments, western commercial banks could undertake part of this risk without any major negative impact and with major public relations benefits.

There are good reasons for ensuring the development of mutual support amongst older persons and for investing in their empowerment. Historically, the small numbers of older persons meant that the number of institutions specifically devoted to their needs were few, and that older persons were isolated by their membership of different households. The inclusion of older persons within kinship structures and the predominance of the three generation life meant that the intergenerational design of social institutions received little attention. Modern economic and social life has been built upon a rigid social paradigm of birth, education, employment, retirement and death, with each age group confined to a specific role. But longevity and the size of the older cohorts require a new flexibility in the paradigm. Older persons, with their greater endowments of available time, can benefit by participating in and contributing to education. The notion that education is not age appropriate for older persons must be combated. Budgetary recognition of older persons education needs is absent in the financial planning of both Governments and development agencies. Older persons have generational skills such as traditional craft knowledge and cultural history which can enhance the education process. Designing roles for older people into the curricula of the developing world is an important step. Assuming that classrooms are only for children closes the door of opportunity for older persons to gain literacy. Yet lack of literacy on the part of the old often generates educational problems for the young. In societies where age remains the basis of respect, an illiterate elder is often unwilling to permit the young, most particularly girls, to gain the skill.

The intergenerational design of education could do much to benefit developing countries. One clear benefit of opening the education sector to older persons is to bridge the chasm between the young and the old of different educational experiences. A common educational experience is likely to produce in the young a greater identification with the old than would otherwise be the case. This has major benefits in terms of social attitudes towards older persons. The subject of rights and entitlements of the older person has been placed on the school curriculum in Singapore. A further step would be to ensure that such courses are taught by older persons themselves.

Discussion regarding the design and development of intergenerational institutions and facilities has focused most specifically on the intergenerational housing provisions made by Singapore and Hong Kong. Although these attempts to develop an intergenerational housing infrastructure are to be applauded, some problems exist. Firstly, the policy makers' understanding of the intergenerational concept is too truncated; there will soon be more generations than many planners considered. Insufficient attention has been given to developing schemes that combine intergenerational and same age group mutual support features-both kinship and mutual support need to be factored in to the policy approach. Finally policy makers are not designing new intergenerational development programmes, which is what is needed, but rather are relying on the harnessing of the existing intergenerational institution par excellence the family.

However since Hong Kong's major social welfare success in world terms has been the provision of public housing, it is perhaps surprising that specialist accommodation for elderly has only relatively recently begun to be developed. Nevertheless, in view of Hong Kong's leading role in public and low cost housing in the south east Asian region, its current policies and practices in accommodation for elderly persons should be of considerable relevance for Malaysia, Indonesia, Taiwan, Province of China, and the Republic of Korea amongst others. All of these countries expect to experience pressure from increasing numbers and proportions of elderly people by the end of the century, Hong Kong's nearest comparison in housing terms is probably Singapore.
(Phillips, 1992: 46)

Generally the elderly are well supported . This shows that the sense of filial piety and family obligation among adults is still strong in Singapore. The Government has an important role to play in encouraging and fostering strong ties among intergenerational families through its implementation of appropriate social policies.
(Cheung and Vasoo, 1992: 102)

Alternative housing options are few for the old and young alike. Housing comes at a very high price in the densely populated, mountainous nation. Under these circumstances, intergenerational co residence becomes a cost effective method of attaining satisfactory housing for all generations involved. The traditional ethics surrounding filial piety give legitimacy to filial care. Reciprocity norms entailed within this traditional code, that foster the informal social security system within the family, provide elderly people with a sense of entitlement to care, and children with a sense of obligations of care.
(Hashimoto, 1992:42 on Japan)

The intergenerational design of housing cannot mean simply the provision of sufficient accommodation spaces for the generationally-extended nuclear household, nor adjacent apartments for the different generations of the same extended family. It must also mean that the needs of the older person are met within this infrastructure. This may include the design of social spaces where older persons can meet such as common sitting areas, social clubs or courtyards; an environment that preserves the autonomy of older persons—fewer stairs, lower cupboards, etc.—or partnering young and old in arrangements outside of kinship altogether in order to permit the inter-generational exchange of services. Simply building inter-generational provision onto the kinship structure will not do because it prevents the development of neighbourhood and community participation and exchange. Loading everything onto the family is likely to lead to a future crisis in kinship arrangements.

Well-designed housing arrangements, both in terms of architecture and accessibility to goods and services, are clearly a cornerstone of care in the community policies. In many developing countries, older persons rely on the services of the very young to perform key tasks such as water carrying, fuel collection, refuse disposal and shopping. Promoting housing design that reduces the dependence of older persons on the young will be increasingly necessary as family size is reduced. The use of solar energy for cooking, for example, would greatly reduce fuel requirements. Older persons' ownership of solar stoves would represent a great asset within the households of the developing world and enhance their bargaining power. With traditional patterns now under erosion, appropriate technology projects can lead the way towards new patterns of sustainable intergenerational exchange.

With demographic change, traditional assumptions of age appropriateness, role and social function have to be reassessed. Reciprocity is at the heart of all social functioning and new bases of reciprocity need to be established. Can the volunteer activities of older persons improve the quality of educational and social services? Can older persons provide escort services for the young rather than requiring them from the middle generation? Can the time endowment of older persons be harnessed to improve the households information on available resources within the society? Can older persons improve their bargaining within intergenerational households without major welfare loss to younger generations? The tradition of development assumes that resources must enter the society through the learning child and economically active adult. But there is another paradigm available -funneling resources through older persons will restore lost reciprocities. In the context of an ageing society, development agencies should make reinforcement of the social and economic resources of older persons a priority.

Finally, attention has to be paid to the mainstream design of relationships in society so as to provide for the inclusion of older generations in mainstream activity. Evidence from a wealth of sources testifies to the many socially and physically constructed barriers of participation in everyday activities (McCallum,1989). Inadequate transport and lack of information are two recurrent blocks to the participation of older persons in everyday activities.

Malaysia: *the general population is served by a comprehensive health care system. However availability alone does not guarantee use of services and facilities*

and elderly people are rarely specifically targeted. There are other factors to be considered in the case of elderly people than availability alone. For instance, incapacity with attendant access problems and other difficulties may cause delay in seeking treatment. Confusion of symptoms with a wrongly perceived understanding of the ageing process may also make individuals ignore the need for attention, until the condition becomes acute.
(Sushama, 1992:174)

The emphasis is to encourage elderly people as much as members of any other group who may require assistance to maintain their independence.... The active involvement of the family and of the community in their care is implicit.
(Sushama, 1992: 177 on Malaysia)

Inadequate access to transportation has very real consequences for older persons with regard to their ability to utilize services both in the developing and the developed world. The physical design of transport plays a key part in the situation. There has been insufficient attention placed on how technology can be modified to benefit the older person. The needs of older drivers are being addressed in the United States and Japan (Axhausen and Grieco, 1991; Grieco, 1992) through high-tech research and development programmes, however, such benefits are unlikely to reach the low income countries of the world in the foreseeable future. In the developing world, two transport options are of relevance: a) the decentralization of public services such as health and construction, and; b) the development of community transport initiatives and options. The decentralization of facilities will better enable the older rural population to participate in the benefits of key modern services such as health and communications. The development of community transport initiatives, with adequate design assistance, creates the possibility of special sectors of the community being served. The link between the individual transport needs of older persons and broader community issues needs to be addressed. The participation of older persons in development designs is one way of ensuring that necessary measures are taken.

Research for action

The objective, then, is not simply to reallocate economic resources in order to accommodate the social and economic participation of the new older generations. It must be the creation of a larger agenda which ensures that these new older generations are fully and usefully integrated into social and economic life. It is a view that is beginning to emerge in several forums repeatedly, although major advocacy and research is still required before policy makers confront these issues.

Much of the research on ageing has been disproportionately concerned with medical and physiological considerations at the cost of the full and proper exploration of social policy issues. The medical and physiological focus has encouraged an approach to ageing, which sees older persons as separate from society or at the very least as a separate category in society. With the import of longevity and demographic change, focusing on older persons as a distinct category is no longer sufficient.

In the main, even social gerontology has something of a traditional focus—it focuses on the problems of the old rather than on the problems of the design of society. Even here the paradigm needs to shift. Despite the limitations of existing social gerontology, it still has an important function to play in identifying the circumstances and social processes affecting older persons. Although social gerontology has become relatively commonplace as an approach and discipline within the industrial world, the lack of such research in the developing world has consequences for those very societies that are most dependent upon kinship structures but lack sufficient knowledge of the social processes involved. The need for social gerontology and social policy research in the developing world, however, is beginning to receive attention.

Most aspects of the work presented here could conveniently be collated under the title of social gerontology. As outlined by Warnes (1989), gerontology itself is a fairly young field of study in many countries, in North America it is better established than in Britain or some other European countries. It is certainly new in this Asian region but is gathering impetus.
(Phillips, 1992:1)

Not only is there a need to collect better descriptive data on the social support systems around ageing in the developing world, but there is also a need for a radical review of the policy options open to Governments, development agencies and society in tackling the social and economic requirements of massive demographic change.

Rapid social and structural changes associated with development and modernization have strong implications for the well-being of aged populations in terms of social support, housing, health care and other needs. Countries in east and south-east Asia still have time to assess future needs and demographic projections in order to formulate appropriate programmes and policies. There is, however, a clear need to go beyond past efforts aimed at collecting purely descriptive data and to explore ways of building a developmental dimension into research on population ageing. Such an approach is needed to underpin the development of economically feasible models of support as a need to avoid reinventing the wheel in both research and policy in the re-

gion—experiences of other countries can be drawn on and, by implication, intra-regional experiences can be compared.
(Andrews, 1992: 33)

Collecting information, even on policy options, is not sufficient. Information has to be readily available to policy makers and to the public to be useful in shaping a new paradigm for an ageing world. Typically, even where established research has been undertaken on ageing in a locality or region, the availability of the research results is limited. Information that could usefully be provided on an online basis is sometimes held back for inclusion in final research reports for specific clients.

The recent substantial efforts in the region and elsewhere in the world in ageing research should be drawn upon so that unnecessary "reinvention of the wheel" and duplication is avoided. Existing resources and experience, especially that available in the more developed countries of the region, should be fully utilized. Some effective means of monitoring relevant activities and assessing programmes should be established on a region-wide basis, but in such a way that scope for innovation and creativity is maintained. Finally, it will be essential for the success of the efforts that research is shown to be relevant to the decision makers at the national level and that policy formulation, programme development and review considerations benefit from information gained through research efforts. To implement these objectives there is a need to develop effective mechanisms of regional coordination and cooperative effort between the various international agencies involved in ageing research within the region. One way to achieve this would be through a consortium approach to the funding of major regional projects.
(Andrews, 1992:31)

Just as there has to be a shift in the paradigm through which we view ageing, so to in the way we report, communicate and cooperate on the topic. The imposition of inappropriate social policy models on developing countries has been a repeated far too many times. It is important that the same mistake not be made in respect of "gray" social policy. Differences between the circumstances of the developed and developing world that require care be taken; the experience of the western world is not always appropriate and its solutions not always applicable.

Despite academic recognition that the developing world will need a different range of policy measures in its approach to ageing, the number of national studies that have been commissioned is very small. Within the developing world, Asian countries have been the most proactive and fortunate in receiving external resources to conduct research (Phillips, 1992). Few national studies on the circumstances of older persons have been undertaken in developing countries where profound differences exist in culture and region. The absence of national studies precludes the possibility of cross-cultural comparison and thus the evaluation of practical policy options. In many instances cross cultural comparisons are difficult in developing countries because of the scarcity of comparable data. It is often feasible to illustrate certain factors only by reference to a particular country that has assembled the relevant type of data, which is typical of countries where no accurate data exists.

> *In many instances cross cultural comparisons are difficult in developing countries because of the scarcity of comparable data. It is often feasible to illustrate certain factors only by reference to a particular country that has assembled the relevant type of data as typical of a number of countries where no accurate data exists.*
> (Tout, 1989: 26)

Apart from establishing crude demographic outlines, there has been insufficient research into the specific and predictable requirements of ageing in the developed world.

> *There is extensive knowledge in developed countries about proportions of disability and impairment that might be expected among older people (non-industrialized or otherwise), but much less is known about the health status and health problems of elderly people in the developing countries. Indeed, as a rule, it seems that the less developed the country the less is known about health needs, and in particular those of the older segments.*
> (Phillips, 1992: 11-12)

The studies which have been undertaken reveal the significance of poverty as a problem faced by older persons.

> *The report of a cross national seminar to review the results of studies noted that most of the problems of the aged identified are related to poverty and decreasing availability of care for the aged.*
> (Andrews, 1992:26)

Poverty is not of course a necessary consequence of ageing, but a reflection of the current social and resource allocation processes. The predominance of poverty raises the issue of how entitlements for older persons are enhanced at the social policy level. The economic disenfranchisement of sizeable cohorts of contemporary society is not a sustainable option either in the developed or developing world. The next section considers concrete policy options that may provide initial steps for producing the social and economic relations necessary to an ageing world.

3. A NEW PORTFOLIO OF CREATIVE APPROACHES: DEVELOPMENT OPTIONS FOR OLDER PERSONS

> *Returning to our thesis on the nature of human relations, we have postulated that human relations, including those within the family, are based upon reciprocity. If this is true, then one may go a step further and state hypothetically that if the aged person's reciprocal relationships in the family are unbalanced, his role, status and authority within the family will suffer.*
> (Azer and Afifi, 1992:104)

The field is wide open; experts agree that the traditional approaches adopted to address ageing in the developed world are not appropriate for the developing world. Governments are casting around for policy solutions but have focused on the three generational families as the main remedy. Moreover, development agencies have been slow to realize the investment opportunities and requirements that an ageing developing world presents. Participation and empowerment have become part of the seniors' agenda of the developed world, and the signs are increasing that this approach will find an audience in the developing world. Empowering and supporting indigenous support structures appears to be a policy path that matches developing world constraints on resources. In this context, this section will identify a range of creative approaches and solutions that have been adopted in particular localities and that could be expanded and more widely implemented. At the core of the approach is the need to develop new forms of social reciprocity. In a world where older persons have seen this erode between the generations, there is a need to restore, accentuate and reinforce the social and economic resources of the older generations to enable them to participate more strongly in social exchange.

The first key to improving the situation of the older person is to ensure their participation in social and community decision-making. In the same way that care should be taken to ensure that both genders are adequately represented in social and community decision-making, so the interests of older cohorts should enjoy the same representation.

Banking on development

Within the developing world, resources exist that could, with a slight change in perspective, be better harnessed by older persons in meeting their developmental needs. A good starting place is the Nasser Bank in Egypt. The Egyptian Government established the Nasser bank in 1971:

> *...to contribute to the formation of a society based on the principles of sufficiency, justice and solidarity. The bank achieves this goal by offering financial aid to needy persons and by providing loans without interest*

to those who wish to set up small productive projects or who encounter social and or/ economic difficulties. (Azer and Afifi, 1992:71)

The Bank is partly funded by the *zakat* contributions of the Egyptian people. *Zakat* is a traditional Islamic welfare provision whereby individuals allocate a part of their income for the welfare of the community. Through the establishment of the Nasser Bank, the Egyptian Government has enabled individuals to meet their religious *zakat* obligations without being involved in its administration. The Nasser Bank provides enterprise assistance for those with low income, but the number of elderly beneficiaries of *zakat* who receive aid or loans is unknown, as the distribution of beneficiaries is not publicized. Clearly, the model of developing a micro-banking service through the channeling of Islamic religious charity obligations is relevant to the developing world and could be expanded within Egypt and elsewhere.

The development of new communication technologies open up greater prospects for micro-banking. Already in Bangladesh, the Grameen Bank, a leader in the area of women's development banking, has brought new computer-based technologies for banking into the field. Grass roots organization are increasingly able to access leading donors and banking institutions for financial support and assistance, and the new communication channels make monitoring of accounts over a distance a much simpler process than was historically the case. Organizations of older persons need to be proactive in gaining access to these new communication channels. Donors and institutions such as the Nasser Bank could assist older persons groups to gain this access by providing gateways within their own technology provisions. Agencies such as the World Bank and the United States Agency for International Development (USAID), who enjoy the benefits of new technology at their own resident missions in the developing world could provide gateway facilities for bona fide grass roots organization within these missions. Placing a communications facility for grass root organization within a public information centre is a viable option with potentially great benefits.

Another area that the development community could usefully focus upon is the goal of developing more migrant friendly banking services. The importance of remittances from family members working in the developed world to their kin in the developing world has long been recognized. Similarly, within regions and countries the same practices of remittances occur. But the literature also points to the difficulties that many migrants experience in remitting resources to their kin and to the fact that such difficulties often result in a breakdown of this flow from the migrant to the home community. Migration removes many of the human resources necessary to care for the older person. With new technologies and with greater commitment, better migrant banking services could be developed. Easier transfer of resources would serve to retain the link between migrant and community. New technologies can provide a transparency that assures the migrant that the resources did in fact reach their kin. Harnessing migrants' resources for the welfare of older persons in their home community is a viable and important development goal, one which, to date, has received scant policy attention.

In Africa, informal savings associations are a well established feature of social and economic life. These associations operate within a major gap left by the formal banking services, micro-banking. Frequently, women are highly active in these informal savings associations, but have very poor access to formal banking services in Africa and elsewhere. Moreover, these savings associations tend to be the province of the younger generations—the economically active—with women traders featured strongly in their composition. However, recently in Ghana, a new development has taken place, which could be replicated elsewhere. In a particular community in Ghana the older women of Shama came together, and with the help of the NGO HelpAge International, negotiated a loan for the younger generations of the community in order to finance local enterprises. By accessing these resources from an outside world they increased their own power and standing in the community, re-inserted themselves back into the economic life of the community and generated a truly intergenerational banking innovation. The home page of the Centre for Social Policy Studies at the University of Ghana supports the older women of Shama. This pairing of a grass roots and policy institution permits the grass roots organization to piggy back the technology resources of national or international institutions.

Enterprising intergenerational arrangements

The notion of funding enterprise development through inter-generational structures has also been adopted in Malaysia though in a very different form. Families with older members can obtain funding to enable them to set up their own enterprises. The enterprise capital grant enables families to create opportunities for the fuller economic and social participation of older persons, who without doubt provide part of the labour force for the running of such family-based enterprises. This approach can be extended and adopted by development agencies.

Every effort is currently being made to maintain the old person within the community. In cases where relief is sought by an elderly person who is part of an extended family experiencing hardship, steps are taken to improve the family situation. For example, a capital grant can be considered for such a family to allow them to embark on a small scale business such as a food stall where financial constraints have previously precluded such a venture. Assistance towards placement in employment for a member of the family who is in the working age group is another alternative. Fostering of older persons with families willing to take them into care because of long association is also considered as a substitute for institutional care, especially if the individual is in need of some supervision. The foster family is paid by the department, but it is safe to State that the reimbursement is more often a token than full payment for the service rendered.

(Sushama, 1992:177 on Malaysia)

Housing participation

Another innovative development emerging from Malaysia is the concept of building rural homes for the elderly. The homes vary from two to 20 persons in size. Their construction is financed by the Central Welfare Council, and the labour for their construction is provided by the community. This scheme has distinct advantages: older persons remain within the community they know—they are ageing in place; the community becomes directly involved in the provision of accommodation without overly stretching its resources; and the State benefits from sustainable provision of facilities at a minimal cost. Kin are clearly involved in the provision of community labour, but those without kin can still be provided for under such a scheme. The division and sharing of responsibility evidenced in Malaysia's rural homes for older persons could be replicated elsewhere.

In Malaysia, the intergenerational element of rural housing design is provided by the labour of the younger generations within the community. In urban Hungary, a different intergenerational arrangement has emerged. In order to obtain lodging within the Headstart public housing programme for youths in Hungary, youth had to agree to share accommodations with an elderly person (Sundstrom, 1994). Twinning youths with older persons, most especially where older persons have no kin, could be an effective housing strategy in developing countries, especially where there are high levels of rural-urban migration. From a developing country perspective, an older person can be a very useful resource in ensuring the security of the home—a domestic anchor (Grieco, Apt and Turner, 1996)—and the younger person has both greater mobility and employability with which to secure household income.

The Hungarian arrangement is unusual in that the intergenerational residential relationship is not based on kinship. The key experiments in intergenerational residential design are those of Singapore and Hong Kong where special provision has been made to support and consolidate the inter-generational family (Phillips, 1992). Provisions include the construction of adjacent apartments for the nuclear family and older generations in each

housing project. Establishing intergenerational protocols for housing allocation and infrastructure sends a message to society that responsibilities can be met. Although much of the developing world does not enjoy the public housing resources of Singapore or Hong Kong, there are lessons to be learned from these pioneers.

Priority schemes for the allocation of public housing units to families with elderly members, units for single elderly persons in public housing, shared flats in public housing for unrelated elderly persons and compassionate rehousing...To encourage families to look after their elderly relatives at home, a priority scheme for families with an elderly member was introduced in late 1982. Families with one or more elderly members were allocated housing one year ahead of their normal waiting time (this incentive was increased to 2 years in 1990 - general waiting time is 7 years). By 1991 some 5,500 families had benefited from this scheme which indicates a fair degree of success....Since 1990 a new application scheme has allowed young families to apply with their elderly parents or dependent relatives for separate flats in the same public housing blocks in new towns.

(Phillips, 1992: 54)

Most of the policy attention has been on the inter-generational characteristics of these pioneer activities. There are some same age mutual support features of Hong Kong's housing policies, however, which should claim our attention.

The Housing Authority has another priority scheme under which elderly couples or single elderly persons applying in groups of two or more will be allocated public housing within two years. This enables unrelated elderly folk to join together to apply for public housing units. A group tenancy agreement can be taken out for what would normally be a family flat, and tenants can subdivide it themselves according to normal Housing Department regulations. This scheme was started in 1980 because at that time there were no specific units being set aside for single elderly people.
(Phillips, 1992: 54)

The suggestion implies a default arrangement within the social provision of housing to "catch" those older persons who did not have families. However there is a case to be made for older persons' group tenancies becoming an established feature of housing policy. These arrangements enable mutual support and have been recognized as beneficial within the industrial world.

In Copenhagen a group of old women who wanted to live together and help one another succeeded in obtaining their own apartments grouped around a central stairway with a common room on the ground floor

where they meet cook and eat together.
(Tinker, 1994: 60)

This Danish example brings up a topic which has had little airing in the development literature, that of the need for the active participation of older people in their own housing design. Within the industrial world, there is growing recognition of the need to preserve the autonomy of older persons in the design of homes and their domestic equipment. World Wide Web pages catalogue available designs and home developers are beginning to experience pressure to design with these lifetime residence requirements in mind. Correspondingly, older people have become involved in decisions regarding housing design; a process already well advanced in Canada.

The involvement of Canadian older people in housing is an example where a group of people assume that they will be consulted and have set up mechanisms for this.
(Tinker, 1994:59)

That Denmark and Canada have recognized the importance of involving older persons in housing design raises the issue of whether their development agencies abroad operate with the same standards. Ageing is a global issue and there needs to be a carry over from policy development in the industrial world to the developing world. This is not to say that exactly the same measures are required but rather to recognize that the processes of participation that are deemed appropriate and healthy for the older persons of the first world have their place in the third.

Volunteer labour: a new social resource

Older persons from the developed world very often choose to live in separate households from their kin, whilst simultaneously living close to them and participating in intergenerational activities and organization. Mutual support within the same age group and intergenerational living are not either/or policy options, for both are necessary; their presence in an older person's life makes each more sustainable.

In Brisbane, Australia, older women were involved in a volunteer educator's project where they imparted forgotten skills to school children. This project had considerable benefits for these women in terms of their sense of worthiness, higher self esteem and sense of well-being, although changes in social network membership or health status were not reflected. Interestingly, the evaluation of this project did not examine the impact of participation in the forgotten skills project on the children involved. Important questions were not addressed, including: how was their view of older people affected by the experience; were there clear educational benefits emerging out of the programme; and, did the presence of volunteers reduce teacher stress. Within the project, it was discovered that women volunteers experienced considerable pressure to perform a standby kinship function (caring for children at short notice when a daughter's schedule changed). This has a bearing on older women's willingness and ability to participate in volunteer activity.

In this project the school personnel responded well to learning more about the lives of older women and were able to change their structures to accommodate and respect the needs of older women.
(Setterlund and Abbott, 1996)

Clubbing together

The new paradigm of ageing moves older persons in the direction of providing mutual support and services to each other rather than as predominately receivers of services. The focus is moving towards self help and mutual help as opposed to reliance on paid staff to perform functions that the old can adequately perform themselves; if not as individuals then as a social group. Older volunteer groups are already a feature of the developed world as the Australian example shows, and will increasingly be a feature of the developing world as they experience growth in their older populations. There are signs from the developing world that the social infrastructure necessary for the development of such mutual support is emerging.

Egyptian clubs for the aged: *In 1977, the Ministry of Social Affairs set up five clubs in four governates with a grant from the American Government. Later the Nasser Bank provided funds for setting up 25 more clubs. There are 44 clubs in 25 governates with 100 to 200 members each.... Fathia Ali, a widow who lives alone and enjoys economic independence, was persuaded by a friend to join a club for the aged. She goes regularly twice a week to meet friends. The club offers various services: it organizes seaside trips, provides medical examinations for a modest fee, has a lounge with a television set and offers possibilities for other activities, such as a savings club to offer assistance to members in times of financial need. Fathia Ali relates that because of the existence of a play school nearby, some of the male members participate in teaching the children and amusing them with anecdotes. This gives a sense of satisfaction.*
(Azer and Afifi, 1992: 75-76)

In Bolivia: *The National Committee was involved in setting up a Grandparents Club and project for multiple activity centres for elderly persons providing the circumstances for mutual support.*
(United Nations, 1991)

In Malaysia: *Another development worthy of note is the establishment of clubs for senior citizens, which began in the early to mid 1980s. They are active in the larger towns throughout the country. The largest has approxi-*

mately 750 members and the membership is now frozen in this particular club. The majority of those who join are healthy and vigorous. The focus of interest is mainly directed towards health and recreational activities, although a caring element is integrated through services to other elderly people in the community.
(Sushama, 1992:181)

Three issues are raised with regards to mutual support clubs: over segregating older persons from other parts of the society; the need to develop mixed function facilities for older persons so that the older person can work, play or rest within the same set of facilities; and ensuring that clubs are designed in such a way that older persons want to join them. Singapore has had real problems attracting a membership for its government-sponsored older person clubs. Clubs can be used as bases for guaranteeing employment opportunities and loan facilities; pooling of effort by a group of older persons provides each individual with a greater level of certainty and flexibility. Development agencies should research the prospects of providing development resources through such forms of community association.

Religious order

In terms of life time participation, the most effective public counterpart of the private three generational structures—the family—is that of religion. It has been widely recognized that for many older persons in developing societies, religion is a key activity; the devoutness of the old is frequently noted.

For many a retired person, religious practice is a compensatory activity: the daily five prayers fill their otherwise long, tedious days. For some of the aged, each of the five prayers marks the time of day and all of their activities are organized around these times; thus a new daily routine is created after retirement...Hassan Abdel Moteleb describes his daily routine: he wakes before dawn prayers, goes to the mosque, returns home for breakfast, goes back to bed until 10 a.m., then sits in front of the house to talk to neighbours and passers by until midday prayers. After lunch he talks to the family or does an odd job in the house until afternoon prayers. This is followed by a visit of one of his children or a neighbour. After evening prayers in the mosque, he often attends an assembly organized by the Hamdia Shazlia religious group. Then he goes to bed.
(Azer and Afifi, 1992:77)

Devoutness provides a schedule to life for many older persons when many of the other social functions have been stripped away—spirituality and piety remain respectable social goals. Praying for the younger generation is a form of social exchange and one that has been greatly

valued at many times in many societies. Religion not only provides a social function for the older person but it also provides them with a network of friends and fellow worshippers and a guaranteed social timetable. Lack of a schedule is psychologically disorientating for individuals whether they are old or young. Religious institutions provide a schedule for older persons that alleviates the disorientation that can occur with the loss of the economic function. In terms of development projects and operations, it is important to ensure that these indigenous scheduling arrangements are not fundamentally disrupted.

An agenda for action

From this review, it is already clear that best practices exist which can be adopted—practices that move us beyond a simple reliance on either the family or the State in the development of new social relationships that are necessary for an ageing world. Part of a creative approach must be to find ways of opening new communication and dissemination channels. The Japanese Government, for example, is considering the possibility of using Post Office staff to help service the needs of older persons. Postal workers would simultaneously be care givers and mail deliverers. This concept of a dual role could be adopted in the developing world with the assistance of agricultural or health extension workers. Clearly the time has arrived for the development of a clearing house of best practice as it affects older persons.

4. THE GROWING POLITICAL POWER OF OLDER PERSONS: DEVELOPING POLITICAL MUSCLE

The ageing of populations is producing a new political dynamic which can and should be harnessed to produce a better quality of life for the older person. The growing numbers and proportion of older persons will increasingly guarantee them electoral power if they are well organized. The electoral power of older persons will assist in ensuring that older persons are consulted at the more local and micro-levels of decision-making. The automatic representation of older persons in decision-making on mainstream issues has not yet occurred, but in some developed countries such as Canada, older persons' interests are being strongly integrated into the political process.

Canada: newly established Minister of State (seniors). *The Minister's mandate is to communicate with seniors and the public, to focus public discussion on issues of concern to older Canadians and to advise the Government of Canada on how to improve the federal programmes to make them more responsive to the real needs of older Canadians.*
(United Nations, 1991: 26)

This governmental recognition is itself a result of the lobbying activities of seniors for better recognition within the political and social process. It is a virtuous spiral. Lobbying for recognition brings about older persons' visibility both to others and to one another.

> *Yhetta Gold, speaking on behalf of the Canadian seniors network, argues that Governments must insist that where issues of concern to seniors are being discussed, seniors will play an integral part in the discussion and decision processes.*
(Tinker, 1994; 59)

Visibility solicits further membership to the ranks of older persons, which promotes further recognition and inclusion in decision- making. Promoting gray power is itself a participatory and empowering process. Although participation produces great benefits, it is not a free good. Those involved in the early stages of promoting gray power clearly pay the greater costs. Lobbying and financing the research that supports the cause costs both time and money, but the greater the numbers participating, the lower the individual cost. These matters seem self evident, but in the case of the developed world, there were sufficient numbers of older people with disposable resources to permit the emergence of gray power. For the developing world, however, it is clear that a significant part of the resources needed to achieve the initial momentum for gray power must come from outside.

There are some structures which can and have been used to place ageing on the development agenda. With the International Plan of Action on Ageing, adopted by the World Assembly on Ageing in 1982—the benchmark event in the initial recognition of the imminence of an ageing world—United Nations agencies have been actively engaged on the issue, working to promote national committees on ageing. Seventy national committees were formed in 1982; there are now close to 100, many of these are in developing countries. Evaluation of the performance of these committees, as well as cross-country links appear to be relatively weak. In addition, there is little to suggest that the majority of countries have taken a participatory approach to ageing. The old gerontological models of the need for care and assistance rather than the new models of empowerment seem to be in play. There are a few notable exceptions where new technologies have enabled the increased vocalness of the older generations. The predominant view is that whilst awareness of ageing has been increased, concrete action has still to take place.

Awareness that participation is a fundamental requirement of effectively addressing ageing has largely been absent up until now. While local schemes focus on action against learned helplessness, these will have little success if social resources are not reorganized to support the full participation of older persons. Both national and international agencies have to do a better job of making information on resources for mutual support available. It would be interesting, for example, to know how many grass roots organizations are aware of the United Nations Trust Fund for Ageing. The tendency to put resources in the hands of large administrators rather than to make use of new technologies to reach out to grassroots organizations, is prevalent.

> *National coordinating mechanisms are uniquely positioned to tap the reservoir of international development aid, including the United Nations Trust Fund for Ageing, which supports catalytic and innovative projects in such areas as policy formulation and self help activities.*
(United Nations, 1991)

Social theory (Scott, 1990) stresses the importance of creating venues, forums and circumstances where the marginalized can develop their own discourse and negotiate with the conventionally more powerful interests in a society. Older persons in the industrial world have created such a venue in cyberspace. In the developing world, the discourse will largely have to be created within the context of more traditional arrangements such as community associations, local societies and national NGOs. However, even here there is space for the incorporation of new technologies. Video technologies can be used by older persons, with some technical support from donors and policy agencies, to develop authentic advocacy materials. These can be readily disseminated and can serve to amplify messages by incorporation on national television or radio.

As Ping Kwong Kam (1996) noted:

> *Elderly services need to promote elderly peoples political consciousness and help them learn how to relate to politicians and develop their ability to counteract the manipulation of political parties.*

Donors and elderly services also need to promote the utilization of appropriate new technologies vis-à-vis the use of social resources. The assumption is sometimes made that new technologies are the province of the rich and have no place in social provision for the poor. Accepting this assumption is a certain path to creating a widening divergence between the political prospects of the poor and the rich. The policy focus must be on adjusting the organizational arrangements around new technologies so that the poor, and those who serve them, can indeed have access. Access to new technologies can provide both detailed information on medical conditions and treatments for those who serve the needs of an ageing world. Moreover, it can simultaneously provide inhabitants of the developing world with an outlook on arrangements elsewhere, as an alternative way of doing things that is likely to furnish the call for improvement.

Grey power has clearly arrived in the developed world; its arrival is still awaited in the developing world. The signs are there of an awakening, but better systematization of information is necessary both at the technical and political levels. The use of the internet, the creation of dedicated development and web sites for older people and the attraction of sponsorship for grass roots organizations through these new technical forms are all important in development operations that commence from the active participation of older persons in the developing world.

5. TIME TO RETHINK SOCIAL RELATIONSHIPS

The urgency of rethinking inter-generational social relationships in the third world in order to meet the challenges of ageing societies must be recognized. The traditional extended family is breaking down, yet Governments are relying on the family as the key social structure upon which ageing policy is to be based. A key area for policy research must be the ways in which the movement from three to four and five generational demographies will affect the balance of reciprocity within the intergenerational family. Recognizing that the family is likely to experience considerable strain under this expanded generational demography, attention must be given to the development of same age mutual support institutions that can share the responsibilities for the full participation of older persons within the family. Assuming that these structures will automatically appear or that the interaction between family and mutual support institutions will evolve naturally is to ignore the evidence of history. There is need for clear social policy thinking about, and a visible investment of, social resources in the development of appropriate social relationships for the new demographic reality facing the world.

One feature of the new demographic reality will be expanded senior power. This has already taken place in the most developed countries and signs of other societies following the same path are beginning to occur. Amongst older people the demand for active participation in social and political decision-making has already begun and the electoral weight of seniors will increasingly ensure that this demand is met. These demands will increasingly begin to affect the way in which the mainstream environment is designed so as to permit the full participation of older persons. Technology has played a major role in the articulation of seniors demands within the industrial world and has a role to play in creating an awareness of the problems and capacities of older persons in the developing world. Neither the provision of services for older persons nor their participation in the design of development projects has occurred on any sizeable scale within the developing world. However, the ageing of the developing world will undoubtedly bring ageing onto the development agenda in the near future. It is important that this not simply be seen in terms of the economic costs of ageing, but rather in terms of the development of new social relationships. There is indeed considerable scope for incorporating older persons in development goals rather than simply viewing the existence of large numbers of older persons as a constraint on development.

To conclude, there are three main requirements in rethinking social relationships for an ageing world: integrated policy research must be undertaken, and in the very near future; the social and physical infrastructure must be put in place for an ageing world; and finally, thought must be given to the distinctive sociability needs of older persons in the context of large amounts of unscheduled time.

We have been decidedly innovative in our approach in order to combat and balance out the over simplistic focus of the literature on the economic costs of ageing. Economic costs are the costs within a particular social structure. A change in structure will change the profile of costs. A truly intergenerational society would see lowered economic costs associated with an ageing demography. In the words of a 68-year-old female American senior who has offset many of the effects of Parkinson's through the use of a computer:

I feel like I'm with it and connecting with the present and the future.

REFERENCES

Andrews, G., "Research directions in the region: past, present and future", in *Ageing in east and south-east Asia*, Edited by David R. Phillips, London, Edward Arnold, 1992.

Apt, N.A., *Coping with old age in a changing Africa*, Avebury; Aldershot, 1995.

Apt, N.A. and Grieco, M.S., "Urbanization, caring for elderly people and the changing African family: the challenges to social policy "*International Social Security Review*, Vol. 47. 3, 1994.

Apt, N.A., Koomson, J., Williams, N. and Grieco, M., "Family, finance and doorstep trading: the social and economic well-being of elderly Ghanaian female traders", *Southern African Journal of Gerontology*, vol. 4 (2), 1994.

Adel Azer and Elham Afifi, *Social support systems for the aged in Egypt*, United Nations University Press, 1992.

Axhausen, K. and Grieco, M.S, "The older driver: emergent trends in the European policy environment". VTI report 1991.

Bulmer, M., *The social basis of community care*. London, Allen and Unwin, 1987.

Cheung, P. and Vasoo, S., "Ageing population in Singapore : a case study", in *Ageing in east and south-east Asia*, Edited by David R. Phillips. London, Edward Arnold, 1992.

Chen, A.J. and Jones, G., *Ageing in ASEAN: its socio-economic consequences*, Institute of South East Asian Studies, Singapore, 1989.

Chi, I. and Lee, J.J., *A health survey of the elderly in Hong Kong*, Department of Social Work and Social Administration, University of Hong Kong, research paper, No 14, 1989.

Chow, N., "Hong Kong: Community care for elderly people" in *Ageing in east and south-east Asia*, Edited by David R. Phillips, London, Edward Arnold, 1992.

Grieco, M.S., "Breaking the ice: the contribution of new transport information technologies to improving the quality of life of the elderly in a cold climate"; report commissioned by the Prefecture of Niigata, Japan, 1992.

Grieco, M.S., "Older people's role in development", in *In spite of poverty: The older population builds towards its future*, American Association of Retired Persons, Washington, D.C., 1996.

Grieco, M.S., Apt, N.A. and Turner, J., *At Christmas and on rainy days: transport, travel and the female traders of Accra*, Avebury, Aldershot, 1996.

Hashimoto, A., "Ageing in Japan.", in *Ageing in east and south-east Asia*, edited by David R. Phillips, London, Edward Arnold, 1992.

Hong Kong Government, *Report of the Working Group on Care for the Elderly*, Hong Kong, Government Printer, 1994.

Ping Kwong Kam, "Empowering elderly people: a community work approach", *Community Development Journal*, Vol 31. No. 3, 1996.

McCallum, J., *The dynamics of community involvement in old age: the syndrome of underuse*, National Centre for Epidemiology and Population Health, Australian National University, Australia, 1989.

OECD, *Caring for frail elderly people: new directions in care*, Paris: Organization for Economic Cooperation and Development (OECD), Social Policy Studies no. 14, 1994.

Open Management Software Incorporated, Senior Citizen Computer Literacy Programme, Too old for computers? *World Wide Web, 1996.*

Phillips, D., "East and south east asia: issues of ageing in the region." In *Ageing in east and south-east Asia*, edited by David R. Phillips. London, Edward Arnold, 1992.

Phillips, D., "Hong Kong: Demographic and epidemiological change and social care for elderly people", *Ageing in east and south-east Asia*. Edited by David R. Phillips. London, Edward Arnold, 1992.

Scott, J.C., *Domination and the arts of resistance*, New Haven, Yale, 1990.

Setterlund, D. and Abbott, J., "Older women participating in the community: pathways and barriers", *Community Development Journal*, Vol. 30, No. 3, 1996.

Strietland, P.H., "Mutual support arrangements among the poor in South Asia", *Community Development Journal*, Vol.31, No. 4, 1996.

Sushama, P.C., "Health and welfare: services for elderly people in Malaysia", in *Ageing in east and south-east Asia*, edited by David R. Phillips, London, Edward Arnold , 1992.

Thomas, D., *The making of franchisal development*, London, Allen and Unwin, 1983.

Tout, K., *Ageing in developing countries*. OUP for Helpage: Oxford, 1989.

United Nations, 1991, *Profiles of national coordinating mechanisms on ageing*. United Nations Office at Vienna, Centre for Social Development and Humanitarian Affairs, United Nations, New York, 1991.

World Bank, *Averting the old age crisis*. World Bank, Washington D.C., 1994.

III. AGEING OF RURAL POPULATIONS IN SOUTH-EAST AND EAST ASIA*

*Ronald Skeldon***

1999 was the United Nations International Year of Older Persons. As part of the Food and Agriculture Organization of the United Nations contribution to the year it was thought that it would be of interest to focus on the ageing of rural populations in a region where this process was rapidly advancing. Furthermore, ageing is not only of interest per se, but is important in relation to the changes in agriculture in the countries covered.

BACKGROUND

The ageing of human populations has emerged as one of the most significant and universal demographic processes as we move into the twenty-first century. By the year 2000, almost one in ten individuals in the world will be aged 60 years or over, but considering the more developed countries only, that proportion will jump to virtually one in every five persons.[1] The implications of having such a large proportion of the populations above the traditional age of retirement are not yet fully understood. Although the proportion of older people is clearly highest in the more developed parts of the world, and hence in those areas most financially capable of supporting them, in terms of absolute numbers there are more elderly people in the developing world simply because that is where the bulk of the world's population is to be found. By 2000, it is estimated that there will be 229.5 million people 60 years of age and over in the more developed regions of the world compared with 373.3 million in the less developed regions.

The proportion in this category for East and South-east Asia in 2000 are estimated to be 11 and 7.2 per cent, respectively, up from 7.3 and 5.3 per cent in 1960. These relatively small increases over 40 years in percentage terms mask substantial increases in absolute numbers, with an increase from 60 million in east Asia in 1960 to 163.8 million in 2000, and from 12 to 37 million in south-east Asia.

The principal reason for this increase in the proportion of older people in the world has been the sustained decline in fertility over the last 30 to 40 years. The fact that each cohort of women has fewer children does not initially give rise to fewer children as a whole because, given prior rapid rates of population growth, there are more women entering reproductive age groups. Put another way, more women in the reproductive age groups can give rise to greater numbers of total births, even when each one of them is having fewer children than their mothers. However, when sustained over the medium-term, declining fertility must give rise to fewer births, decreasing the size of the younger cohorts and bringing about the increasing proportion of older age groups. When combined with declining mortality at older ages giving increased survivorship to older populations, the result is a marked ageing of the human population.

Countries in east and south-east Asia have witnessed some of the most dramatic declines in fertility among all countries over this period as shown in table I. By the late 1990s, not one area in east Asia (excluding Mongolia) had a total fertility rate (a period measure defined as the number of children the average woman would be expected to have had by the end of her reproductive life) above the replacement level of 2.1. Fertility rates in south-east Asia were significantly higher, with the poorest countries of the former Indo-China, the Lao People's Democratic Republic, and Cambodia showing

---

*The paper covers the countries of east and south east Asia, excluding the Democratic People's Republic of Korea, Mongolia and Taiwan, Province of China. Hong Kong, China , and Singapore are only briefly considered, as their rural populations are negligible.

** Ronald Skeldon is an independent consultant and Adjunct Professor at the Institute for Population and Social Research, Mahidol University, Thailand. The comments of Jacques du Guerny, David Iaquinta, Guillaume Lanly and Alain Marcoux on an earlier draft of this paper are gratefully acknowledged.

[1] Unless otherwise stated, all numbers and proportions for global and regional populations come from the medium variant estimates as published in United Nations, *The Sex and Age Distributions of the World Populations 1996 revision*, New York, Department of Economic and Social Affairs, Population Division, ST/ESA/SER.A/162, 1997. This paper follows the definition of the elderly population as adopted by the United Nations: the population 60 years of age and older.

the highest fertility and the larger countries of south-east Asia more moderate levels.

The difference in proportion of elderly populations between east and south-east Asia observed earlier is largely explained by these patterns of fertility, and inter-country differences in the proportion of elderly population can be seen largely in terms of the date of the onset of fertility decline (compare tables I and II). The pattern for Japan is unique among the countries under consideration. It last saw a total fertility rate of over 5 children per woman in the mid-1920s and had essentially reached below-replacement-fertility by the late 1950s, a time when fertility was generally peaking in the other economies in the region.

With the exception of the poorest countries of the region of the former Indo-China, a decline in fertility was under way throughout the region from the first half of the 1960s, being most marked in Singapore, followed about five years later by Hong Kong and the Republic of Korea, and five years after that by China and Thailand. This highly generalized pattern obscures a host of intra-country variations. The reasons accounting for the onset and magnitude of the fertility declines are too complex to summarize here and have been examined at length elsewhere. Suffice it to say here that government policy was a not insignificant factor among the matrix of explanatory variables.

Throughout the region under consideration, the proportion of the population that was aged 60 years and older in 1960 was less than 10 per cent of the total population, and typically between 4 and 6 per cent (table II). By the mid-1970s, only in Japan had that proportion risen to over 10 per cent of the total population. For several countries in the region that proportion had even declined somewhat over the 15 years from 1960, reflecting the impact of the high fertility of the time. The 15-year period from 1975 saw an increase in the proportion of the elderly populations of all countries in the region, with that increase being most marked in those areas where fertility decline had either been earliest or most rapid and pronounced. Only in Japan, however, had the numbers of elderly approached one in five individuals in the population, and for the majority of the countries in the region the numbers were still fewer than one in ten members of the respective populations in 1990. The ageing of the populations of the east and south-east Asian region is thus recent and, with the exception of Japan, had yet to make a truly major impact on the age structure of the populations, until 1990 at least. This overall trend, as we will see, hides significant differences between rural and urban sectors.

The basic patterns of fertility decline, of changing demographic structure and of the ageing of the populations, as described above, are well developed in the existing literature. A substantial literature, too, already

exists on the ageing of Asian populations, as documented by United Nations studies in 1991, 1993, 1994, 1996 and 1997; Knodel and Debavalya (1992; 1997); Phillips (1992); and Chen and Jones (1989) (see references). Most of these articles focus primarily, and very correctly, on the demographics of the process or on the availability of family support systems or private or public welfare provision for the elderly. While recognizing that significant intra-country variation by region and by urban and rural sector exists, the literature has relatively little to say about sub-national differences in the pattern of ageing or on the consequences of ageing for particular subregions or sectors. An exception is the demographic description of ageing on the rural sector of developing countries by Marcoux (1994). This paper will continue that study, but focus on the differential patterns and consequences of ageing for the rural sector in countries of east and south-east Asia, and particularly upon the role of migration in modifying the effects of changes in fertility and mortality.

TWO SCENARIOS

At the risk of overgeneralization, the interpretations of the impact of migration on rural areas can be broadly divided into two types. The first would see the migration as essential for development and its impact as positive. Among these approaches are the neo-classical, two-sector models of urbanization, migration and development, which saw excess population removed from a labour-surplus rural economy of a developing country through migration to a labour-deficit urban sector. Once a critical threshold had been reached and the marginal productivity of labour in the rural sector ceased to be zero, real wages in that sector would rise, eventually to reach those of the urban sector. Migration from the rural sector to the urban sector would then slow to reach a new equilibrium. This idealized model seldom, if ever, described the real experience of developing countries and has been the subject of modification and refinement. The critical point is that, in this scenario, migration is generally seen to be positive for development and, presumably, the ageing rural populations would eventually benefit from the movement of people from rural to urban sectors.

The above simple model ignores the selective nature of migration, that it is the youngest and the brightest who tend to leave the villages for the towns, albeit with spatial and temporal variation in the specific patterns of selectivity. Thus, a second very different interpretation builds in a demographic component. In this scenario, migration not only exacerbates the ageing effects of fertility decline by removing the youthful and most energetic cohorts, but it also removes those with initiative who are most likely to improve the condition of the rural and increasingly elderly poor. In this scenario, migration is negative for development and is likely to lead to the erosion of rural production and a deterioration in the welfare of the elderly village populations. The exodus of the youthful cohorts ultimately reduces the capacity of the village to reproduce itself, leading to a stage of decline and depopulation as the remaining elderly population dies off.

These two scenarios are clearly ideal types that try to capture the essence of what is occurring while ignoring the detail. As will become apparent in subsequent discussion, there is an element of truth in both viewpoints, depending upon the development potential of the area concerned and upon the stage of a hypothesized development sequence. That sequence is related to the phases of the demographic transition as reflected in the patterns of fertility decline. However, although all societies are experiencing a transition towards ageing populations, that transition is variable in both its pattern and its impact. Populations with different proportions of elderly will be examined before a more general assessment of an ageing transition model is made in the conclusion.

Before the relative impact of ageing on rural societies at the country level can be attempted, a major difficulty underlying the analysis of the patterns of rural and urban ageing needs to be examined. This difficulty is essentially methodological and goes some way to explaining why the issue of differential rural ageing and the impact of migration have been poorly developed in the literature. The methodological difficulties relate to problems of data availability and to definition.

METHODOLOGICAL ISSUES

Although the majority of countries in the east and south-east Asian region publish data on population by age and sex by sector, there are several important qualifications that have to be borne in mind. The first relates to the well-known issue of the lack of a common definition of rural (or urban) from country to country. Hence, direct comparisons from country to country of proportion of rural population can be deceptive. The changing definitions of urban and rural for a single country over time can also complicate any analysis of sectoral change, and China is a particular case in point in Asia (see Chan 1994; Zhang and Zhao 1998). Nevertheless, despite the definitional difficulties, distinct rural and urban sectors exist in each country. It is not at all clear, however, that distinct rural and urban populations exist. In every census and large-scale survey, respondents are allocated to a rural or urban sector of residence, depending upon rules of enumeration, giving the impression that it is in that sector that they live and work. In reality, there is tremendous interchange of population between the two sectors, not just of long-term ru-

ral-to-urban migration, or the converse, but of a multitude of more short-term movements of human circulation. These migrations are paralleled by flows of goods and money in the form of remittances.

Thus, substantial numbers of those living in the urban sector may return to the villages at weekly, monthly or more long-term intervals and regularly send remittances in cash or kind back to their families in the rural sector. The short-term circulation of people is generally not captured in the majority of censuses or large-scale surveys. Hence, simply comparing the population structure of a rural sector, as derived from such data sources, may give a very misleading impression of the very real dependency relationships that exist across sectors. The problem will be more acute in those countries adopting *de jure* systems of census and survey registration, where the population is enumerated where it "usually lives" and significant numbers are recorded in their places of registration rather than where they normally live. This problem is particularly acute in China but is also present in other countries in south-east Asia that follow a *de jure* census enumeration strategy such as Indonesia, the Philippines and Thailand. A more refined definition of migration adopted in the *National Migration Survey of Thailand*, for example, virtually tripled the proportion of the migrant population of Bangkok from 8 to 22 per cent when the survey results were compared with those of the 1990 census of population (Chamratrithirong et al. 1995 (pages 18-19). Using these different definitions of migrants brought out a difference between the wet and dry season populations of Bangkok, a city of some 6.6 million in 1994, in the order of 10 per cent.

One could perhaps argue that where the population is enumerated at place of registration rather than where it is actually living at "census moment", may give a better impression of commitment to place of enumeration and thus of dependency relationships. That is, the *de jure* system, although omitting a greater proportion of short-term mobility than the *de facto* system of census enumeration, may in fact give a better impression of the "real" structure of the population based in the rural sector. Unfortunately, such a hypothesis must remain not proven at this stage as we do not have the data to test the idea adequately. In the following discussions, the available data on the rural population structure will be used but readers must be aware of the weaknesses inherent in the application of such data. Deficiencies in the data, however, must not be used as an excuse for lack of analysis and, despite their weaknesses, the existing data certainly suffice to allow the broad trends of the impact of migration on rural populations to be drawn out.

RURAL-URBAN DIFFERENCES IN POPULATION STRUCTURE[2]

In all the east and South-east Asian countries for which data exist, the populations of rural areas are older than those of urban areas (table III). It is in Japan and the Republic of Korea, those two most developed countries, with the highest proportions of elderly population, that the greatest differences between the proportions of populations 60 years of age and over in urban and rural sectors are to be found. The Republic of Korea is perhaps an extreme case, with almost one in five of the rural population classified as elderly, compared with only about one in every 14 in the urban population. In the Asian countries under consideration, fertility, while declining overall, as we have seen, is generally higher in the rural than the urban sectors (table IV below). Although the differences in several countries are hardly pronounced, they are enough to suggest that the variations in the sectoral patterns of ageing should, if fertility decline were the only factor and other factors were equal, be in the opposite direction to that observed. Other factors are not equal, however, and migration from rural to urban areas is clearly critical in transferring youthful cohorts from the villages to the cities to generate the observed patterns. Urban areas are made youthful by accretion and rural areas age as residual populations through migration. That this statement requires some qualification will become clearer in the discussion south-east Asia below.

It is also interesting to observe that in several countries where there is little observed difference between urban and rural patterns of ageing, such as China and Viet Nam, the censuses there too severely underestimate the volume of population mobility. In China, census enumeration through the system of household registration tends to omit vast numbers of the "floating" population, perhaps as many as 100 million, who have left their places of registration to look for work in the largest towns. As most of these "floaters" are young adults, the impact of migration upon the age structure of the rural populations of these countries is underestimated in the figures. However, as implied above, the question about the commitment and continued attachment to origin areas by the more short-term migrants becomes a critical issue in the assessment of the impact of migration on rural populations and areas. As we will see below, the volume of remittances sent by the young adults in the towns and cities of Asia to the villages may be an important factor in the continued viability of the rural economies and of the survivorship of the increasingly elderly populations.

Migration can also influence the age structure of rural populations in another way, not simply in terms of the exodus of the young adult cohorts. Return movements of those who have spent several years away, either overseas or in the urban sector, will contribute to the replenishment of older age cohorts and the aggravation of potential problems of supporting older populations in the villages by local sources of labour. Such potential problems, however, must be balanced against any wealth, knowledge or other resources, such as pensions, that they may bring back to the village communities. Return migrants, although older, also have learned skills that may encourage them to invest in small businesses or in land development.

The effects of the changing age structures are clearly reflected in the dependency ratios, or the ratio of the potentially economically active population 15 to 59 years old to those who are assumed to be dependent, or those 0 to 15 and 60 years of age and older. The dependency ratio is primarily a demographic index and it is well recognized that, in the rural areas of developing countries in particular, many of those 60 years of age and older (together with many younger members of those populations) are truly "economically active". This proviso and the accepted close interrelationship between urban and rural sectors apart (through which the urban-based economically active can support the rural-based elderly), the older age and youth dependency ratios for urban and rural sectors give some idea of where the burden of ageing is falling in the countries of the region (table V). Looking at the rural areas, it is clear that Japan and the Republic of Korea are in a class by themselves, with a very high proportion of elderly relative to the numbers of economically active in that sector. There are considerably larger numbers of rural old relative to rural youth in Japan, while the proportion in the Republic of Korea is virtually equal. In all the other countries, the pattern is still one of the large proportion of youthful dependants, and ageing as an economic burden has not yet emerged as a significant issue. As might be expected, overall dependency in the urban areas is considerably lower than in the rural sector except in the cases of Brunei Darussalam and Viet Nam. Excluding Japan, there is also much less variation in the pattern of old age dependency. Thus, ageing as a potential burden is primarily to be found in the rural sectors of the most developed economies of the region.

The ageing of the rural sector also has a gender dimension. That women live longer than men is virtually a universal characteristic of human populations, even if there are certain exceptional areas where this is not the case. All the elderly populations in the countries under consideration, excluding Brunei Darussalam, follow this generalization and have a greater proportion of women, with that trend being most emphasized in the

---

[2]Singapore and the Special Administrative Region of Hong Kong, China are not further considered in this paper because their rural populations are either non-existent or negligible.

populations of highest longevity and greatest ageing, Japan and the Republic of Korea. There are slightly fewer elderly men than elderly women in the rural sector of Japan when compared with the urban sector, while that situation is reversed in the Republic of Korea. The clearest difference, as far as the gender of the elderly population is concerned, is found in Malaysia, the Philippines and Thailand. There, the elderly in the rural sector are much more balanced in terms of sex ratio than are the populations in the urban sector, which are much more female-dominant. This difference may be due to a greater incidence of return of male rural-to-urban migrants to the rural sector, although why this pattern should not also be evident for Indonesia, where the phenomenon of male retirement migration back to the villages has been identified as being important (Hugo 1992: 216), is not clear from the data presented here (table VI).

An alternative scenario would involve differential migration of the elderly women themselves. In Indonesia the data suggest a lower propensity for older women to migrate to towns than in Malaysia, the Philippines or Thailand. The migration of the elderly is always going to affect a very small minority of total movers but some attention may need to be given to the relative provision of traditional support services for elderly women in south-east Asian countries, where, upon the death of their spouse, elderly women may have to seek support from urban-based family in some of these countries. More positively, grandmothers can also provide babysitting and other domestic services for their sons and daughters in town that would allow the adult female members to pursue urban employment. This situation might apply particularly where fertility decline has been marked and there are few children to look after younger siblings. Perhaps significantly, fertility in the major urban areas of Malaysia, the Philippines and Thailand is lower than in Indonesia. Hence, the differential migration of elderly women may indeed be a factor in explaining the observed differences and their migration and social situation warrant further study.

Clearly, the impact of ageing in the rural sector is not going to be evenly spread, either within the region or within any particular rural sector in any single country. We will now consider the impact of ageing on the rural populations of the east and south-east Asian region, looking first at the countries where ageing is most pronounced and then moving on to those areas where the impacts are as yet more potential than real. Particular attention will be given to the situation in the Republic of Korea and in Thailand.

Advanced ageing: cases from north-east Asia

By the mid-1990s in the Republic of Korea, the proportion of the population in the rural sector that was elderly was virtually one in five compared with only one in ten for the population as a whole. If we consider the current difference between the ageing in rural areas and that for the total population from another point of view, the population as a whole of the Republic of Korea is not projected to reach a proportion of one in five elderly population until around the year 2017. Thus, in terms of ageing, the rural population is some 20 years ahead of the population as a whole. The rapid increase in the proportion of the elderly in the rural sector is recent. In 1975, only 8.5 per cent of the rural population was aged 60 years of age or older; this figure rose to 10 per cent in 1980 and 12.4 per cent in 1985 before reaching 17.9 per cent in 1995 (United Nations 1993, table I; United Nations 1998).

The Republic of Korea, as one of the "tiger" economies of Asia, is atypical of the region as a whole. Although it experienced a rapid decline in fertility in common with several countries of the region, this was accompanied by a dramatic shift in population from rural to urban areas. In 1960, the Republic of Korea was still primarily rural, with only 28 per cent of its population classified as living in urban areas. By 1975, this proportion had increased to 48 per cent and, within another 20 years, to over 78 per cent. While most of the rapid growth in the cities of Asia could still be attributed to rapid rates of natural increase, in the Republic of Korea, well over half of that growth during the years of most rapid urbanization could be attributed to net rural-to-urban migration. For example, 60.5 per cent of urban growth in the Republic of Korea between 1960 and 1970 could be attributed to net migration and reclassification, the highest for all countries in Asia for which data were available except for Japan (United Nations 1980). The comparable figures for the decades of the 1970s and 1980s were 56.3 and 55 per cent respectively (data cited in Skeldon 1998: 9). Young adults were being transferred from the rural to the urban sector of the Republic of Korea faster and in larger numbers than in almost any other country in the Asian region, clearly contributing to the rapid ageing of the rural population in that country. The rural population has experienced absolute declines in population since the mid-1960s.

The critical questions revolve around the implications that this population transfer out of the rural population, and the consequent ageing of that population, have had for the rural population, as well as for the population as a whole. Did the loss of such a large part of the rural labour force have negative implications for the agricultural economy and society at a time when the

Republic of Korea was experiencing a transition from an agrarian to an industrial society? The evidence suggests otherwise. Overall grain production has steadily increased over the last 20 years and, although rice production has fluctuated and has been on a downward path since the early 1990s, it has consistently exceeded demand (table VII). Government policies to ensure self-sufficiency have been an important factor in the persistence of rice production and, since the 1970s, grain prices were raised to improve farm incomes and to stimulate production (Mason et al. 1980: 234). Gross agricultural income increased more than tenfold between 1977 and 1996.

In June 1996, the Government introduced a comprehensive plan to maintain the cultivation of rice in an increasingly high labour-cost economy. Part of the package included measures to ensure a specific income level for older farmers nearing retirement. Those farmers 65 years of age and older who wished to retire from farming and who sold their paddy land to households actively engaged in rice cultivation would receive an income subsidy of around $322,500 per hectare of paddy land sold. The only stipulation was that the land sold had to have been under rice cultivation for at least three years prior to the sale (see Korea 1997).

Government figures indicate that the total area of cultivated land (including orchards and hill land) declined by about 12 per cent between 1977 and 1996, with the area under paddy rice declining by 9.7 per cent. The farm population, on the other hand, declined by 57 per cent between 1979 and 1996. The decline in rural population was accompanied by a shift in the structure of landholding. Holdings larger than 3 hectares more than doubled in number, from 32,887 in 1976 to 70,353 in 1996, while those smaller than 0.3 hectares declined from 308,775 to 222,744 over the same period. Non-agricultural income increased as a proportion of average farm household income from about 20 per cent in 1976 to around 30 per cent in 1996. FAO data for the Republic of Korea, using different definitions and sources, suggest a 15 per cent decline in arable land between 1980 and 1996, while, at the same time, food production increased by over 20 per cent (see the data in FAO 1998). The consolidation of holdings allowed greater economies of scale, which resulted in improved production.

Thus, in the Republic of Korea, conditions in the rural sector appear to have improved at the same time as the population has aged. Also, no negative impacts can be seen on the overall situation of food security at the national level. As the country industrialized, the agricultural sector was transformed as holdings became larger and more responsive to the needs of an increasingly urban society. The whole relationship between rural-to-urban migration, ageing of rural populations

and changing land tenure requires much further investigation. The Republic of Korea appears to support the case that the exodus of surplus rural population to the cities generates improved standards of living in both rural and urban sectors. Government policy has also been a significant factor in ensuring continued food security in the rural sector throughout the transition in age structure of the rural labour force.

This is not to say, of course, that conditions improved because rural populations have aged, but that the improvements occurred despite the ageing. Almost certainly, localized pockets of deprivation came about because of the ageing of rural populations and the exodus of the younger most productive members of those populations. Rural depopulation is part of the transition towards an urban society and outmigration can lead to the point where a community loses its reproductive capacity and only the elderly are left, eventually to die off and leave a landscape of deserted villages and abandoned fields. Such a process tends to occur in more marginal environments where commercial agriculture is not viable as, for example, in the *kaso*, or severely depopulating districts in Japan—to be considered below—or in the more isolated parts of the New Territories of Hong Kong, China.

Incipient ageing: cases from south-east and east Asia

The proportion of elderly in the rural sector of Thailand in 1990, at around 8 per cent, was similar to that for the rural sector of the Republic of Korea in 1975. That proportion in Thailand had risen from 6 per cent in 1980. The persistent decline in fertility will ensure the continued ageing of the rural population in Thailand although, given the present age structure, it is difficult to see any immediate repercussions of ageing on the rural economy or society of the country. The pattern of ageing, however, can give us some insight into how the process evolves during its early phases. If we compare a map showing the distribution of the elderly population by small geographical area in Thailand with maps of fertility decline, we can see a virtually identical pattern: the areas with the highest proportions of elderly are, with few exceptions, those areas where the decline in fertility began earliest.[3] The largest concentrations of districts with the highest proportions of the elderly are to be found in the central plains and in the north, which are precisely those areas where the decline in fertility began and from which it rapidly extended outwards during the 1970s. The north-east region remains an area of relatively high fertility, and, although it is known

---

[3] Unfortunately, the electronic compilation of this paper did not permit ready reproduction of the relevant maps. The map of the distribution of the elderly can be found in NSO (1994) and those of decline in fertility in ESCAP (1988).

that this region is a major source of migrants to Bangkok, the impact of the movement on the age structure of the places of origin has, as yet, been partly offset by the higher fertility.

Two additional factors must be borne in mind, however. First, there is more migration from the Central Plains to Bangkok than from the north-east, even though that flow is matched to some extent by a significant counterflow (Thailand 1993). Return migration from Bangkok to the central plains may also be of older migrants returning home after finishing their work in the capital city. The age composition of the five-year migration flows into regions of Thailand other than Bangkok, for example, were older than those to Bangkok (Thailand 1993). In the central plains, the impact of migration on the age structure has reinforced the impact of fertility decline, while in the north-east the impact of migration on age structure has been muted by higher fertility. Second, it is likely that, as outlined earlier in this paper, much of the migration out of the north-east in particular is seasonal, or some other form of short- or long-term circulation that is largely unrecorded by large-scale data-recording systems. Thus, the real impact of migration on the age structure of large parts of the rural sector of Thailand may be understated.

A survey in the Mun River basin in the southern part of the north-east revealed that, in 10 of the 11 provinces covered by the survey, 40 per cent or more of the economically active population in every district were migrant workers (Thailand 1995, annex G). While considerable variation existed among the districts, there was an overall bias towards males among the migrant workers from the region, which implied a feminization of agricultural activities as well as an ageing of the labour force. The outmigration allowed some consolidation of landholdings on the better land and abandonment of more marginal holdings. The future rural labour force in the region would be smaller, older and increasingly feminized. Rural development policies hence needed to be adjusted accordingly and the survey envisaged rural depopulation by the 2020 in several parts of the region covered (Thailand 1995, annex G: 39).

There are several aspects of this process that warrant closer examination. Unfortunately, however, many of the data to make such analyses are just not available. The impact of the return migrants upon the nature of the agricultural economy is a critical element of rural transformation and the capital earned, as well as the experience of the wider world gained by villagers, has been fundamental to the spread of commercial agriculture in parts of the Pacific as well as elsewhere (Connell 1985, Long and Roberts 1984). More speculatively, one could argue that ageing rural labour forces might act as a stimulus for the adoption of labour-saving technologies as heads of household become increasingly unwilling or unable to undertake backbreaking agricultural tasks. Thus, there are several dimensions to the impact of ageing on agricultural production. All, however, will depend upon the potential of the local area for the introduction either of commercial agriculture or of new technologies. Such innovation would not be a realistic proposition in isolated, marginal areas.

Much of the present movement in Thailand is of a short-term or temporary nature and the links between destination and origin areas through regular return visits and remittances are likely to be strong. A national migration survey taken in 1994 reported that over 40 per cent of migrants to Bangkok, for example, had sent money back to their home areas (Thailand 1997). In common with migration elsewhere, population movement from villages to towns initially acts as a support for the household economies in origin areas. See, for example, the debates of the impact of migration on villages in France in the late nineteenth and early twentieth centuries (Chatelain 1976). Those households receiving remittances are generally better off than those that do not. Thailand, with its large independent peasantry with access to land (Pasuk and Baker 1995), and its intense circulation between rural and urban sectors, would be unlikely to have yet experienced any negative impacts as a result of the changing age structure of its population. Dependency ratios calculated separately for the rural sector would be deceptive owing to the importance of younger family members, particularly women, based in towns who are an integral part of the rural household economy. Although fertility decline ultimately tends to favour a trend towards smaller nuclear families, there is the other critical dimension of spatially extended families, in which resources in urban as well as rural sectors are incorporated into the peasant household economy. It is only in the later stages, when the migration is increasingly permanent, that depopulation is observed, as we have seen above in the cases of the Republic of Korea and Japan.

Thailand is fortunate to have had sufficient land to allow the extension of an agricultural frontier until fairly recently which has given the peasantry a degree of independence that may not be found in all countries of the region. Movement to escape exploitation by local elites or to search out new resources has been a traditional part of Thai rural life. A detailed discussion of agriculture and the position of the peasantry in Thailand is given in Pasuk and Baker (1995). Unlike the Republic of Korea, the rural population of Thailand is still rising, with the number of agricultural households having increased from 4.7 million in 1983 to 5.1 million in 1992. The area under paddy rice actually decreased over almost the same period from 11.7 million hectares in 1984 to 10.9 million hectares in 1993, while the agricultural GDP grew at between 2.5 and 3.4 per cent per annum through this period. Thus, Thai farmers have shifted to more intensive land-saving technology and to crops that have brought higher income per unit of land (FAO 1996: 4). Where the option of opening up new agricultural land is not available or the adoption of more intensive technologies is not viable, circulation to urban areas becomes an even more important means of ensuring rural food security. I have argued elsewhere that migration, by linking rural and urban economies, acts to alleviate rather than to exacerbate poverty in the rural sector (Skeldon 1997).

One of the dangers, however, is that if and when a downturn affects an economy, as in the current crisis in Asia, the repercussions will very quickly be passed down to the rural sector. Just as the benefits of the incorporation of an additional resource niche in an urban economy support village households, so the loss of that resource may intensify hardship in those same households. For example, families may come to depend upon regular remittances from towns or they may have taken on loans or other commitments that cannot be supported once a family member loses an urban job and has to return to the village.

The case of Thailand is again a useful illustration. Although the share of wealth of the poorest of the poor declined even during the years of rapid growth, the incidence of poverty declined markedly from almost 30 per cent in 1986 to less than 10 per cent in 1994, with the steepest declines in the poorest region, the north-east (Warr 1998: 61-2). That region, as we have seen, has been one of intense human circulation to the major cities and to Bangkok in particular. The rate of economic growth at which poverty levels remain constant has been shown to be at least 6 per cent per annum (Warr 1998: 62); that is, growth rates above that level will tend to reduce the incidence of poverty while those below it will see an increase in poverty. With growth in Thailand forecast to be at least -3.5 per cent in 1998, the implication is that the incidence of poverty may rise to almost 20 per cent by the end of 1998. Tens, if not hundreds, of thousands of retrenched workers, both male and female, have returned to their villages. The ageing of the age structures of the rural sector will thus be reversed, over the short term at least, as greater numbers of people must survive on a spatially concentrated and more limited resource base. The implications of this process for rural food security are not yet evident, but it is clear that the incidence of poverty will rise.

The option of a return to the village is at least open to a certain number of Thai rural-to-urban migrants. In some other countries where rapid demographic growth has persisted to generate a strain on rural resources, this option may not be so viable. Indonesia may be a case in point here. Circulation between city and village has in-

tensified over the last 20 years (Hugo 1997), but rural population densities in Java and Bali are significantly higher than in Thailand and the sudden reincorporation of large numbers of retrenched workers may indeed create problems of food security. Although rice production in Indonesia has trebled at a time when the population increased by three-quarters, that expansion in rice production "has been achieved through increasing inputs other than labour" (Hugo 1997: 227). Given that ageing is not yet a major concern in rural Indonesia, any reversal of that trend may create more problems for food production than would its continuation. The urban informal sector may have to bear the brunt of absorbing the retrenchments in Indonesia.

China, which has followed a rigid policy to restrict the number of births, has the highest proportion of elderly in both urban and rural sectors of all the countries under consideration, except the highly developed economies of Japan and the Republic of Korea. Some 8.7 per cent of the rural population is 60 years of age or older. China is also recorded as having the highest proportion of elderly urban population of east and South-east Asia after Japan. The relatively small difference between urban and rural sectors, however, should not be taken at face value simply because so much migration towards the cities is not recorded. Ageing in the rural sector is thus likely to be more pronounced than the data suggest while, conversely, the urban populations are likely to be more youthful.

It is accepted that there are somewhere between 70 and 100 million floating migrants in China—those whose places of actual residence do not match their places of registration—the majority of whom are young adults. Overall, almost one tenth of China's vast population may be unrecorded migrants, although there will be clear areas of regional concentration. For example, in 1990, the floating population accounted for between 11 and 27.5 per cent of the real population of eight of China's largest cities (data cited in Ma and Xiang 1998: 546). The nature of their linkages with home communities is, as yet, little understood, although it would be surprising if the situation were to be significantly different from that elsewhere in Asia. Millions of workers, laden with the fruits of their labours, return to their home villages every year at Chinese New Year, for example. Thus, again, ageing rural populations are likely to find support in the migration of family members to the urban sector.

Like China, Viet Nam is also facing a recent and rapid increase in the proportion of elderly consequent upon the decline in fertility. Again, like China, much of the increasing domestic migration to the major cities, Hanoi and Ho Chi Minh city, goes unreported in official sources. A survey of migration to Ho Chi Minh City showed that virtually three-quarters of those who

45

had moved to the city after 1991 had done so without officially changing their registration (Anh et al. 1996). They were, in effect, illegal migrants and were still officially in the rural sector, inflating the more youthful *de jure* cohorts of that sector while spending most of their time in the town. Yet again, the linkages between town and village are likely to be maintained through circulation, dampening the economic impact of ageing in the rural sector.

Fertility remains relatively high in Viet Nam, as well as in the Philippines. It has hardly begun to decline in Cambodia and the Lao People's Democratic Republic. Throughout much of south-east Asia, the ageing of the population structures remains a problem of the future which, in terms of food security, pales into insignificance when compared with the current economic and political issues facing the region. The incidence of human circulation throughout the region, whereby the youthful cohorts shift back and forth between town and village, will act to ameliorate the immediate effects of the increasing numbers of elderly in the rural sector. Over the longer term however, and particularly in more marginal environments, the ageing of rural communities does indeed imply significant social and economic problems that require policy intervention. Here, we must return to the most developed economies of north-east Asia, and particularly to that of Japan.

Severely depopulating rural areas: the case of Japan[4]

In Japan, almost two-fifths of "cities, towns and villages" are classified as "*kaso*", or severely depopulating areas, but these account for only 6.3 per cent of the total population. These areas account for virtually half of the land area of the country (figure 1 below). In 1995, 20.5 per cent of Japan's population was aged 60 years and over: for those areas classified as *kaso*, the equivalent figure was 33.2 per cent. In 1975, some 18. per cent of the kaso area populations fell into that elderly group compared with 11.7 per cent for the population as a whole. Data for comparable age groups for earlier periods are not readily available, but taking the elderly as those over 65 years of age as the accepted definition of the elderly in Japan, the differences in the ageing between *kaso* and total population in 1960 is not marked. Only 6.9 per cent of *kaso* districts in 1960 were 65 years of age and over compared with 5.7 per cent for the population as a whole. It is perhaps worth bearing in mind that the proportion of elderly in Japan just 40 years ago is not very different from the proportions of the elderly in most of the countries in east and south-east Asia today.

A critical point in the evolution of the *kaso* areas came in 1987 when the annual number of deaths began to exceed the number of births. The natural increase of the *kaso* areas has gone from -1,409 in that year to -34,939 in 1996. The process had reached a stage where the *kaso* areas had lost their reproductive capacity through the continuous exodus of younger cohorts and they had entered into the last phases of depopulation. By the mid-1990s, too, the volume of population migration had slowed as the populations declined. In 1980, with a total *kaso* population of 9.21 million, there had been an in-migration to these areas of 404,441 and a migration from these areas of 507,346, for a net balance of -102,905. By 1995, with a population of 7.97 million, the annual inflow had been reduced to 272,297 and the outflow to 319,308, for a net balance of -47,011. Thus, there had been a much more rapid decline in population movements than for the population as a whole. The *kaso* populations have become increasingly residual, gradually atrophying through mortality.

Clearly, in a developed and wealthy society such as Japan, national and regional food security are not being threatened by the depopulation of rural areas and small towns, even if these areas do cover half of the land area. The concerns are more over the costs of supplying adequate social infrastructure, clinics, hospices and so on, to isolated areas that have limited revenue-generating potential. *Kaso* areas are primarily in mountainous or other marginal areas and depopulation, as in many parts of Europe, is a logical spatial adjustment of the population to an economy based on industry and, increasingly, services which are located in accessible, highly urbanized areas.

Certainly, overall food production indices in Japan, according to FAO (1998) estimates, have remained fairly constant or declined marginally over the last decade, while the arable area declined by 8 per cent between 1980 and 1996. The area under permanent crops declined more markedly by one third over the same period. However, these changes are more logical macroeconomic adjustments in a high labour-cost economy as it is brought more fully into a global system than any simple response to declining productive capacity of the rural labour force. That said, however, agricultural incomes are clearly lower in *kaso* areas than in other agricultural areas and these differences have increased over time. In 1995, agricultural income of *kaso* areas was just over 70 per cent of the national average. These *kaso* areas are pockets of relative deprivation in a prosperous country but are neither sunk in rural poverty owing to their ageing populations, nor are they significant positive or negative contributors to national development trends.

---

[4]The information in this section comes largely from Japan (1998).

DISCUSSION

The information presented in this paper shows that the ageing of populations in east and south-east Asia is advanced in relatively few areas as yet. The growth in the numbers of older people is, however, faster than for the populations as a whole and projections for the countries in the region to 2020 show marked increases in the proportions of populations 60 years of age and older (compare tables II and VIII). United Nations projections also show substantial increases in the proportion of the urban population over the same period, although, by the year 2020, only Brunei Darussalam, as well as the Republic of Korea and Japan, are projected to be over 80 per cent urban. Brunei Darussalam is projected to have the most striking shift towards an ageing population over the 30 years from 1990, with the proportion of the population 60 years of age and older projected to increase from 4.1 per cent in 1990 to 15 per cent by 2020. Taking the slightly longer time horizon to the middle of the twenty-first century, the process of ageing is projected to rise markedly with between one in four and one in five of the populations of most of the countries in the region being 60 years or older at that time. The proportions of elderly are projected virtually to double in several countries in the 30 years between 2020 and 2050 (table VIII). Only in the two countries that are currently the poorest in the region, Cambodia and Lao People's Democratic Republic, is the proportion of the elderly still seen to be at relatively low levels.

The sectoral shift in the structure of ageing is not available in the United Nations projections; nor would it be particularly meaningful given the complex mix of the three factors in urbanization: natural increase, net migration and reclassification. The latter two are virtually impossible to project accurately. However, from the experience of countries undergoing the process as described in the cases in this paper, we can see that ageing will increasingly be a rural issue. It is there that ageing as a social problem will be most deeply felt as younger family members move to the cities leaving the elderly to look after themselves. This is not to say that the elderly in urban areas do not face problems of isolation and loneliness too, but the costs of providing basic support services for the elderly are likely to be greater and more difficult to implement in rural areas. In 1990, in Japan, some 463,203 men and 1,702,163 women aged 60 years or over were living alone, 10 per cent of the total number of Japanese in that age group. Unfortunately, the rural-urban breakdown is not available. Information from *kaso* areas for 1997, however, revealed that the proportion of household heads of 65 years of age and over who lived alone was, at 9.6 per cent, just over double the proportion for non-*kaso* areas.

The decline in fertility throughout the Asian region means that there are fewer children available per person to look after the population when they become old. Urbanization and the transition to industrial societies might be seen to weaken family ties, spatially if not emotionally, and residual rural populations without adequate welfare systems are likely to suffer relative , if not absolute, deprivation. Studies on the living arrangements of the elderly in south-east Asian countries have shown that, despite the rapidity of economic and social change that has occurred over the last decades, the familial system of care for the elderly has been maintained. (see the essays in Knodel and Debavalya (1997)). Very few of the elderly live on their own or without seeing their children on a regular basis. Only 4.5 per cent of the elderly in rural Thailand (and 3.5 per cent in urban areas) in 1990 lived on their own, for example.

Change can certainly be expected in the future as fertility change and migration impact further upon the family. While most Asian societies are unlikely to develop welfare systems as comprehensive as those found in Europe, for example, they may choose to rely on the promotion of "community care" approaches. There is still time to plan for the type of future care to be provided for the elderly in the region. Even in 2020, the proportion of elderly in the countries under consideration will rarely be above one in six of the population. However, as we have seen in the cases of Japan and the Republic of Korea, the ageing of the rural population can be many years ahead of that for the population as a whole. If the linkages between urban and rural sectors are to weaken as rural migrants spend longer at their destinations, the time for action may be shorter than might be suggested by the figures for ageing for the populations as a whole.

While the ageing of the rural populations can be related to the spatial spread of fertility decline, migration is the key factor in intensifying regional and sectoral patterns of ageing. The exodus of the younger cohorts and the return of older migrants upon retirement accelerates ageing in the villages. Return migration, through the introduction of more modern ideas into the communities, may help to diffuse the idea of a small family norm and the contraceptive practices that foster the decline in fertility and, ultimately, promote the ageing of the local population. Initially, however, migration acts to support the rural populations by extending the resource base of peasant households to include other opportunities. Thus, although a village population, *sensu stricto,* may be ageing, to consider that population in isolation is deceptive as it is but part of a much wider economic system that transcends the rural sector itself.

This logic can be extended to the rural sector as a whole. Nevertheless, over the longer term, migration can act to undermine the village communities as the number of outmigrants increases and they spend progressively longer away. As the reproductive capability of a community is eroded, depopulation is the end result, as we saw in the cases of the *kaso* areas in Japan. For most countries in east and south-east Asia, such a scenario is unlikely to evolve in the near term except in the Republic of Korea and perhaps in parts of China. Rural depopulation, nevertheless, cannot be simply dismissed as an unlikely development outcome by other countries in the region. Labour shortages are already prevalent in the rural sectors of Malaysia and Thailand and these are presently being met by immigration from neighbouring countries, much of which is illegal. The transformations that are being wrought by rural-to-urban migration and by the decline in fertility far transcend those of demographic structure and raise questions about the integrity of the nation States themselves. Situations in which at least one in five of the labour force is a foreign worker, as in the case of Malaysia, must ultimately bring about change in the nature of the society.

It is clear from the data presented that no macro-level, or even regional, economic difficulties appear to be the result of the ageing of the rural populations. Agricultural production overall increased as more economically rational holdings could be created and more marginal lands were taken out of production as greater numbers left for the cities. The ageing and ultimate decline of the rural populations tends to be associated with increasing wealth at the national level. Ageing, as the primary result of the decline in fertility, is a direct consequence of the developments that brought about that decline, both in terms of policy intervention and in the complex matrix of economic and social development variables. The ageing of human populations was obviously not a direct policy goal of Governments, but an outcome of other governmental policies as well as of global economic and political forces. Governments in the region now need accommodate the consequences of those processes, even if no negative impacts can yet be observed at the macro-level. There are clear local difficulties as marginal areas embark on the process of depopulation engendered through outmigration. Thus, as wealth accumulates at that national level, it is incumbent upon the State to ensure that ageing populations in isolated rural areas are adequately provided with services and care. There may be much to learn for countries in the region from the policies followed by Japan towards its *kaso* areas. The provision of basic medical services in *kaso* areas over the recent past, for example, has outpaced that for the population as a whole.

CONCLUSION

This paper has attempted to highlight important sector differences in the pattern of ageing in east and south-east Asia. It has attempted to show that ageing and, ultimately, declining rural populations are a definite possibility for many countries in the region. Few major negative economic consequences of this trend can be identified, however, as the driving forces behind the transition emanate increasingly from the urban sector, or through the urban sector from overseas. The idea of a transition does imply that, like the sequence outlined for Japan and the Republic of Korea, other Asian countries will follow in their footsteps. This is unlikely to occur throughout the region, however, as uneven development intensifies. Over the time horizon of the next 50 years, rural depopulation and the stagnation of small and medium-sized towns are likely to characterize increasingly larger parts of the region as younger people are drawn internally and internationally towards regional growth centres that are experiencing labour deficit as a result of persistent low fertility.

Thus, the principal issues of ageing in the region under consideration are likely to revolve around the social conditions of the elderly in isolated rural areas. How are poor States in the region going to provide these areas with services and care, particularly in a context of declining family concerns where close family members are permanently absent? Once remittances sent back home by family members in towns begin to decline as the urban commitment of the migrants grows, difficult questions will be posed for the State, as well as for the elderly in the rural sector. Even in Japan, many elderly must move to the towns where at least they can have family support. Such an alternative may not be open to the elderly in less affluent societies, especially where a transnational movement might be involved.

While most previous work has focused on the overall trends of the ageing of Asian populations, this paper has emphasized the importance of adopting a sectoral perspective. The ageing of the rural sector is likely to anticipate by several years the kinds of consequences that are implied by the data for the populations as a whole. This paper has also identified unknown and unresolved issues, many of which the result of the unavailability of data. The issue of ageing, depopulation and land tenure, for example, remains poorly understood, as does the issue of the gender implications of ageing in the rural sector. Policy issues, too, require much more detailed examination, particularly with respect to the funding of services for the aged in more isolated rural areas which have limited local potential and have become cut off from family support systems through remittances. Marginal areas are unlikely to be high in a country's priority for social development, but it is incumbent for modern nations and States to ensure that the elderly do not become marginal peoples, in isolated regions and elsewhere.

REFERENCES

Anh, T.S., P. Gubry, V.T. Hong and J.W. Huguet, "Ho Chi Minh-Ville: de la migration à l'emploi", Les dossiers du Centre français sur la population et le développement (CEPED) No. 40, Paris, 1996.

Chamratrithirong, A., K. Archavanitkul, K. Richter, P. Guest, V. Thongthai, W. Boonchalaksi, N. Piriyathamwong and P. Vong-Ek, *National Migration Survey of Thailand*, Institute for Population and Social Research, Mahidol University, 1995.

Chan, K.W., "Urbanization and rural-urban migration in China since 1982: a new baseline", *Modern China* 20(3), 1994.

Chatelain, A., *Les migrants temporaires en France de 1800 à 1914*, Presses Universitaires de Lille, 1976.

Chen, A.J. and G. Jones, *Ageing in ASEAN: Its Socio-economic Consequences*, Singapore, Institute of South-east Asian Studies, 1989.

Connell, J., "Copper, cocoa and cash: terminal, temporary and circular mobility in Siwai, North Solomons", in M. Chapman and R.M. Prothero (eds.), *Circulation in Population Movement: Substance and Concepts from the Melanesian Case*, London, Routledge and Kegan Paul, 1985.

FAO, *FAO Yearbook: Production. Vol.51, 1997*, Rome, FAO Statistics Series No. 142, 1998.

FAO, "Thailand, World Food Summit Follow-up", draft strategy for national agricultural development, Horizon 2000, Rome, 1996.

Hugo, G. "Population change and development in Indonesia", in R.F. Watters and T.G. McGee (eds.), *Asia Pacific: New Geographies of the Pacific Rim*, London, Hurst, 1997.

Hugo, G., "Ageing in Indonesia: a neglected area of policy concern", in D.R. Phillips (ed.), *Ageing in South East Asia*, London, Arnold, 1992.

Japan, *Kaso Taisaku no Genkyo* (Current Policy Towards Depopulation), Tokyo, Kokudo-cho, Chiho Shinko-Kyoku, Kaso Taisakushitsu, 1998.

Knodel, J. and N. Debavalya (eds.), "Living arrangements and support among the elderly in South-east Asia: an introduction", *Asia-Pacific Population Journal* 12 (4): special issue, 1997.

Knodel, J. and N. Debavalya (eds.) "Social and economic support systems for the elderly in Asia: an introduction", *Asia-Pacific Population Journal*, 7(3): special issue, 1992.

Korea, *Korea Annual 1997: A Comprehensive Handbook on Korea*, 34th annual edition, Seoul, Yonhap News Agency, 1997.

Long, N. and B. Roberts, *Miners, Peasants and Entrepreneurs: Regional Development in the Central Highlands of Peru*, Cambridge, Cambridge University Press, 1984.

Ma, L.J.C. and B. Xiang, "Native place, migration and the emergence of peasant enclaves in Beijing", *The China Quarterly*, No.155, 1998.

Marcoux, A., "Ageing rural populations in the developing countries: patterns, determinants and implications", in United Nations, *Ageing and the Family*, New York, Department for Economic and Social Information and Policy Analysis, (ST/ESA/SER.R/124), 1994.

Mason, E.S., M.J. Kim, D.H. Perkins, K.S. Kim and D.C. Cole, *The Economic and Social Modernization of the Republic of Korea*, Cambridge, Harvard University Press, 1980.

National Statistical Office, *Statistical Atlas of Population and Housing, 1990*, Bangkok, , Office of the Prime Minister, 1994.

Pasuk, P. and C. Baker, *Thailand: Economy and Politics*, Kuala Lumpur, Oxford University Press, 1995.

Phillips, D.R. (ed.), *Ageing in East and South-east Asia*, London, Arnold, 1992.

Skeldon, R., "Urbanization and migration in the ESCAP region", in *Asia-Pacific Population Journal* 13 (1), 1998.

Skeldon, R., "Rural-to-urban migration and its implications for poverty alleviation", *Asia-Pacific Population Journal* 12 (1), 1997.

Thailand, *Report of the Migration Survey 1994*, National Statistical Office, Bangkok, Office of the Prime Minister, 1997.

Thailand, *Mun River Basin Water Resources Development Master Plan: Final Technical Report*, Royal Irrigation Department, Royal Thai Government, 1995.

Thailand, *1990 Population and Housing Census. Subject Report No.1: Migration*, National Statistical Office, Office of the Prime Minister, 1993.

United Nations, *1996 Demographic Yearbook*, New York, Department of Economic and Social Affairs, (ST/ESA/STAT/SER.R/27) 1998.

United Nations, "Some problems and issues of older persons in Asia and the Pacific", *Asian Population Studies Series No.144*, New York, Economic and Social Commission for Asia and the Pacific,(ST/ESCAP/1735), 1997.

United Nations, "Added years of life in Asia: current situation and future challenges", *Asian Population Studies Series No.141*, New York, Economic and Social Commission for Asia and the Pacific, (ST/ESCAP/1688), 1996.

United Nations "Annotated bibliography on productive ageing in Asia and the Pacific", *Asian Population Studies Series No.143*, New York, Economic and Social Commission for Asia and the Pacific (ST/ESCAP/1695), 1996.

United Nations , "Implications of Asia's population future for older people in the family", *Asian Population Studies Series No.145*, New York, Economic and Social Commission for Asia and the Pacific (ST/ESCAP/1736), 1996.

United Nations, "Population ageing and development", *Asian Population Studies Series No.140*, New York, Economic and Social Commission for Asia and the Pacific (ST/ESCAP/1680), 1996.

United Nations, *Population Ageing in Asia and the Pacific*, New York, Economic and Social Commission for Asia and the Pacific (ST/ESCAP/1594), 1996.

United Nations, *The Ageing of Asian Populations*, New York, Department for Economic and Social Information and Policy Analysis (ST/ESA/SER.R/125) 1994.

United Nations , "Productive ageing in Asia and the Pacific", *Asian Population Studies Series No.129*, New York, Economic and Social Commission for Asia and the Pacific, (ST/ESCAP/1302), 1993.

United Nations, "Population ageing in Asia", *Asian Population Studies Series No.108*, New York, Economic and Social Commission for Asia and the Pacific (ST/ESCAP/1120) 1991.

United Nations , "The geography of fertility in the ESCAP region", *Asian Population Studies Series No. 62-K*, New York, Economic and Social Commission for Asia and the Pacific, 1988.

United Nations, *Patterns of Urban and Rural Population Growth*, New York, Department of International Economic and Social Affairs, Population Studies (No.68, ST/ESA/SER.A/68), 1980.

Warr, P.G., "Thailand", in R.H. McLeod and R. Garnaut (eds.), *East Asia in Crisis: From Being A Miracle To Needing One?* London, Routledge, 1998.

Zhang, L. and S.X.B. Zhao, "Re-examining China's 'urban' concept and the level of urbanization", *The China Quarterly* No. 154, 1998.

TABLE I.   PATTERNS OF FERTILITY DECLINE: TOTAL FERTILITY RATES, SELECTED COUNTRIES, 1950-1995

	1950-1955	1955-1960	1960-1965	1965-1970	1970-1975	1975-1980	1980-1985	1985-1990	1990-1995
China	6.11	5.48	5.61	5.94	4.76	3.26	2.50	2.41	1.95
Hong Kong	4.44	4.71	5.31	4.02	2.89	2.32	1.80	1.31	1.21
Japan	2.75	2.08	2.01	2.00	2.07	1.81	1.76	1.66	1.50
Republic of Korea	5.18	6.07	5.40	4.52	4.11	2.80	2.40	1.73	1.73
Brunei Darussalam	7.00	7.00	6.72	5.94	5.40	4.40	3.80	3.40	3.07
Indonesia	5.49	5.67	5.42	5.57	5.10	4.68	4.06	3.31	2.90
Malaysia	6.83	6.94	6.72	5.94	5.15	4.16	4.24	4.00	3.62
Philippines	7.29	7.09	6.61	6.04	5.50	4.96	4.74	4.30	3.93
Singapore	6.40	5.99	4.93	3.46	2.62	1.87	1.69	1.71	1.73
Thailand	6.62	6.42	6.42	6.14	5.01	4.27	2.96	2.57	2.10
Cambodia	6.29	6.29	6.29	6.22	5.53	4.10	5.06	5.25	5.25
Lao People's Democratic Republic	6.15	6.15	6.15	6.15	6.15	6.69	6.69	6.69	6.69
Viet Nam	6.05	6.05	6.05	5.94	5.85	5.59	4.69	4.22	3.87

Source: United Nations, 1995, *World Population Prospect: (1994 Revision)*, New York, Department for Economic and Social Information and Policy Analysis, Population Division, ST/ESA/SER.A/145.

TABLE II.   UNITED NATIONS ESTIMATES OF THE PROPORTION OF PERSONS
60 YEARS OF AGE AND OLDER, SELECTED COUNTRIES, 1960-1990

	1960	1975	1990
China	7.2	6.9	8.6
Hong Kong	5.9	8.8	12.6
Japan	8.9	11.7	17.4
Republic of Korea	5.3	5.8	7.7
Brunei Darussalam	6.1	5.6	4.3
Indonesia	5.2	5.3	6.3
Malaysia	5.3	5.6	5.8
Philippines	4.9	4.3	5.1
Singapore	3.7	6.7	8.4
Thailand	4.5	4.7	6.9
Cambodia	4.5	4.6	4.7
Lao People's Democratic Republic	4.1	4.6	4.9
Viet Nam	6.9	6.4	7.2

Source: United Nations, 1997, *The Sex and Age Distributions of the World Populations (1996 Revision)*, New York, Department of Economic and Social Affairs, Population Division, ST/ESA/SER.A/162.

TABLE III. TOTAL POPULATION, PROPORTION URBAN, AND PROPORTION OF ELDERLY IN URBAN AND RURAL POPULATIONS,
VARIOUS COUNTRIES, LATEST AVAILABLE YEARS

	Total population	Proportion urban (%)	Urban population: proportion 60 years and older (%)	Rural population: proportion 60 years and older (%)
Japan (1995)	125,570,246	78.1	19.5	25.4
Republic of Korea (1995)	44,553,710	78.5	6.9	17.9
Brunei Darussalam (1991)	260,482	66.6	3.5	5.3
China (1990)	1,130,510,638	26.2	8.1	8.7
Indonesia (1995)	194,754,808	35.9	5.6	7.4
Malaysia (1991)	17,498,091	50.6	5.3	6.7
Philippines (1990)	60,559,116	48.6	5.0	5.5
Thailand (1990)	54,532,300	18.7	6.3	7.7
Cambodia (1996)	10,702,329	14.4	5.0	5.4
Lao People's Democratic Republic (1995)	4,574,848	17.1	5.7	
Viet Nam (1992)	69,175,080	19.5	7.4	7.7

Source: United Nations,1998 *1996 Demographic Yearbook*, New York, Department of Economic and Social Affairs, ST/ESA/STAT/SER.R/27, Table 8. Incomplete data for Lao People's Democratic Republic from "A demographic perspective on women in development in Cambodia, Lao People's Democratic Republic, Myanmar and Viet Nam", *Asian Population Studies Series No. 148*, New York, Economic and Social Commission for Asia and the Pacific, ST/ESCAP/1869, table 39.

TABLE IV. PATTERNS OF URBAN AND RURAL FERTILITY, VARIOUS COUNTRIES, MID-1970s

	Total fertility rate: rural	Total fertility rate: other urban	Total fertility rate: major urban
Indonesia	4.9	4.3	4.6
Malaysia	5.0	4.5	3.5
Philippines	6.0	4.0	3.5
Republic of Korea	5.0	4.2	3.3

NOTE: The three categories, rural, urban and major urban, come from definitions adopted in the World Fertility Survey. Urban areas were identified through individual national definitions, while major urban centres included cities exceeding 1 million population, all national capitals regardless of population, and the largest city in any country where no city exceeding 1 million inhabitants existed.
Source: United Nations, 1987, *Fertility Behaviour in the Context of Development*, New York, Department of International Economic and Social Affairs, Population Studies No. 100, ST/ESA/SER.A/100.

TABLE V.   OLD AGE AND YOUTH DEPENDENCY RATIOS, BY URBAN AND RURAL SECTOR, LATEST YEARS

	Rural		Urban	
	Old age dependency ratio	Youth dependency ratio	Old age dependency ratio	Youth dependency ratio
Japan (1995)	44.1	29.1	29.4	24.1
Republic of Korea (1995)	29.0	32.6	10.0	34.2
Brunei Darussalam (1991)	8.5	57.8	5.7	55.3
China (1990)	14.1	48.0	11.7	32.1
Indonesia (1995)	13.0	62.2	9.1	48.9
Malaysia (1991)	12.1	74.7	8.7	55.1
Philippines (1990)	10.5	80.7	8.7	63.2
Thailand (1990)	11.3	48.4	9.0	32.5
Cambodia (1996)	10.7	88.8	9.3	74.2
Lao People's Democratic Republic (1995)	11.8	nd	9.7	nd
Viet Nam (1992)	14.5	75.0	14.0	74.4

NOTE: Old age dependency ratio is the ratio of the population of 60 years and older to the working population 15-59 years old. Similarly, youth dependency is the ratio of the population younger than 15 years old to the working population 15-49 years old.

Source: United Nations, 1998 ,*1996 Demographic Yearbook*, New York, Department of Economic and Social Affairs, ST/ESA/STAT/SER.R/27, table 8; United Nations 1998 "A demographic perspective on women in development in Cambodia, Lao People's Democratic Republic, Myanmar and Viet Nam", *Asian Population Studies Series No.148*, New York, Economic and Social Commission for Asia and the Pacific, ST/ESCAP/1869, tables 7 and 8; and *Lao Census 1995: Country Report*, Ventiane, 1997, National Statistical Centre.

TABLE VI.   SEX RATIO OF POPULATIONS 60 YEARS OF AGE AND OLDER BY SECTOR, LATEST YEARS

	Urban	Rural
Japan (1995)	77	74
Republic of Korea (1995)	64	69
Brunei Darussalam (1991)	101	122
China (1990)	95	89
Indonesia (1995)	85	87
Malaysia (1991)	83	95
Philippines (1990)	82	95
Thailand (1990)	79	96
Cambodia (1996)	248	75
Lao People's Democratic Republic (1995)	90	92
Viet Nam (1992)	70	77

NOTE: The very high masculinity for urban areas in Cambodia is a result of the recent tragic events in that country which saw the virtual emptying of the cities during the Pol Pot years. Men have been among the first to enter the urban sector with a return to more stable conditions.

Source: United Nations, 1998, *1996 Demographic Yearbook*, New York, Department of Economic and Social Affairs, ST/ESA/STAT/SER.R/27, table 8; United Nations, 1998,"A demographic perspective on women in development in Cambodia, Lao People's Democratic Republic, Myanmar and Viet Nam", *Asian Population Studies Series No.148*, New York, Economic and Social Commission for Asia and the Pacific, ST/ESCAP/1869, tables 7 and 8; and *Lao Census 1995: Country Report*, Ventiane, 1997, National Statistical Centre.

TABLE VII. OVERALL FOOD GRAINS SUPPLY AND DEMAND (IN THOUSAND M/T), REPUBLIC OF KOREA, 1983-1996

Year	Total	Rice	Barley	Wheat	Corn	Soybean	Potatoes	Corn
				Supply				
1983	16 591	6 814	1 304	2 228	4 484	1 020	357	1 404
1984	17 052	6 922	1 412	2 973	3 580	1 047	401	1 764
1985	16 947	6 929	1 158	3 256	3 443	1 226	391	1 770
1986	17 580	7 054	715	3 716	4 027	1 274	358	1 710
1987	19 183	6 856	681	4 628	5 183	1 357	302	1 533
1988	19 995	6 732	711	4 744	5 892	1 465	257	1 659
1989	19 838	7 174	805	2 839	6 555	1 338	302	825
1990	19 939	7 470	833	2 477	6 891	1 450	275	543
1991	21 298	7 631	822	4 922	6 027	1 312	226	358
1992	22 190	7 525	813	4 551	6 927	1 597	251	526
1993	22 347	7 330	827	4 897	7 228	1 383	250	432
1994	22 549	5 670	714	6 968	6 112	1 578	203	404
1995	23 093	6 216	713	3 697	9 402	1 820	192	1 053
1996	22 901	5 469	677	3 398	9 838	1 889	234	1 396
				Demand				
1983	13 786	5 297	680	1 924	4 279	907	357	1 249
1984	14 372	5 526	814	2 724	3 305	960	401	1 602
1985	14 667	5 501	896	2 988	3 245	1 130	391	1 646
1986	15 422	5 805	550	3 315	3 749	1 247	358	1 645
1987	16 624	5 617	531	4 129	4 654	1 225	302	1 391
1988	17 047	5 611	537	4 198	4 971	1 298	257	1 473
1989	16 934	5 602	452	2 602	5 983	1 232	301	762
1990	16 282	5 445	427	2 005	6 425	1 254	274	452
1991	17 467	5 490	457	4 228	5 561	1 202	221	308
1992	18 322	5 526	380	4 056	6 209	1 503	237	411
1993	18 336	5 510	426	3 981	6 520	1 274	237	388
1994	19 530	5 414	455	6 058	5 678	1 347	203	375
1995	19 974	5 557	421	3 335	8 066	1 558	192	845

Note: Rice year is calculated from 1 November to 31 October .
Source: Korea ,1998, *Korea Statistical Yearbook 1997*, Seoul, National Statistical Office.

TABLE VIII.   PROJECTED PROPORTION URBAN AND OLDER POPULATION, 2020, AND PROJECTED OLDER POPULATION, 2050

	Projected proportion urban in 2020 (%)	Projected proportion 60 years and older in 2020 (%)	Projected proportion 60 years and older in 2050 (%)
Japan	83.2	31.3	36.0
Republic of Korea	92.7	18.6	28.8
Brunei Darussalam	80.1	15.0	23.8
China	49.1	15.9	26.2
Indonesia	55.4	11.1	21.6
Malaysia	68.5	10.8	21.1
Philippines	69.9	9.5	18.7
Thailand	32.5	15.1	28.1
Lao People's Democratic Republic	36.0	5.5	11.0
Cambodia	36.2	7.6	14.6
Viet Nam	27.3	9.7	22.1

Source: United Nations, 1997 *The Sex and Age Distribution of the World Populations, (1996 Revision)* New York, Department of Economic and Social Affairs, Population Division, ST/ESA/SER.A/162; and United Nations, 1998, *World Urbanization Prospects, (1996 Revision)*, New York, Department of Economic and Social Affairs, Population Division, ST/ESA/SER.A/170.

Figure 1.   Distribution of kaso districts in Japan, 1997

Source: *Kaso Taisako no Genkyo (Current Policy Towards Depopulation)*, Tokyo, Kikudo-cho, Chiho Shinko-Dyoku, Kaso Taisakushitsu, 1998.

IV. SITUATION OF OLDER PERSONS IN THE NEWLY INDUSTRIALIZED COUNTRIES OF EAST ASIA[1]

*Poo Chang Tan**

1. INTRODUCTION

This paper discusses the situation of older persons in the newly industrialized countries of east Asia. Four areas of policy concern are highlighted in the discussion to address the United Nations Principles for Older Persons, namely, the principles of independence, participation, care, self-fulfilment and dignity for older persons. They are

(i)   Older persons as a valuable resource;

(ii) Social security benefits;

(iii) Strengthening family support systems;

(iv) Promotion of community support systems and inter-generational relationships.

A discussion of these issues centers on the experiences of the newly industrialized countries of the Republic of Korea, Taiwan, Province of China, Hong Kong and Singapore and serves at least two purposes. First, the newly industrialized countries are far advanced economically and demographically in relation to population ageing. Hence, countries that are less advanced can learn from the experiences of these countries, especially as they have less resources to commit and may only be able to adopt those programmes that they can afford. Secondly, a discussion of these issues will highlight their importance and the need for Governments to think ahead and consider existing approaches, or seek new ones to prepare for the ageing of their populations. This is especially important as the growth rate of the population 60 years and over is faster than those of other ages because of a decline in fertility rates and the improvement in life expectancy. Moreover, ageing will take place at a much faster pace in many of these developing countries, which are projected to have large absolute numbers of older persons because of their already large population base. It is pertinent to mention however that older persons are a heterogeneous group and a successful policy or programme in one locality or country may still have to be adapted to suit different local and cultural conditions.

2. THE SITUATION OF THE AGEING POPULATION[2]

The age structure of the populations of the Newly Industrialized Countries indicate a burgeoning proportion in middle age, with ageing likely to proceed much faster than comparable socio-economic growth, an unprecedented development in world history (see figure 1 below). For both the male and female populations, the Korean and Taiwan, Province of China population structures indicate equally high percentages of above 8 per cent in the five year age groups from 10-39 years, while Singapore and Hong Kong register more than 10 per cent in the five year age groups from 30-39 years.

The share of older population has been higher and will continue to be higher in the more developed countries of Asia (see figure 2 below). For example, Japan, which experienced a sharp decline in fertility immediately after the Second World War, has an older population 60 years and over whose share in the total population increased from 7.7 per cent in 1950 to 20.1 per cent in 1995, and is expected to increase to 31.1 per cent by 2020, an increase of more than 50 per cent. The newly industrialized economies of Hong Kong, Singapore and Taiwan, Province of China, which have experienced a rapid decline in mortality rates (and also fertility rates in Singapore and Hong Kong), currently have an older population of 14.5 per cent, 10 per cent and 11 per cent of their total populations. By 2020, they

[1]The present report was prepared prior to the economic crisis of the late 1990's in Asia.

*Professor Tan Poo Chang is with the Faculty of Economics and Administration at the University of Malaya, in Kuala Lumpur. The author would like to acknowledge the assistance of Miss G.L. Chwee, Miss Ng Sor Tho and Mr. Brian Tan in the preparation of this paper. The information provided on Taiwan by Mr. Teng of the Taipei Economic and Cultural Office in Malaysia and Mr. Huang Hai-tung, Director of Population, Ministry of the Interior, Taiwan Province of China, is gratefully acknowledged.

[2]Figures in this section for Taiwan, Province of China are largely based on the Council of Economic Planning and Development, Province of China (1996) and those provided by Ministry of the Interior, Taiwan, Province of China, (1997), while figures for other countries are based on United Nations (1994), unless otherwise specified.

Figure 1.   The Age-Sex Structure of Selected Populations, 1995

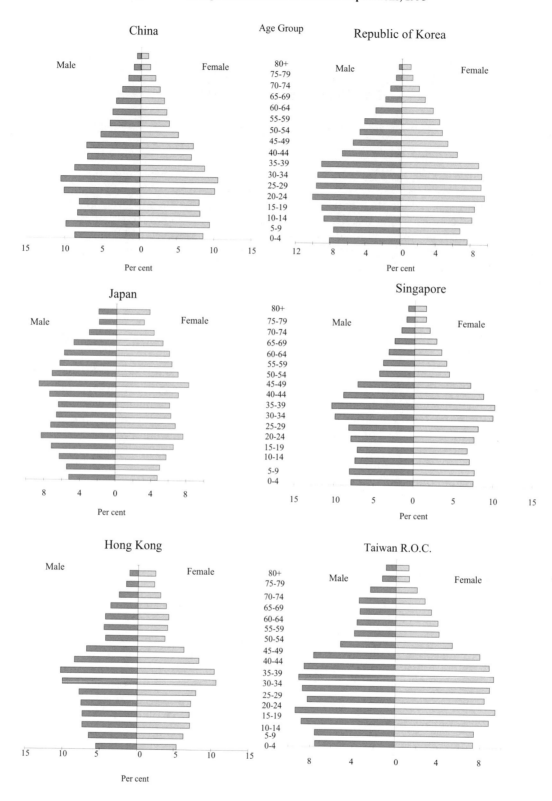

Source: United Naitons, 1994.

Figure 2. Proportion of Older Persons (60+ Years) in Selected Populations, 1995-2020

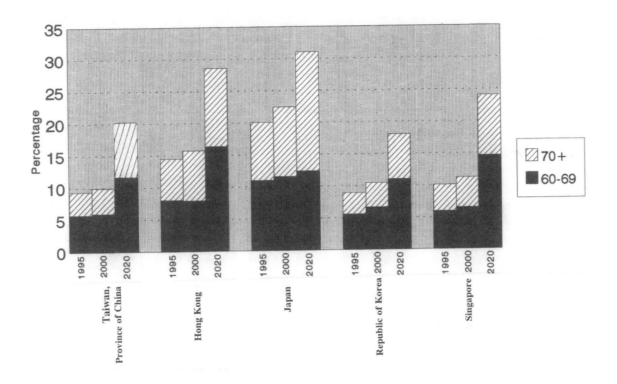

Source: United Nations, 1994; Ministry of the Interior, Taiwan, Province of China, 1997

are expected to reach 28.6 per cent, 25 per cent and 20 per cent of their total populations, respectively (Chang and Ofstedal, 1991). For the other Newly Industrialized Countries that moved into a phase of declining mortality and fertility one or two decades later and at varying rates, population ageing is still at an early stage. For example, the share of older persons in the total population is currently 8.9 per cent in the Republic of Korea; by 2020, the figure is expected to reach 18 per cent.

The increase in the relative size of older populations do not reflect the absolute magnitude of the populations involved. In 1995, Japan had 25.1 million aged 60 and over, while countries like Hong Kong and Singapore had 0.8 million and 0.3 million, respectively. The Republic of Korea and Taiwan, Province of China, reported 4 million and 2.3 million respectively in 1995. In the year 2020, countries like Japan are projected to have 38.5 million of older persons while Hong Kong and Singapore will have 1.7 million and 0.8 million, re-

spectively. In the Republic of Korea, there will be 9.6 million and in Taiwan, Province of China, 5 million.

Continued improvement in life expectancy has also resulted in older persons living longer after reaching old age. The expectation of life at birth of the various countries indicates that it has been improving over the years (see table I below). Today, persons 70 years and over account for close to 40 per cent or more of the ageing populations in the Newly Industrialized Countries in east Asia and, by 2020, the percentage would be slightly higher, and this proportion will probably rise further. For example, taking the experience of Japan, by 2020, persons 70 year and older are expected to account for about 60 per cent of the ageing population, and would actually outnumber those in the 60 to 69 age group in that country.

The decline in mortality has also resulted in increased female over male longevity, resulting in increased feminization of the older population, an

57

57

TABLE I.   LIFE EXPECTANCY AT BIRTH OF SELECTED POPULATIONS, 1995-2020

Country	1995		2000		2020	
	Male	Female	Male	Female	Male	Female
Taiwan	72.6	78.1	73.7	79.3	76.0	82.0
Hong Kong	76.2	82.3	76.8	83.0	78.5	84.6
Japan	76.8	82.9	77.4	83.5	79.0	85.1
Republic of Korea	68.8	76.1	70.6	77.6	74.3	80.7
Singapore	73.5	78.6	75.0	80.1	78.2	83.2

Source: United Nations, 1995; Ministry of the Interior, Taiwan, Province of China 1997.

Figure 3.   Male and Female Share of Older Persons (60+ Years) in Selected Populations, 1995-2020

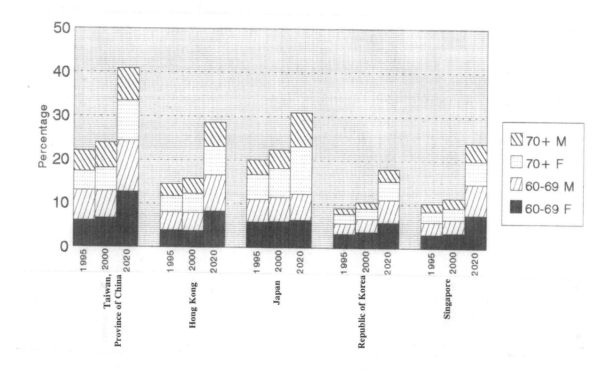

Source: United Nations, 1994; Ministry of the Interior, Taiwan, Province of China, 1997

imbalance that is more pronounced in the older ages (see figure 3 below). The female advantage in life expectancy is expected to continue, with a preponderance of female over male older persons beyond 2000.

It is relevant to mention here that subnational disparities exist in all countries and generally, due to rural-urban migration of the young, a larger older population is found in the rural than in urban areas, except perhaps for Hong Kong and Singapore (which is all urban). Also, within each country, ageing is likely to affect some groups more rapidly than others owing to differential decline in fertility and mortality. Policies and programmes should take cognizance of these differences when being considered for implementation.

3. AREAS OF POLICY CONCERN

This section will discuss four areas of policy concern by drawing on the experiences of the newly industrialized countries. The paper will allude to the diverse policies and programmes existing in the four countries, in particular those that have proved successful and received considerable support. In this regard, both governmental and non-governmental policies and programmes will be discussed. A bias may arise in highlighting particular policies and programmes as this paper will rely completely on secondary data sources and materials, in particular those published by the United Nations and the Economic and Social Commission for Asia and the Pacific. As such, information on Taiwan, Province of China, is relatively scarce compared with the other countries.

(i) *Older persons as a valuable resource*

It has been established that the large majority of older persons in every country, developed and developing, are still capable of participating actively in society. More often than not though, older persons have been viewed as dependent and in need of assistance. In many instances, there is a need for policies and programmes to promote older persons as a valuable resource and involve them in economic, educational, social and recreational activities (Tan, 1996).

Promotion of economic and community participation

Older persons may find it difficult for various reasons to continue in economic employment. Among others, age discrimination is a common practice and a retirement age is widely utilized to terminate an older person's continued participation in the labour force. While the society may need to provide for the upward mobility of younger members and promote retirement as a macroeconomic device to deal with problems of slow growth and unemployment, it nevertheless should

consider and implement alternative employment prospects to benefit older persons.

There are a number of reasons for promoting the continued economic participation of older persons. In some instances, there may be a real need to improve unsatisfactory economic situations (such as those found in a number of studies, see Lee et al., 1996, p. 29, and Chow, 1995, p. 3). For others, work provides a psychologically important source of satisfaction and self-fulfillment as well as providing them a status within the society. Older workers are also a potential resource for increasing output by enlarging the work force. They can also form a pool of expertise to train younger workers. Four major mechanisms have been utilized to assist older workers:

(i)   skills/job training;

(ii) job redesign and job creation assistance programmes;

(iii) introduction of flexible work schedules;

(iv) improving job search information and procedures.

In the Republic of Korea, welfare centres have been established in 22 places to consult and provide job opportunities for older persons (Choe, 1992, p. 96). There are three job placement programmes jointly organized by voluntary organizations and the Government to provide older persons with an opportunity to earn income—Elderly Ability Bank and Elderly Person Bank (started in 1981), Elderly Workplace (started in 1986) and Elderly Employment Promotion (started in 1992) (Park, 1996, p. 12-13). In Singapore, efforts are being made to upgrade the skills of mid-career workers by the National Productivity Board so that middle-aged workers can remain longer in the workforce (Mehta, 1996, p. 7). The Skills Development Fund in the Ministry of Labour has also raised subsidies for such purposes. The long-term aim is to increase the official retirement age from 60 to 67 years by the year 2003. The 1988 Advisory Council on the Aged has advocated fundamental adjustments in the existing seniority-based wage system to a flexible wage system linked to productivity rather than seniority to facilitate the continued employment of older workers (Cheung, 1995, p.10-11). In addition, employers are urged to allow greater work options such as part-time or flexi-time work. In 1993, a special programme called Training Initiatives for Matured Employees (TIME) was started to retrain workers aged 40 and above who have below primary education to equip them with relevant skills.

Raising the present retirement age or considering a flexible retirement age will be a step that should be considered in all countries. A retirement age sends a signal that a person is unable to contribute fully after this age. In fact, many have a life expectancy of at least 20 years or more upon retirement and the valuable resources of these older persons will be lost if not fully utilized. With rising education and late age at marriage, many older persons may need to continue working, otherwise they would not have the necessary accumulation of wealth for old age security. Many may also have fairly young children to care for when they retire and, perhaps, provide care and support for more than one generation of older persons. In the Republic of Korea, extension of retirement age and re-employment of older persons have taken place recently in the private sector, partly due to the shortage of labour.(Choe, 1992, p. 99).

Older persons may be mobilized as latent potential resources to participate in community development projects. As they are key beneficiaries, they need to participate at the planning stage to share their knowledge of the local environment and constraints. Their training, experience and maturity also put them in good stead to deliver the necessary social services.

Older persons may, *inter alia*, inculcate moral and religious values and acquaint children and young people with local history and socio-cultural traditions and help to resolve intra-family tensions. Because of their wide experience, older persons can effectively perform in such spheres through play and story-telling, and in preventive health care and nutrition and many other spheres. They can also be effective agents of change, such as fighting social ills, promoting the quality of life of those in disadvantageous positions and care of the environment. Older persons therefore should volunteer their expertise and form a core group providing such services and advice, perhaps through a volunteer registry. In Singapore, a retired and senior volunteers' programme is being considered by the National Council of Social Services (Mehta, 1996, p. 16).

The vast majority of older persons who remain capable in their later years should be mobilized to organize and run community and residential service centres. The decline in employment opportunities for older persons can now be offset by options for part-time employment in these centres and elsewhere. Child support services for working women can also be provided by such older persons.

Training and education

In order to participate actively in society and to have the confidence and ability to undertake new tasks, older persons may need increased educational exposure. Informal adult education, including functional literacy and training in new technologies is necessary and relevant. Where possible, older persons should be encouraged to participate in activities of this nature and to

bring in those less able and confident through community schemes.

It is found that, in Hong Kong, efforts by Non-governmental organizations to organize education programmes for the elderly are not popular, as many Chinese elderly believe that to be wise one need not necessarily be learned (Chow, 1995, p. 11). In Singapore, this area is still relatively undeveloped although there are classes in calligraphy and other artistic endeavours (Mehta, 1966, p. 17). Plans are underway for an Elders' Village where social and recreational pursuits are organized for older persons, with provision for a hostel where they can stay for short periods. An Elders' College is also being considered. In the Republic of Korea, there are currently 800 senior schools in operation by voluntary organizations and local community centers to promote cultural, educational and recreational programmes for older persons (Park, 1996, p. 15). Hence, such educational programmes have to take into account local interests, with perhaps a focus on areas that would enable older persons to generate other forms of income and continue to contribute usefully to society.

Older persons may have to assume new and varied roles in society and in the home. However, many may find these new roles foreign to them and may require special reorientation courses not only for themselves but for others in the family and society. Towards this end, specialized training and reorientation courses, including the training of care givers, should be implemented at the local level. However, even in Singapore, the training of care givers (professional and family) is still relatively undeveloped. Nevertheless, various support groups are available and training of care givers is provided by some hospitals for family members. Educational forums are also held for the public by various voluntary organizations.

While parents are working or when they emigrate to work elsewhere, children are often entrusted to grandparents. In this regard, older persons may require training in childcare and home economics to keep up with the rapid changes in knowledge, attitudes and practices related to family care and home economics.

Common societal perceptions of older persons are largely negative stereotypes that lead to subjective and biased images of them being weak and dependent. Many older persons themselves are also likely to confirm this negative perception; those who are active do not want to be considered as "old" for fear that they would be negatively stereotyped as "useless, weak or dependent". It is pertinent that these perceptions be changed to accept older persons as being able to maintain an active life and contribute to society. A whole gamut of policies and programmes can be proposed: from educational materials in school and in the media targeted at the society at large to those targeted specifically at older persons. There should be preparations made for life in old age through anticipatory role orientation and role transition. In many cases, the performance of new or continuing roles would require education, orientation and counseling, including reestablishing social contacts and socialization. A number of countries, including Singapore, promote an annual senior citizens' day or week, to promote the recognition of the contributions and status of older persons.

Overall, there is perhaps a relative lack of focus in promoting the positive image and roles of older persons in Newly Industrialized Countries. There has been some progress made but the impact is not widespread and, from recent international conferences, the focus seems to be still very welfare-oriented, with insufficient emphasis on the developmental aspects of productive ageing.

Health and a healthy lifestyle

The lifestyle changes that one has to make from young as well as at older ages to maintain continuous good health is another area of focus. While education and the mass media can promote and emphasize this aspect, it is necessary to institute sports, exercise and recreational programmes for both the young and the old. Of particular focus are programmes for those in the middle and older ages. Many who are middle aged may not find time for recreational and sporting activities and there may not be many programmes for those who are older. It may be necessary for all private and public agencies to emphasize and carry out such exercise or sporting activities on a regular basis for all employees. For self-employed and non-working older persons, there is a need to encourage group and specialized programmes for them at the local level and to provide the necessary facilities to as many as possible. Older persons should be encouraged to coordinate such activities for other older as well as younger persons. Activities of this nature may also become income-generating for the older persons as participants may be charged a small fee. Alternatively, they can also be voluntary and older persons would gain not only through involvement but also through the opportunities to socialize with others.

Singapore, for example, emphasizes developmental and preventive strategies in keeping older persons physically and mentally active so that they can remain in their usual living arrangements for as long as possible (Mehta, 1996, p. 8). From time to time, such as during senior citizens' week in November, the Ministry of Health organizes health screening to raise awareness of preventive care amongst older persons. A Healthy Lifestyle Unit at the Ministry of Health promotes a healthy lifestyle, designed for both young and older participants.

Older persons need to be informed of ways to prevent common and unnecessary illnesses and accidents. With the participation of women in the labour force, care in the home has been left increasingly in the hands of older persons. They need to update themselves on recent developments in health practices in caring for themselves as well as other family members.

(ii) *Social security benefits*

Besides ensuring that older persons continue to pursue and involve themselves in economic activities and in the community, adequate social security benefits are equally important. This covers pension, provident fund and other security benefits, including medical and housing.

It is found that economic support from pensions, provident funds and other social security schemes are likely to cover only a very small proportion of the older population and only those in the formal sector and in the urban areas (see, for example, Choe and Lee, 1991, p. 62; Chow, 1995, p. 3). In the Republic of Korea, it is reported that only some 6 per cent of the population are covered by pension. A social insurance programme to provide pension benefits was implemented in 1987 and it will be 2008 before adequate old age pension benefits are received. In Hong Kong, contributory retirement pension is only available to government employees and the few who are employed by large enterprises. It was only in July 1995, that a mandatory provident fund scheme was established to protect old age. Taiwan, Province of China, plans to institute national health insurance (which is likely to include some provision for life insurance) by 1995 and is debating the details of a national pension scheme (Li et al., 1994, p. 22). It has a pension scheme for both government and private workers (Shih and Chuang, 1995 p. 17). Among the Newly Industrialized Countries, the estimated prevalence of life insurance shows Singapore and Taiwan having higher coverage than the Republic of Korea and Hong Kong (Table II).

Unlike pensions, payments of provident funds are usually in the form of a lump-sum upon retirement and are usually inadequate and quickly spent. Consequently, many older persons work to advanced ages and depend almost entirely upon the informal system during their later years. The informal system is wholly voluntary, buttressed by children caring for aged parents and other safety nets provided by local NGOs and the Government. Support may be in the form of shared housing, food and other necessities and less often in the form of direct transfers of income. These transfers or remittances are, however, more likely to be received

TABLE II. ESTIMATED PREVALENCE OF LIFE INSURANCE IN SELECTED COUNTRIES

Country	Prevalence of Life Insurance
Taiwan, Province of China (1993)	47%
Hong Kong	10%
- below 65 years (1992)	18%
Republic of Korea	30%
Singapore (1993)	57%
Japan	>100%
United States of America	90%
- aged 50-69 (1992)	73%
- aged 70+ (1994)	57%

Source: Li et al., 1994, table 2.

from those children who live apart or who have migrated. The persistence of such an informal system is likely to remain for some time owing to the strong Confucian influence and the Asian values of filial piety and care of family members. Increasingly, less reliance is placed on children, as reflected in the low percentage of people who wanted another child to support them in old age (see table III). Financial help is expected more from sons than daughters and is still prevalent in the Republic of Korea and Taiwan, Province of China, although not in Singapore (see table IV). Nevertheless, it has been observed that, as families become smaller and more women participate in the labour market, older persons may have to place less reliance on children or may want to maintain their own independent living arrangements, as evidenced in the Republic of Korea (see Choe, 1992).

However, with rapid industrialization, urbanization and changing expectations and attitudes, reliance on a more formal and mandatory system that links benefits with contributions and risk is unavoidable. Singapore's fully-funded Central Provident Fund (CPF) is well-known. Nevertheless, a brief discussion is in order.[3] Started as an old age social security scheme, CPF took over public as well as many private sector pension schemes and extended its provisions beyond social security. The 1990 census indicates that 67 per cent of the labor force is covered by CPF (Shantakumar, 1996, p. 56). Among others, housing or home ownership is considered essential, as a roof over one's head provides a lot of security in old age. CPF was initiated in 1968 for a public housing scheme, but was subsequently extended to private residential properties in 1981. Health provision is in the form of approved hospitalization expenses covered by a portion of CPF funds. Medisave was launched in 1984, promoting health care as a necessary basic need to avert high medical care costs at advanced ages. The savings in this account can also be used for medical expenses of an ill parent. Liberalization of CPF funds for tertiary education took place in 1989. Although not directly contributing to old age security, this move is expected to improve economic welfare of older persons. The Education Scheme is in the form of loans, which are repayable upon graduation, together with interest. In addition, a number of protective insurance schemes, such as medical and housing insurance and some form of unemployment insurance are available. CPF funds have also been liberalized for approved investments, such as purchase of shares, stocks, unit trusts and gold. Old age savings is safeguarded as all principal sums for investments must be returned to the CPF account, although the dividends may be withdrawn. For those with insufficient funds, a safety net is provided by the Government through CPF top-up from budgetary surpluses. The CPF withdrawal age is still at 55 years or upon retirement but the total amount cannot be withdrawn, so that after age 60, the member would receive a monthly income. It may be a while yet before people can be persuaded to leave their CPF savings until they are older. Recently, provision has been made for a working member to open an account for a non-working relative by starting with a $50 deposit, and, moreover, adult children may top up the CPF accounts of their parents (Mehta, 1996). The savings accumulated in CPF under a government-managed but individual financed scheme is in principle a welfare system which may be difficult to replicate to a large extent in other countries because Singapore is a small country with a

---

[3]The features of the Singapore CPF is largely based on Low (1996).

TABLE III. PERCENTAGE OF RESPONDENTS FOR WHOM HELP IN OLD AGE IS
A "VERY IMPORTANT" MOTIVE FOR WANTING ANOTHER CHILD

Country	Male	Female	Total	Urban Mid	Urban Lower	Rural
Japan	na	na	12	2	7	21
Republic of Korea	12	18	16	3	26	43
Singapore	43	48	46	na	na	na

Source: Arnold et al., 1975, and Kagitcibasi, 1982, as reported in World Bank, 1994.

completely urban population that is small in size. Nevertheless, some features of CPF may prove favourable for other populations and adapted accordingly.

Remedial programmes, such as residential care for those who are chronically ill, are carried out jointly by governmental and non-governmental organizations (Mehta, 1996, p. 8). Health services for older persons may be subsidized by the Government, and there is a hospital run by the Government with a day hospital that also provides care givers. There are also six health care centres for older persons within the government-run polyclinics. Such centres provide subsidized rehabilitative services and day care. Domiciliary health care service, known as the Home Nursing Foundation, reaches out to those who are house-bound and need nursing care, where charges are on a sliding scale. In addition, there are commercial or other voluntary nursing homes, community and private hospitals, as well as shelters and residential homes which cater to ambulant elderly with no family. Voluntary organizations also operate mobile clinics. The Government subsidizes and promotes other health care services and programmes. A public assistance scheme under the Ministry of Community Development provides monthly allowances for the needy, in addition to those provided by voluntary organizations (Cheung, 1995, p. 8).

In Taiwan, Province of China, an average Taiwanese retires at the age of 65, but the Elderly Welfare Law implemented in 1980 covers only those aged 70 years and over. Among the benefits covered by the Government are:

(*a*) To provide and assist private funded:

(i) shelters for elderly who have no means for independent living;

(ii) institutions for the elderly with chronic diseases;

(iii) programmes to promote leisure and social activities;

(iv) service organizations;

(*b*) To subsidize health care and transportation costs for the elderly.[4]

In the Republic of Korea, a Social Welfare Law for the Aged was enforced in June 1981 to promote and improve living arrangements and health for the elderly.[5] A social welfare system giving preference to the elderly started on Parents' Day in May, 1980. Public aid provides benefits to older persons over 65 who are living alone whose families do not have the capability of supporting them. Among the benefits are provision of nursing homes, cash benefits and medical aid and special measures for disabled veterans over 65 and their families. Medical examinations for the elderly began in 1983 and are now provided to 200,000 older persons per year. Such examinations are provided free of charge once every other year to low-income persons. The provision of a second detailed examination began in 1989. Government aid also covers compensation support, medical care and resettlement funds to disabled veterans over 65 (about 4,900 of them). Medical aid is provided by the Government for the poor, which includes quite a number of older persons. A range of health and social service programmes for older citizens are available from Multipurpose Senior Centers established in 1985 (Park, 1996, p. 16). Two public assistance programmes are available—Livelihood Protection Program and Old Age Allowance. The Livelihood Protection Programme provides financial assistance to poor persons aged 65 years and over with no supporting relative. The Old Age Allowance is provided to poor persons aged 70 years and over who are not covered by any kind of public pension.

In Hong Kong, care and support of older persons outside of the family was recognized as early as 1977 where, instead of committing the Government to meet all the needs of older persons, a "care in the commu-

[4]See Shih and Chuang, 1995, p. 19.
[5]This is based largely on Choe, 1992.

TABLE IV. PERCENTAGE OF PARENTS WHO EXPECT FINANCIAL HELP FROM SONS AND DAUGHTERS

Country	Mother son	Mother daughter	Father son	Father daughter
Republic of Korea	85	46	78	42
Singapore	39	31	31	25
Taiwan, Province of China	85	39	76	29

Source: Adapted from Kagitcibasi, 1982 as reported in World Bank, 1994.

nity" approach was proposed.[6] The adoption of this approach is based on the premise that older persons would be most satisfied in the care of their families and that institutional care would be second best and should only be considered when the older persons are too frail to take care of themselves or when their families are unable to do so. Other than the old age allowance, which is regarded as an entitlement of all older persons,[7] all other public services are provided on a needs basis and for some, a means test is required. The needs of the older persons vary from service to service but are measured, in general, by the degree of urgency for support and the extent to which they can be met by the older persons themselves or their families. Another organization known as the Association for the Rights of the Elderly was formed by a group of social workers in the late 1970s to fight for the rights of older persons. In the mid-1980s, a group of professionals working in the field of gerontology formed the Hong Kong Association of Gerontology. At present, the activities of the Association include the publication of journals, the organization of seminars and the promotion of research on ageing issues. Care of older persons has also been a focus of many debates in the Legislative Council, which is a law-making body in Hong Kong. Provision of housing and hospital services are administered by two quasi-government organizations, the Housing Authority and the Hospital Authority, which have their own criteria for determining the needs of the older persons. A poor older person is also entitled to receive support from the comprehensive social security assistance

scheme, which enables him/her to live above subsistence level.

Housing for older persons was set up in the form of a hostel in the late 1960s and since then, a great variety of housing resources have been developed. While hostels are the major form of housing resource for older persons who were alone and without family prior to 1985, those requiring accommodation since then were placed in "sheltered housing" managed by either the Housing Department or non-governmental organizations. In addition, older persons can also apply for accommodation in public housing estates either through the Elderly Persons Priority Scheme or the Compassionate Rehousing Scheme. Two or more unrelated persons reaching the age of 58 years or over who agree to live together can also apply for rehousing (Chow, 1994, p. 68). These two schemes are intended mainly for the older persons who are capable of self-care or in need of only minimum assistance. For those older persons who cannot manage on their own, two types of residential care are available. The first is homes for older persons while the second consists of care and nursing homes that cater to older persons requiring different levels of nursing care. It is reported that there has been an upsurge in demand for nursing care places. Demand often exceeds availability, forcing some to turn to the more expensive private sector.

Families with an older member have a shorter waiting period when applying for public housing. Despite Government efforts to provide housing for all older persons, there are still several thousand older persons who, for various reasons, including wanting to be near their place of work and being unwilling to move to another district, are occupying just a bed-space in dilapidated private tenement blocks and are often referred to as "caged men". There are also about a thousand homeless older persons sleeping in the streets; plans are under way to house them in a few specially designed hostels located in the urban areas.

It is pertinent to highlight that services for older persons in Hong Kong have been developed largely from

---

[6]This is based largely on Chow (1995).

[7]Old age allowance is available to residents of Hong Kong reaching the age of 65, but if they have not attained 70 years of age, they have to declare that they have neither income nor assets above certain prescribed levels to be eligible. The allowance for those aged 70 and over is higher than for those below 70 years. This allowance is non-means tested and non-contributory and hence is small so as not to overburden the Government. It was first introduced in 1973 as an incentive to encourage families to take care of their own older members.

the efforts of the non-governmental organizations, with resources coming first from local and overseas donations and now from governmental subsidies. The fees charged for use of the various public services are either nominal or at an affordable level for the majority of the older population. In addition, private nursing and other home-based services are also available for those who can pay higher fees.

Very few older persons in Hong Kong are covered by private medical insurance and the majority of them utilize public medical and health services. Besides preventive health care, a wide range of domiciliary and institutional services are available for the older population, including community nursing and community psychiatric nursing services, infirmaries, priority medical consultation, psychogeriatric services and hospice care. While the quality of services is generally acceptable, such services are often in such short supply that they are available only to those in urgent need (Chow, 1995, p. 8).

An issue of concern therefore is the rising cost of health care and the ability of older persons or their family members to pay for such services. This issue will become critical as health care costs rise further and health services increasingly extend beyond the reach of more and more older persons. Related to this is the availability of specialized medical care and services, with appropriate medical staff and expertise to cater to the needs of older persons, such as geriatric care. Perhaps some form of health insurance, possibly from young, should be encouraged and implemented. For those in the disadvantaged groups, both the public and private sectors should provide some form of concessions so that the older persons in these groups have access to good quality medical care. In Singapore, the Government subsidizes varying levels of health services for the older persons.

Many insurance policies discriminate against older persons. It is timely to review such policies, at least to reduce the burden of health costs of those most likely to be in need. For example, in Singapore, Medishield, which is an optional medical insurance scheme, covers a person until 70 years of age (Mehta, 1996, p. 5). In the Republic of Korea, since 1989, all Koreans have been covered by medical insurance or medical assistance programmes (Choe, 1994, p. 100-101).

In Singapore, three hospitals and a number of community hospitals have geriatric facilities (Cheung, 1995, p. 9). In one hospital run by the Government, a geriatric Centre has been established with a Day Hospital for recently discharged older patients, especially those who have suffered from stroke (Mehta, 1996, p. 9). Temporary day care is also available for ex-patients. The Republic of Korea has 11 geriatric hospitals (Oh, 1995, p. 5).

(iii) *Strengthening family support systems*

There is a need for policies and programmes to strengthen family support and care of older persons. This is despite the fact that older persons now generally have a place to live with their children (Chen and Jones, 1989; Andrews et al., 1986; ESCAP, 1992; World Bank, Lee et al., 1996,). However, with high growth and urbanization rates, massive rural-urban migration and changes in family structure, family support of older persons has shown signs of weakening (World Bank, 1994,). Single person households are also becoming more common, as evident from surveys in Hong Kong, Japan, Republic of Korea and other countries (Tan, 1993). As argued elsewhere (see Tan, 1993, for example), due to these and other changes, the family may not automatically provide for the care and support of older persons. It is therefore necessary for a support system to be established to enable families to continue being the main care provider of older persons. Public and private housing and other social infrastructure should provide for the requirements of older persons within an extended family system, or, for ageing parents to live close to their children. This may include housing facilities catering to the needs of older persons, tax concessions or special allowances provided to children who live with their aged parents or who live fairly close by. In the case of Hong Kong, those families with an older member are given a shorter waiting period when applying for public housing (Chow, 1995, p. 9). Children who support elderly parents can apply for a dependent parents' tax allowance, which is increased if the parents also live with them. In the Republic of Korea, the Government provides various benefits to those who take care of their aged parents, through tax deductions, housing loans and special monthly allowances for government officials (Oh, 1995, p. 6). The Government has given an annual reward in recognition of such filial care since 1982.

Partly because 90 per cent of Singapore's population lives in public housing, the Government is able to ensure that parents and married children are allocated flats next to each other, or are allowed to exchange flats with others so that they can live in close proximity to one another (Mehta, 1996, p. 14). Families living in the same household are also given special privileges and concessions, and there is a special government grant for parents and adult children to live within the same housing estate. Housing facilities are also being upgraded with non-slip tiles, handle bars in the toilet and an alarm system (for single elderly) for emergency help and elevators.

To foster family care and support, special grants may also be established for family-based income-generating projects. It may be appropriate to introduce policies and programmes that encourage children to make regular contributions for the care of aged parents. Near-by day care centres may be another option well worth considering for working children, as such centres can provide temporary relief for carers as well as the older persons. Home nursing and rehabilitative day care are other essential services.

In Singapore, a recent legal measure called the "Maintenance of Parents Act" provides an avenue for elderly parents who are not receiving financial assistance from children to seek redress (Mehta, 1996, p. 7). Adult children can be legally bound to financially support parents until their demise. This measure, however, may be difficult to enforce and may cause a lot of resentment. Children also may grudgingly comply creating a lot of family conflict and tension. In my opinion, this should be a measure of last resort. Perhaps other less extreme measures could be considered, even one in which compulsory monthly deductions from each worker are sent to a common fund (since everyone has parents) for use by those in the disadvantaged categories.

(iv) *Promotion of a community support system and inter-generational relationships*

The importance of reciprocal care and support between generations, including the sharing of accommodation and caring for grandchildren, should be encouraged and emphasized. There is also a need to formulate or strengthen policies/programmes aimed at enhancing family relationships across generations, such as having "family day", where both the young and old can participate. Instead of homes for the aged, a more positive alternative is to adapt a social health delivery system that would include hospice and community care to supplement family care. Communities should be encouraged to form voluntary and mutual aids organizations in providing support of older persons and their families.

It is reported that, in the Republic of Korea, older persons often spend their time in community centres for older persons, but, owing to insufficient social services, often feel alienated (Choe, 1992, p. 94). A "Charter for Older People " which promotes the well-being of older persons, led to the formation of the Korea Senior Citizens' Association in 1982. About a third of the older persons in the Republic of Korea are members of this association. It is reported that the various activities and programmes that enhance the well-being and integration of older persons into their community are still in the trial stage (Choe, 1992, p. 97).

In Hong Kong, community support services consisting of home help services, social centres, multi-service centres and day care centres constitute an important part of the social support network. To assist older persons in remaining in the community, supportive medical and health services such as respite service and various kinds of community programmes are available. In 1991, an outreach service for "elderly at risk" was targeted at older persons in need of support who would otherwise not seek the service. In addition, mass programmes such as health education and festivals are held regularly to encourage the active participation of older persons in community activities. Older persons have an opportunity to associate with other members of the community through a great variety of indigenous organizations, including mutual help associations and religious bodies.

In the Republic of Korea, home care services, day care centres and short-stay centres are provided (Oh, 1995, p. 5). Nursing homes and facilities for older persons are operating in 8,942 places (Park, 1996, p. 12). Community, religious and other voluntary organizations can play a major role in organizing these arrangements to meet emerging needs. In Singapore, under a new funding scheme that began in 1992, voluntary welfare organizations are eligible for governmental financial assistance (Cheung, 1995, p. 8). Under this scheme, the Government provides capital grants of up to 80 per cent of approved building costs and recurrent grants of 50 per cent of the annual operating expenditure.

In addition, concessions should be provided to all older persons, especially those who cannot afford to obtain basic aids such as spectacles, dentures and hearing aids as well as other implements needed to continue to interact and participate fully in the home and community. Public facilities and services should ensure that priority lines are created for older persons and that their needs and comfort are attended to. In Hong Kong, concessionary fares for limited community facilities and public transport services are available to encourage older persons to participate in community activities (Chow, 1995, p. 12). In the Republic of Korea, the Elderly Special Treatment Program provides older persons aged 65 years and over with free bus coupons and discounts on public transportation (Park, 1996, p. 12). Social welfare centers and counseling services operated by volunteers working through the private sector, have a preferential system for older persons that includes discounts on fees or free admission to public facilities such as parks, museums and theaters.

A number of services have been set up to enable older persons to continue to participate in the mainstream of society. In Hong Kong, supportive services are provided to enable older persons to remain in the community for as long as possible, either by themselves or with their families (Chow, 1990). Such services include community nursing, home help, day care, laundry and food services, social and recreational activities, hostel accommodation and sheltered employment. Most older persons spend their leisure time in family-related activities, such as watching television programmes (Chow, 1995, p.10-11). Many who stay with married children revealed that they are too busy with household chores and looking after their grandchildren to have much time left for their own. There seems to be a cultural resistance as Chinese older persons seldom engage in activities outside of the home environment and with non-family members. For those older persons who want to spend leisure time outside their homes, social centers provide the most convenient venue. In these centres, various kinds of social and recreational activities are provided and older persons are encouraged to serve as volunteers for other frail older persons and the handicapped. An increasing number of older persons are also becoming quite religious and they regard religion as their major pursuit in life. Older persons residing in the same housing block or nearby also gather informally to play mahjong or do tai-chi exercises. Chatting with neighbours is commonly regarded as a most convenient way to spend their leisure time, and such companionship is invaluable to older persons.

In Singapore, home visiting, day care, respite care and other supportive services are being offered (Cheung and Vasoo, 1989). Older persons are kept fit and healthy and they are capable of full participation in the mainstream of community life. An Advisory Council on the Aged was established in 1988 and senior citizens' clubs have proliferated with the encouragement of the Government. These clubs, which are run by the Government or para-governmental organizations, offer recreational programmes, health screening, fitness activities and opportunities for community services. There are also advice and counseling services to provide avenues for older persons to settle their personal and family problems and disputes (Cheung, 1995, p. 7). There are also provisions for unrelated older persons to form a household unit and rent a public apartment, thus encouraging older persons to live in the community for as long as possible (Cheung, 1995, p. 8). Retirement villages are being considered to house older persons together so that they can provide mutual support and assistance to one another. Kim and Choe (1992) reported that the various types of services recently introduced for older persons by the Government of the Republic of Korea are limited in scope and utilized by a small percentage of the population. Nevertheless, the Government subsidizes about 25,000 facilities, where classes for leisure and hobby activities are conducted (Park, 1996, p. 15-16). Home care programmes include home help service, adult day care and short stay service programmes. Older persons volunteer to teach Chinese caligraph, and to provide instruction on filial obliga-

tions and traditional culture to younger persons (Choe, 1992, p. 99). Many Korean older persons visit friends or relatives, listen to radio and watch television and play cards or chess (Park, 1996, p. 7). In Taiwan, Province of China, participation in clubs for senior citizens is rather limited, while watching television or listening to the radio is a favourite pastime, with walking being the main form of exercise of older persons (Lee et al., 1996, p. 34-52).

It is necessary to avoid duplication and ensure that quality services are provided by the various non-governmental, governmental and private organizations. To this end, appropriate law enactment and monitoring should be instituted to protect those vulnerable and in need of such services. There should also be legislation to cover the running of voluntary and commercial old-people's homes to protect those in need of such services. For example, in Hong Kong, even though community support and residential services are operated by different non-governmental organizations, similar criteria are employed in assessing needs as the services are uniformly funded by the Government. Since 1972, the Hong Kong Council of Social Service, a coordinator of non-government organizations, has established a division to monitor their work in the area of services for older persons and to draw up relevant service standards.

Programmes for special groups

Certain groups would require special programmes and assistance. Among them would be women at older ages. Women are economically more vulnerable than men at older ages for a number of reasons:

(*a*) Women do not work in the formal labour force owing to home and childbearing responsibilities and, even if they do, their careers are often interrupted and limited by such responsibilities;

(*b*) Women tend to be at the lowest rung and receive little pay, partly as a result of poor education and training skills;

(*c*) Women are less likely to have pension or other social security benefits, and be less able to have savings or access to credit and other inheritance;

As a result if their inferior economic positions throughout their lives, older women require special programmes to enable them to participate in the mainstream of society. The fact that they live longer than men in most societies suggests that special programmes need to be initiated for women at older ages. Changes in family circumstances affect women more than men largely due to the fact that many women live longer and hence are more likely to face widowhood. In 1980, 75 per cent of women aged 65 years and above in the Republic of Korea were widowed compared with 64 per cent in Singapore (United Nations, 1991,). A widowed, divorced or abandoned woman is likely to receive a reduced income when her husband leaves her (due to death or divorce), resulting in the majority of widows/divorcees being poor (World Bank, 1994,).

Older women are disproportionately represented amongst the poor, which has implications on their nutritional status and access to adequate medical care and their physical well-being. Coupled with low income and poor education, many older women are very vulnerable. Unlike older men, who may depend on their wives when they fall ill, older women are quite likely to have to rely on children and other relatives.

Widowhood/divorce is also often associated with depression and deterioration in physical and mental health. Women facing such a situation therefore would require special programmes to enable them to return to the mainstream of society and enable them to cope.

Women remain largely the main care providers in the family. Largely because of increased life expectancy, women in the "middle" face the additional burden of having to cope with young children (due to later age at marriage) and work outside the home (due to rise in educational level) as well as care for aged parents and relatives. The men in the "middle" may also share the financial burden and care for the young and old, and they also require special support from the community and society to enable them to cope. One such service is respite care that provides some relief and support to care givers by giving them time off and relieving their stress of having to provide continuously to the care and demands of those sick and less abled persons. Employment policies that respond to the care responsibilities that workers must assume over and above their job responsibilities have been developed in some countries.

4. CONCLUSION

The review of the situation of older persons in the newly industrialized countries of east Asia therefore indicates that a welfare rather than a developmental approach has been adopted in many aspects of the policies and programmes for older persons. While it is certain that some amount of care and support would be required by all older persons, with rising education, improved nutrition and better care, more and more older persons would remain fairly healthy until advanced age. This, coupled with the fact that the vast majority of older persons would remain able and capable for quite a number of years in all countries, calls for an emphasis on policies and programmes that promote older persons as a valuable resource, be it in economic, social or community participation. Older persons then are likely to maintain independence, participation, care, self-fulfillment and dignity, when they have a choice—and they are likely to have the support and care, when they need

it. Developing countries with limited resources would also benefit by promoting a developmental rather than a welfare approach to population ageing. This is especially as the former promotes ageing issues as concerning persons of all ages and encourages older persons to remain in the mainstream of society, while not ignoring the need for their care and support.

REFERENCES

Andrews, G., A. Esterman, A. Braunack-Mayer and C. Rungie eds, *Aging in the Western Pacific: A Four-Country Study*, Manila, Western Pacific Reports and Studies, No. 1, Manila, 1986.

Arnold, Fred et al., *The Value of Children: A Cross-National Study,* Vol. 1, East-West Population Institute, East-West Center, Honolulu, 1975.

Chang, Ming-Cheng and M.B. Ofstedal, *Changing Attitudes Towards Old-Age Support in Taiwan: 1973-1985*, Comparative Study of the Elderly in Asia Research Report No. 91-8, Population Studies Center, University of Michigan, Ann Arbor, 1991.

Chen, A.J. and Gavin Jones, *Ageing in ASEAN: its Socio-Economic Consequences*, Singapore, Institute of Southeast Asian Studies, 1989.

Cheung, Paul P.L., "Population Ageing in Singapore", Paper presented at the Evaluation Meeting for the United Nations Population Fund-supported project; Promotion of Awareness and Policy Formulation on Aging', Japanese Organization for International Cooperation in Family Planning, 21-22 September, 1995, Japan 1995.

Cheung, Paul P.L. and S. Vasoo, "Country Study on the Elderly: Singapore", report prepared for the Economic and Social Commission for Asia and the Pacific, Singapore, 1989.

Choe, Ehn Hyun ,"New Role of Elderly in Newly Industrializing Countries" in ESCAP, *Productive Ageing in Asia and the Pacific*, Asian Population Studies Series, No. 129, United Nations, New York, 1992.

Choe, Ehn Hyun, "Programmes and Policies for the Aged in the Republic of Korea", in United Nations, *The Ageing of Asian Populations*, Proceedings of the United Nations Round Table on the Ageing of Asian Populations, 4-6 May, 1992, Bangkok, 1994.

Choe, Ehn Hyun and Lee Jung Sup,"Future Directions for Ageing Policy in Asia" in ESCAP, *Population Ageing in Asia*, Asian Population Studies Series, No. 108, Bangkok, 1991.

Chow, Nelson,"Ageing in Hong Kong" in B.K.P. Leung (ed.), *Social Issues in Hong Kong*, Oxford University Press, Hong Kong, 1990.

Chow, Nelson, "Ageing in Hong Kong", in United Nations, *The Ageing of Asian Populations*, Proceedings of the United Nations Round Table on the Ageing of Asian Populations, 4-6 May, 1992, Bangkok, 1994.

Chow, Nelson , "Ageing in Hong Kong", Paper presented at the evaluation meeting for the United Nations Population Fund-supported project 'Promotion of Awareness and Policy Formulation on Aging, Japanese Organization for International Cooperation in Family Planning, 21-22 September, 1995, Tokyo, 1995.

Council for Economic Planning and Development, Republic of China *Taiwan Statistical Data Bank, 1996.*

Statistical Yearbook of the Republic of China, 1996.

Department of Health, Taiwan Provincial Government *Health in Taiwan Province*, 1993.

Economic and Social Commission for Asia and the Pacific , *Asia Pacific Population Journal*, Vol. 7, No. 3, Bangkok, 1992.

Kagitcibasi, C., "Old Age Security Value of Children: Cross National Socioeconomic Evidence", *Journal of Cross-Cultural Psychology*, Vol. 13, 1982..

Kim, Ik Ki and Choe Ehn Hyun "Support Exchange Patterns of the Elderly in the Republic of Korea" in *Asia-Pacific Population Journal*, Vol. 7, No. 3, 1992.

Lee, Meiling, Kaunjeng Cehn and Chingli Yang, "Quality of Life for Elderly in Hsin-chuan City, Taipei Country, Taiwan", Paper presented at the International Symposium on Aging People in Transition, : comparative study of three cases in Asia: Korea, Taiwan and Japan', 14-15 November, 1996, Tokyo, 1996.

Li, Rosa Maria, Laura Duberstein and Hui-Sheng Lin , *An Exploration of Life Insurance among the Elderly in Taiwan,,* "Comparative Study of the Elderly in Asia Research Report No. 94-27, Population Studies Center, University of Michigan, Ann Arbor, 1994.

Low, Linda, "Social Security and Economic Well-being of the Aged in ASEAN", paper presented at the Seminar on Social Security and Economic Well-being of Older Persons in ASEAN Countries, 17-19 October 1996, Kuala Lumpur, Ministry of National Unity and Social Development, Malaysia, 1996.

Mehta, Kalyani, "Social Security and Economic Well-being of Older Persons in ASEAN: The Singapore Scenario", Paper presented at the Seminar on Social Security and Economic Well-being of Older Persons in ASEAN Countries, Kuala Lumpur, 1996.

Oh, Kyung-Seuk, "Current Welfare Programmes for the Aged in Korea", paper presented at the Evaluation Meeting for the United Nations Population Fund-supported project: Promotion of Awareness and Policy Formulation on Aging, Japanese Organization for International Cooperation Family Planning, 21-22 September, 1995, Tokyo, 1995.

Park, Jae Gan , "The Ageing Situation and its Problems in Korea", Paper presented at the International Symposium on Aging People in Transition: Comparative Study of three cases in Asia: Korea, Taiwan and Japan, 14-15 November, 1996, Tokyo, 1996..

Shantakumar, G., "Preparing for the Greying Century: Lessons from an Industrializing Country and Future Developments" in International Federation on Ageing, *Ageing International: Global Ageing - Challenges and Opportunities of the Next Century*, Vol. XXIII, Issue 1, 1996.

Shih, Shiauping Rosa and Yi-Li Chuang, *Opportunities and Constraints for Older Workers in Taiwan*, Comparative Study of the Elderly in Asia, Research Report No. 95-30, Population Studies Center, University of Michigan, Ann Arbor, 1995.

Tan, Poo Chang , "Implications of Changing Family Structures on Old-Age Support in Asia" in ESCAP, *Fourth Asian and Pacific Population Conference*, 19-27 August 1992, Bali, Indonesia, Asian Population Studies Series, No. 124, Bangkok, 1993.

Tan, Poo Chang , "Productive Ageing" in Tan, Ng and Chwee (eds.), *1995 Celebrations National Day for the Elderly*, 7-8 October 1995, Faculty of Economics and Administration, University of Malaya, Kuala Lumpur, 1996.

Tan, Poo Chang , "Productive Ageing" in *Added Years of Life in Asia: Current Situation and Future Challenges*, ESCAP Asian Population Studies Series, No. 141, United Nations, Bangkok, 1996.

United Nations, *The World Ageing Situation* (ST/CSDHA/14), New York, 1992.

United Nations , *The Sex and Age Distribution of the World Populations*, New York, 1994.

United Nations, *World Population Prospects,* 1994 Revision, New York, 1995.

World Bank , *Averting the Old Age Crisis*, Oxford University Press, New York, 1994.

V.   AGEING IN TRANSITION: SITUATION OF OLDER WOMEN IN LATIN AMERICAN REGION

Martha Dueñas Loza*

I.   CONCEPTUAL FAMEWORK: summarizes the main principles, recommendations and conclusions of the United Nations global conferences, trying to include the greatest number of elements relative to the environmental, social, economic, political, demographic, legal, lawful and institutional conditions at the national and international levels, that influence the lives of older persons, particularly, of elderly women.

II.   AGEING IN TRANSITION: deals with different anthropological factors intervening in the transition process of elderly women as individuals and as a group. Due to the limited space available, this section is very condensed. The analysis of the issue should be expanded not only regarding the typology of the processes described, but also, the evaluation methodology according to sector, gender, geographical, historical and cultural conditions, among others.

III.   CONDITIONS OF OLDER WOMEN IN LATIN AMERICA: describes several essential issues relative to the conditions and characteristics of the lives of middle-aged and elderly women in the region. The existing diversity requires a great purge of the reference data, due to the ambiguity of the available statistical data and the lack of reliable and recent information that might permit the verification of the validity of general and anecdotal references in countries lacking specific statistics.

INTRODUCTION

La vejez no es una enfermedad, es una etapa de nuestra vida.

Betsie Hollants[1]

The 1999 International Year of Older Persons has drawn to a close. Several initiatives have begun. These,

in time, increase the need for bibliographic material in order to represent adequately such an important human group. This search is an overwhelming struggle in itself. There is little specialized literature on the subject matter, most of which deals with a variety of social situations in which the elderly are represented as a population group whose growth is an overwhelming challenge to the existing economic and social structures.

In general, the situation of older persons is reflected as complementary to the analysis of: population; gerontology, health care, social security systems and health insurance; labour and income generating activities; censuses and population statistics; migration, refugees and displaced persons. The notion of older persons "as a burden to the social system", as "excessive beneficiaries of pensions and health care not provided to younger people and children in welfare",[2] is becoming much too common. At present, another recurrent comment derives from various articles where the elderly are represented as a demographic time bomb. This is due not only to the decline in fertility levels, but to a disproportionate growth of the old and very old population worldwide, which in time will alter the financial, medical, and social security schema. "Burgeoning elderly populations threaten to overwhelm government benefit programmes in the developed nations, but demographers differ on how great the challenge will be…".[3]

BACKGROUND

The Global Targets on Ageing for the Year 2001 (General Assembly resolution 47/86), primarily aim at strengthening the capacities of the countries to deal effectively with the ageing of the population and with the special concerns and needs of their elderly, and to promote an appropriate international response to the issues of ageing through action for the establishment of a new international economic order and increased international

*M. Dueñas Loza is former acting Direct of The Research and Training Unit of the International Research and Training Unit of the International Research and Training Institute for the Advancement of Women (INSTRAW).

[1]Hollants, Elizabeth (Betsie) M, Belge Journalist, Founder of (i) Centro Integral de Desarrollo Humano en América Latina (CIDHALL); (ii)Asociación Civil para la Vejez en Mexico: Estudio y Acción; (iii) ANSAM Fundación Los Ancianos y sus amigos. CIDHAL Boletín 27 Aniversario, Vol.4 No. 1-2, 1996.

[2]American Association for the Advancement of Sciences, Vol. 273, July 1996.

[3]*The Situation of Elderly Women, Available Statistics and Indicators*, INSTRAW/UNSTAT (INSTRAW/SER.B/44-1000), United Nations publication.

technical cooperation, particularly among the developing countries themselves.

The United Nations General Assembly adopted resolution 50/141 on 25 December 1995, declaring 1999, the International Year of Older Persons, with the theme, "Towards a Society for All ages". Equally important in the United Nations institutional process are resolution 33/52, of 14 December 1978, the celebration of a World Assembly on Ageing in 1982, and resolution 44/76, of 8 December 1989, on elderly women.

The involvement of the International Research and Training Institute for the Advancement of Women (INSTRAW) in this chapter represents another step forward in a long process that began in 1982, when the Institute presented a position paper entitled "Women and the Hidden Economy" in a United Nations University (UNU) project, "Household, Gender and Age". In 1987, INSTRAW developed a statistical data base on selected variables of mid-life and elderly women in Latin America and the Caribbean. This material was made available at a joint meeting of the Pan-American Health Organization (PAHO), American Association of Retired Persons (AARP), INSTRAW and the United Nations Commission on Sustainable Development.

In 1990, INSTRAW provided advisory services to the College of Arts and Sciences of the Kansas State University, drawing up the work plan and design of the survey on productive age in the Dominican Republic. This survey explores the potential of older persons to enhance their contributions to social and economic development and expand their income-generating and services activities.

In 1993, in conjunction with the United Nations Statistics Division, INSTRAW published "The Situation of Elderly Women: Available Statistics and Indicators", on the basis of a study carried out to review and propose measures for improving the concepts relevant to: (a) the position of elderly women in family formation and household; (b) elderly women, learning and education; (c) the economic activity and labour force participation of elderly women; (d) elderly women's economic and social support and, (e) health status of elderly women.

In 1996, at the NGO Panel Committee of Ageing of the second United Nations Conference on Human Settlements (HABITAT II) in Istanbul, INSTRAW presented a position paper entitled "Ageing: A Chronological Process in Life, and the Social and Economic Questions Arising from It".

I. CONCEPTUAL FRAMEWORK: MAIN ELEMENTS

Population ageing is a global phenomenon with important implications for developing as well as developed countries. In 1982, the World Assembly on Ageing adopted the International Plan of Action on Ageing, which affirmed the need for further research in matters of population ageing in developing countries. While this phenomenon is increasingly becoming of universal concern, its problems and/or consequences, as any other economic and social problem of the contemporary world, cannot be resolved without clear reference to adequate and reliable statistics. However, based on the concepts and methods currently being applied in most data collection systems, existing data do not provide sufficient information to carry out a more complete analysis of the status and problems of the elderly.

Ageing can be a nebulous concept, but its contours are undeniable. In the course of building a conceptual framework, chapter IV (Areas of special concern) of the Nairobi Forward-Looking Strategies for the Advancement of Women, adopted in July 1985, provides important background. It briefly describes the major social sectors—health care, employment opportunities, housing, sanitation, family and community participation—that condition the quality of life and the well-being of older women and men. In addition, it makes special recommendations to both Governments and non-governmental organizations relative to the care and protection that should be provided for the elderly.

In order to have a better understanding of the elements that should be incorporated in a conceptual framework accordant to present realities, reference should be made to several important issues engrafted in the programmes, plans and platforms for action of the series of United Nations global conferences held since 1992.

Older persons and the United Nations Conference on Environment and Development[4]

Among the 27 principles of the Rio Declaration on Environment and Development, adopted in June 1992 at the United Nations Conference on Environment and Development (UNCED), there is no specific mention of the status of older persons as a population group, in issues concerning sustainability; farming practices and soil maintenance; food production and conservation; wood and fuel collection; safe water and sanitation services. Neither does it mention the condition of older persons living in slums and in urban destitution; nor the growing millions of homeless older persons in

---

[4]*Report of the United Nations Conference on Environment and Development,* Rio de Janeiro, 3-14 June 1992, (United Nations publication, Sales No. E. 98. I.8 and corrigenda), vol. I: *Resolutions adopted by the Conference.*

industrialized societies; or the consumption patterns of the well-off older population.

However, for the purpose of this analysis, it is relevant that the following principles were adopted:

Principle 1 - Human beings are at the centre of concerns for sustainable development. They are entitled to a healthy and productive life in harmony with nature.

Principle 5 - All States and all people shall co-operate in the essential task of eradicating poverty as an indispensable requirement for sustainable development.

Principle 20 - Women have a vital role in environmental management and development. Their full participation is therefore essential to achieve sustainable development.

In addition, in chapter 5 of the declaration, it was observed that policies should combine environmental concerns and population issues within a holistic view of development whose primary goals should include the alleviation of poverty; secure livelihoods; good health; quality of life; improvement of the status and income of women and their access to schooling and professional training, as well as fulfilment of their personal aspirations. Item 5.22, stated that an assessment should be made of the implications of the age structure of the population on resource demand and dependency burdens, ranging from educational expenses for the young to health care and support for the elderly, and on household income generation. Item 5.32 expressed the need to develop appropriate socio-economic policies for the young and the elderly, in terms of both family and state support systems.[5]

In chapter 6 of the Rio declaration, it was noted that special attention should also be paid to the health needs of the elderly and that it would be advisable to carry out baseline surveys and knowledge, attitude and practice studies on the health and nutrition of women throughout their life cycle, especially as related to the impact of environmental degradation and adequate resources.[6]

Older persons and the World Conference on Human Rights

Neither ageing as a process, nor older persons as a group, are specifically mentioned in the text of the Convention, its protocols, or by the Vienna Conference. Ageing is therefore not a category included in any part of the different instruments, while youth and childhood are incorporated in the Convention on the Rights of the Child. The situation of the girl-child is addressed in the

Beijing Platform for Action and the Cairo Plan of Action.

The Vienna Conference emphasized that action for the promotion and protection of economic, social and cultural rights is as important as action for civil and political rights. This Conference should be regarded both as the culmination of a long process and as the point of departure for a new adventure on behalf of human rights.[7] In his address to the opening meeting of the Conference, the Secretary-General stressed: the importance of the question of the interdependence of all human rights.[8]

The Declaration on the Right to Development, adopted by the General Assembly in 1986 and reaffirmed in 1993 at the World Conference on Human Rights, defined development as a comprehensive economic, social, cultural and political process, which aims at the constant improvement of the well-being of the entire population and of all individuals on the basis of their active, free and meaningful participation in development and in the fair distribution of benefits resulting therefrom. It redefined the objective of economic activity, which was no longer geared towards growth and profit, but towards the attainment of human and social objectives through the improvement of the social, economic, political and cultural well-being of individuals and peoples. It presupposed the participation of the entire people inspired by a common ideal, and individual and collective creativity in devising the most adequate solutions to problems arising from local conditions, needs and aspirations.[9]

In Vienna Declaration and Programme of Action, grave concern was expressed regarding continuing human rights violations in all parts of the world and about the lack of sufficient and effective remedies for the victims. It also expressed concern about violations of human rights during armed conflicts, affecting the civilian population, especially women, children, the elderly and the disabled.

In chapter II (B), Equality, dignity and tolerance, the importance of the enjoyment by women, of the highest standard of physical and mental health throughout their life-span was recognized. In reference to equality between women and men, it reaffirmed a woman's right to accessible and adequate health care and the widest range of family planning services, as well as equal access to education at all levels.

---

[5]Ibid.
[6]Ibid.

[7]*Report of the World Conference of Human Rights,* 1993, Vienna, 14-25 June 1993, United Nations publication, Sales No.E.94.14.1).
[8]Ibid.
[9]The International Covenant on Economic, Social and Cultural Rights. General Assembly resolution 2200A (XXI).

Older persons and the International Conference on Population and Development

Among the fifteen principles included in chapter II of the Programme of Action of the United Nations International Conference on Population and Development, there is no specific mention to the situation of the elderly. Nevertheless, principle I recalled that all human beings are born free and equal in dignity and rights.[10]

Items 6.16 to 6.20 contain concrete references to the condition of older persons, namely, their increase in number as a consequence of the decline in fertility levels and the corresponding changes in the age structure; the economic and social impact and the provision of long-term support systems and safety nets; and enhancing self-reliance mechanisms to better serve this population group.

Older persons and the World Summit for Social Development

The Copenhagen Declaration on Social Development refers to the elderly "as particularly vulnerable to social exclusion, poverty and marginalization" and pledges Governments to make the commitment to create a framework for action to "improve the possibility of older persons achieving a better life" and to "develop and implement policies to ensure that all people have adequate economic and social protection [...] and old age". Furthermore, the Governments also commit themselves to acknowledging and encouraging the contribution of people of all age groups as equally and vitally important for the building of a harmonious society, and fostering dialogue between generations in all parts of society. The Declaration also refers to the promotion of equal partnership between women and men in providing care and support for older family members. .[11]

The Copenhagen Declaration also refers to the need to ensure special measures to protect older persons and to ensure that they are integrated into their communities, and promotes full and equal access to health care for women of all ages, and states that, social protection systems should be based on legislation to protect old age and to ensure that social protection and social support programmes meet the needs of support for older women.[12]

The Declaration emphasises the particular efforts that should be made to protect older persons, including those with disabilities. These efforts are oriented to improve family support for older persons living in rural areas, the so-called working older, those affected by armed conflicts and natural disasters, those subject to all types of exploitation, abuse and/or violence. or victims of serious diseases. Securing the ability of older persons to meet their own basic human needs, creating a financial environment to encourage people to save to be able to provide for their old age; ensuring mechanisms to ensure that retired workers do not fall into poverty, taking into account their contribution to development; and supporting cross-generational participation in policy and decision-making bodies.[13]

Older persons and the Global Conference on the Sustainable Development of Small Island Developing States

The Programme of Action for the Sustainable Development of Small Island Developing States, states that the commitment and genuine involvement of all social groups is critical to the effective implementation of the objectives, policies and mechanisms agreed to by Governments in all programme areas of Agenda 21 and that new participatory approaches to policy-making and implementation of sustainable development programmes will be necessary at all levels. In that regard, the Programme noted that there is a special role for groups that include women, youth, senior citizens, indigenous people and local communities, as well as the private sector, labour and non-governmental organizations. As stated in Agenda 21, and reiterated in the Programme of Action, one of the fundamental prerequisites for the achievement of sustainable development is broad public participation in the decision-making process.[14]

Older persons and the Second United Nations Conference on Human Settlements[15]

According to the Agenda adopted at the Second United Nations Conference on Human Settlements, older persons are entitled to lead fulfilling and productive lives and should have opportunities for full participation in their communities and society, and in all decision-making regarding their well-being, especially

---

[10]*Report of the United Nations Conference on Population and Development, Cario, 5-13 September 1994* (United Nations publicaton, Sales No. E. 95. XIII.18).

[11]Report of the World Summit for Social Development, Copenhagen, 6-12 March 1995 (United Nations publicaton, Sales No. E. 96. IV.8).

[12]Ibid.

[13]Ibid.

[14]*Report of the Global Conference on the Sutainable Development of Small Island Developing States,* Bridgetown, Barbados, 25 April-6 May 1994 *(United Nations publication, Sales No. E. 97.IV.6).*

[15]*Second United Nations Conference on Human Settlements (HABITAT II),* Istanbul, 3-14 June 1996. (United Nations publication, Sales No. E. 97.IV.6).

their shelter needs; their many contributions to the political, social and economic process of human settlements should be recognized and valued. Special attention should be given to meeting the evolving housing and mobility needs in order to enable them to continue to lead rewarding lives in their communities.

The Global Plan of Action contains a comprehensive set of elements related to ageing:

- Paragraph 60 states that "adequate shelter means more than a roof over one's head... Gender-specific and age-specific factors [...] should be considered in this context";

- Paragraph 78 (d) and (g) state that Governments should "develop regularization programmes and formulate and implement such programmes and projects in consultation with the concerned population and organized groups, ensuring the full and equal participation of women and taking into account the needs differentiated by gender, age, disability and vulnerability. Promote mechanisms for the protection of women who risk losing their homes and properties when their husbands die."

- Paragraph 100 states that "given the magnitude of the challenges that human settlements pose, society must value and take advantage of the wisdom, knowledge and skill of every person. Sustainable human settlements development requires cooperative and complementary actions among interested parties [...] As a general matter, interested parties include women and men of all ages."

- Paragraph 121 (f) encourages Governments to "Prepare and disseminate disaggregated data presented by age, sex and work status, set up monitoring mechanisms in government structures and integrate the result into mainstream policies for sustainable human settlements."

- Paragraph 123 (i) states that, "To prevent, reduce and eliminate violence and crime, Governments.. should ..Encourage the establishment of programmes and projects based on voluntary participation, especially of children, youth and older persons, to prevent violence, including violence in the home and crime."

- Paragraph 124 (b) states that "to protect vulnerable and disadvantaged people, Governments should facilitate the participation of local organizations, including elder councils, women's groups..."

- Paragraph 136 (d) and (f) state that "To improve the health and well-being of all people throughout their life-span, particularly people living in poverty, Governments should....Improve shelter conditions so as to mitigate those health and safety risks, particularly risks to women, older *persons*, children and people with disabilities that are associated with activities at home;

- Paragraph 147 reads,: "Transport and communication systems are the key to the movement of goods, people, information and ideas, and to access to markets, employment, schools and other facilities and land use, [...] People living in poverty, women, children, youth, older persons and people with disabilities are particularly disadvantaged by the lack of accessible, affordable, safe and efficient public transport systems";

- Paragraph 184 (c)(ii) and (c)(iii) read, "To facilitate capacity-building and institutional development for the improvement of human settlements planning and management. Governments should [..] train [...] trainers to develop a core capacity for institution-strengthening and capacity-building that includes gender awareness and the needs of children, youth and the elderly as integral components" and develop "local capacity to define needs and undertake or commission applied research, particularly with regard to age and gender-sensitive analysis ...".

Older persons and the World Food Summit[16]

There is no specific reference to the elderly population in the Rome Declaration and the Plan of Action of the World Food Summit

Older persons and the Fourth World Conference on Women[17]

The Platform for Action of the Fourth World Conference on Women notes that "the risk of falling into poverty is greater for women than for men, particularly in old age, where social security systems are based on the principle of continuous remunerated employment..[..]..Moreover, older women also face greater obstacles to labour-market re-entry" (para. 52). Paragraph 92 expresses a women's right, "to the enjoyment of the highest standard of health must be secured throughout the whole life cycle in equality with men..." In reference to health, paragraph 101 states that, "with the in-

---

[16]*Report of the World Food Summit, Rome, 13-17 November 1996, Part I, (WFS/96/3-FAO), Rome, 1997.*

[17]*Report of the Fourth World Conference on Women, Beijing, 4-15 September 1995. (United Nations publication,. Sales No. E. 96.V.13).*

crease in life expectancy and the growing number of older women, their health concerns require particular attention..."

Paragraph 106 requests Governments to "Develop information, programmes and services to assist women to understand and adapt to changes associated with ageing and to address and treat the health needs of older women, paying particular attention to those who are physically or psychological dependent".

Paragraph 113 defines violence against women as "any act of gender-based violence that results in ... physical, sexual or psychological harm or suffering to women..." Paragraph 116 recognises elderly women "as particularly vulnerable to violence." Paragraph 131 refers to the impact of armed conflict impact on the elderly.

The International Year of Older Persons[18]

In 1982, the participating States of the World Assembly on Ageing solemnly recognized that quality of life is no less important than longevity, and that the ageing should therefore... be able to enjoy in their own families and communities a life of fulfilment, health, security and contentment, appreciated as an integral part of society.[19]

The concern with this honourable social group remains unexhausted. Ten years later, the General Assembly declared 1999 the International Year of Older Persons with the theme, Towards a Society for All Ages, demonstrating an interest in ensuring the integration of older persons in all areas and sectors of society, and perceiving older persons as custodians of cultural heritage, knowledge, trades and skills.[20] It is up to the international community, Governments and individual organizations to put it into practice.

II. AGEING IN TRANSITION

"Parce qu'on respecte le passé, on peut esperer a l'avernir"
Danielle Mitterand

To better focus the development of this chapter, it is relevant to quote paragraph 286 of the Nairobi Forward Looking Strategies, which presents a very interesting recommendation: "Women should be prepared early in life, both psychologically and socially, to face the consequences of longer life expectancy. Although, while getting older, professional and family roles of women are undergoing fundamental changes, ageing, as a stage of development, is a challenge for women. In this period of life, women should be enabled to cope in a creative way with new opportunities. The social consequences arising from the stereotyping of elderly women should be recognized and eliminated. The media should assist by presenting positive images of women, particularly emphasising the need for respect because of their past and continuing contributions to society "[21]

Reading different articles on the situation on the ageing population, I sometimes have the impression that the elderly have always been old and that we, the young, have always been carrying them as a burden. It should be clear that as individuals and as members of a social group our cultural richness and ability exist thanks to the preceding generations. It is then that the saying 'to protect the health of future generations, to build peace for the children of our children may have a meaning.[22]

Several demographic aspects of population ageing merit attention. Firstly, as a result of population ageing, the dependency ratio (the non-working age population relative to the population of working age) is raising in the more developed regions. Secondly, since the sex ratio (males per hundred females) tends to be lower at older ages, the ageing of populations implies a greater increase in the number of elderly women as compared to elderly men. Thirdly, the age composition of the elderly population is being altered because of the tendency of the older groups within the elderly population to expand more rapidly. Finally, the greying of populations in the developing regions and their faster population growth in comparison to the developed regions will lead to increasingly larger proportions of the world's senior citizens residing in the Third World. In the next several decades, the current age distribution will have an impact on the ageing of population.[23]

In 1990, the world's elderly population (herein defined as those persons 60 years and older) was esti-

---

[18]International Year of Older Persons: Towards a Society for All Ages, General Assembly resolution 50/141, 21 December 1995. Report A/50/628.

[19]International Plan of Action on Ageing World Assembly on Ageing, 26 July-6 August 1982, Vienna.

[20]Habitat Agenda. Para 153.

[21]*Report of the World Conference to Review and Appraise the Achievements of the United Nations Declaration for Women: Equality, Development and Peace, Nairobi, 15-26 July 1985.* (United Nations publication, Sales No E.85.IV.10), Chap. I, Sect. A. See aksim General Assembly resolution 40/108.

[22]See *Ageing: A Chronological Process in Life, Social and Economic Questions Arising from It,* M. Dueñas Loza, position paper at AARP-BGO Panel: Living Longer, Living Better - HABITAT II, Istanbul, 4 June 1996.

[23]The Situation of Elderly *Women: Available Statistics and Indicators,* INSTRAW/UNSTAT, (INSTRAW/SER.B.44-1000), 1993.

mated at 488.8 million, nearly equivalent to the combined 1950 populations of Latin America, North America and the former Soviet Union. One out of 11 global inhabitants is at least 60 years of age. Out of nearly half a billion elderly, 44 per cent are male, underscoring the higher levels of mortality among the males as compared to their female counterparts. A little over two-fifths of the world's elderly dwell in the developed regions. Of this number, around 10 per cent are found in North America, just under a fifth live in Europe and about 9 per cent are in the former Soviet Union. One in every two of the world's senior citizens resides in Asia. The ageing and feminization of the population is presented in table I below.

Ageing is not an isolated experience that suddenly afflicts human society. As a process, it is a step ahead in the anthropological evolution and social transformation, whose characteristics inescapably depend upon the level of social organization; tradition and cultural values; and access to the benefits of social and economic development. The global population of both genders is as varied (individual condition), heterogeneous (collective condition) and dispersed as younger generations. Population grouping by age is a statistical category, essential for the first approach of the issue, but not sufficient or adequate in itself to reflect the inherent situations. Thus, categorizing and generalizing about the conditions applicable to the ageing population is a great risk, as well as a misleading assumption.

All countries have rural and urban populations that are growing older. The condition of their life and wellbeing, shelter and food security, quality of health care and medical services are going to depend on the level of development and the political, economic and social conditions of each population. The quality of food, hygiene, health, education and housing available to a person or a generation are important elements, which determine in great measure the quality of life and wellbeing of the elderly.

If childhood and adolescence provided positive opportunities to learn social, civic, moral, ethical and cultural values, the person will grow not only with a sense of self respect and dignity, but will be well balanced in the satisfaction of personal needs, seeking and able to find solutions to problems. A person of these characteristics, as an individual or as member of a group, can be perceived as ideal.

This process of growth and development as an individual and as a group is, of necessity, in the amalgam of life and the relations between generations. Changes, dislocation and alterations require a process of adaptation that individuals and generations make in an instinctive and gradual way during their life span. Therefore, change and the overcoming of stereotypes require creative stimuli.

In all societies, the family is the basic social unit, where individuals of both genders and of all ages participate, interact and support each other. It is the social unit that guarantees the procreation, safeguard, care and education of the human species. It is also where changes and adjustments take place at different degrees and levels.

In all societies, the great cultural diversity of the family structure represents the most active community

TABLE I. ABSOLUTE AND RELATIVE FREQUENCIES OF MALES AND FEMALES 60 YEARS AND OLDER: WORLD AND ITS MAJOR REGIONS, 1990-2025 (NUMBERS IN THOUSANDS)

Region	1990		2000		2025	
	Males	Females	Males	Females	Males	Females
World	216887	271870	277529	336607	558909	646428
	[8.1]	[10.3]	[8.8]	[10.8]	[13.1]	[15.3]
Africa	14056	16816	19036	22812	47159	54289
	[4.4]	[5.2]	[4.4]	[5.2]	[5.9]	[6.9]
Latin America	14857	17187	19404	22951	43818	53356
	[6.6]	[7.6]	[7.2]	[8.5]	[11.7]	[14.0]
North America	19486	26758	20769	28797	38825	49696
	[14.5]	[19.0]	[14.4]	[19.1]	[23.9]	[29.3]
Asia	115034	125614	154097	167254	334475	364864
	[7.2]	[8.3]	[8.1]	[9.2]	[13.4]	[15.1]
Europe	38244	54774	43472	59437	61308	77906
	[15.7]	[21.5]	[17.4]	[22.8]	[24.2]	[29.8]
Oceania	1518	1864	1771	2159	3337	3994
	[11.4]	[14.1]	[11.7]	[14.4]	[17.4]	[20.9]

Source: INSTRAW/UNSTAT, 1993, INSTRAW/SER.B/44.

TABLE II.   PROJECTIONS WITH HIGH INDEX VARIABLES

	1995	2000	2005	2010	2015	2020
Percentage aged 60 and over	7.5	7.9	8.4	9.2	10.2	11.5
Percentage aged 65 and over	5.1	5.4	5.8	6.2	6.9	7.8

Projections with low index variables

	1995	2000	2005	2010	2015	2020
Percentage aged 60 and over	7.5	8.0	8.7	9.8	11.3	13.1
Percentage aged 65 and over	5.1	5.5	6.0	6.6	7.6	8.9

Source: *United Nations World Population Prospects, 1996 Revision.*

nucleus, with its own characteristic ecosystem. This cultural diversity is one of the factors that promotes stereotypes based upon each individual and each group's age. Anthropological evidence confirms the male domination in all family structures. The processes of modernization, industrialization and technological changes have placed women in a kind of labyrinth with no way out, trapped in their reproductive and productive roles.

Studies carried out in France related to population behaviour and the perception of the elderly, for periods beginning in mid eighteenth century[24] clearly illustrate the opposed, and often conflictive, evolution of different stereotypes of elderly women and men in the rural and urban sectors. These are marked examples of the perception of gender differences and, regrettably, older and elderly women occupy the worse role.

Transformation induced by exogenous causes derived from industrialization and internal migration resulting from hired manual labour; modernization of production, transportation and distribution of products; consumption patterns; and population movements produced by employment have provoked structural changes of great magnitude. These processes produce very important changes in the composition of the nuclear family and in the relationship between generations, as well as changes in the support structures and the options of personal improvement and fulfilment.

Additional causes are those generated by the macro-political and macro-economic decisions relative to the use of technology in each country. Social security schemes, pensions and retirement plans, medical insurance and hospital care, changes in labour laws and conditions of employment, are factors whose rules and fluctuations have repercussions in the individual circumstances of the elderly.

Long before the globalization phenomenon of the economy, it was possible to examine the impact of global, regional and national issues on populations and individuals. The international tariff agreements on basic products negotiated during the 1970s are a clear example of how the fluctuation and dependence on global markets determine economic, fiscal and political decisions in the countries exporting raw materials. This, in turn, has a direct effect on the level of income of small producers in developing countries, who each day have to produce more at lower prices to continue competing and maybe gain a comparative advantage.

These decisions produce complex changes whose potential benefits generally revert in women and men of middle to high income. They are also the ones to receive the direct benefits of social improvements resulting from increased education, health care, birth control, sanitary conditions, quality of transportation and housing. In these levels, the elderly will have more facilities than those will at lower levels, but will not completely escape the negative stereotypes that modern society places on old age.

The impact of the exogenous causes produces a triple negative impact on older women who live in different levels of poverty. The 1995 *Human Development Report* of the United Nations Development Programme states that, almost a third of the population, about 1.3 billion people, live below the poverty line, 70 per cent of which are women."[25] The triple impact could be defined as: women + poor + elderly.

As mentioned earlier, the individual and collective changes generated by structural changes have an impact in the quality of life and in the status of the elderly, particularly of elderly women. Transition, then, has to be analysed within the dynamic concept of the life span

[24]Bourdelais, P., *L'age de la vieillese*, Editions Odile Jacob, 1993.

[25]The 1995 Human Development Report, United Nations Development Programme, Oxford Press, 1995.

and the interaction between generations in view of the national and global occurrences.

For women, life's practical conditions do not match the stature they were granted in theory. To better illustrate this matter, I quote Dr. Joyce Braak, "From the age of puberty on, women show a marked decline in self-esteem. From puberty on, there's a widening gap between the self-esteem of men, which gets higher and higher, and women, which is low and gets lower. If you superimpose on that the sensations of worthlessness and the inappropriate guilt of depression, you have somebody who has self-esteem in the negative range. And fatigue. Does anybody know a multiple role woman who is not fatigued? I think women live most of their lives fatigued"[26]

The main purpose of research and analysis of ageing in transition should be to mobilize opinion and then to modify behaviour regarding the role of older persons in society. It should not only be explained, but also carefully evaluated and recorded with reliable data in order to be utilised in policy decision-making. Particular concern to very practical issues of social, cultural and economic infrastructure can help to prevent the destructive impact of loneliness, destitution, verbal and physical violence and other unfortunate problems of the modern social organization (Dueñas 1996).

III. STATUS OF OLDER WOMEN IN LATIN AMERICA

"We do not stop working because we are old; we grow old because we stop working"
J.M. Capozzi[27]

"Due to the fact that the general population in the region is relatively young, up to now little attention has been paid to middle aged and elderly women, in investigation activities and in services".[28] For the most part, the last days in the life of older women are marked by loneliness, abandonment and insufficient satisfaction of their economic needs, with little or no employment opportunity and with a limited access to social services.

Population

In 1995, the estimated total population of Latin America and the Caribbean was 476,637 million people, of which 240 million people were women. Of these, 17.5 per cent (18 million) were older than 60 and 5.1 per cent (12 million) were older than 65. Almost half the population is between 15 and 49; approximately 40 per cent is less than 15 years old, especially in the Caribbean and the southern tip of the continent. During the 1980's, in Cuba, Jamaica and Barbados, more than 10 per cent of the population was older than 60. By 2025, all the Caribbean countries, except Haiti, will have surpassed that percentage. In five of these countries, the percentage will be greater than 20 per cent. In Mexico, Brazil and the southern and Andean countries the ratio will be closer to 40 per cent. The rate of increase projected shows that the number of people over 60 is rapidly increasing, representing a sub-group that cannot continue to be ignored.[29]

The principal factors of the demographic transition result from the fluctuations in the fertility and mortality rates of all the countries in the region, but in different periods and of varied intensity. Changes in the education structures in elementary school, as well as in health and medical care no doubt will have foreseeable consequences in the demographic structure.

There is ample evidence in all the countries of the region that a better education allows women to understand, access and practice birth control, overcome traditional stereotypes and thus improve their situation in life. There is also evidence to suggest that middle aged and older women play an important role in the economic development process and in the stability of the family, not only because of the care and support they provide, but also because every day the number of homes headed by women grow.

The statistical data relative to fertility is based upon rather recent estimates and projections of population's census. The studies carried out by the Economic Commission for Latin America and the Caribbean, the United Nations Population Fund and others regarding economic and social conditions, in relation to employment and financial resources basically refer to the poorest sectors of women, who generally bear a greater burden in a patriarchal family and social system. This, in turn, gravely reflects on the status of elderly women. Though the information available is anecdotal, it is also known that women lack control over the distribution and use of their time and the use of their bodies. Moreover, they do not have control over the products of their labour nor access to decisions that affect their daily life.

[26]Braak, J., *Depression: A Woman's Health Perspective.* 1997 Spring Forum, The global Alliance for Women's Health. Edited by Elaine M. Wolfson, PhD. GAWH.

[27]Capozzi, J.M., *If You Want the Rainbow You Gotta Put-up with the Rain*, 1997. JMC Industries.

[28]Sennot-Miller, L., *Mid-life and Older Women in Latin America and the Caribbean*, American Association of Retired Persons.

[29]*United Nations World Population Prospects:1996 Revision.*

There are fewer studies regarding the behaviour of women of economically wealthy classes, who not only have ample access and availability to birth control, but also have quality education, health care, nutrition, employment, and thus, can enjoy better life conditions. This situation is also reflected in older women of the same social strata.

There is evidence of profound differences between urban and rural populations on the one hand, and between the different regions on the other. During the 1960s and 1970s, Latin America and the Caribbean were already one of the most urbanized regions in the planet. The Economic Commission for Latin America and the Caribbean estimates that by 1980, 65 per cent of its population lived in urban areas. Nevertheless, there are substantive differences not only in the urban-rural demographic configuration, but above all, in fertility rates; mortality and morbidity; illiteracy based on gender and age; and political participation and access to paid employment. There is evidence that points to women encompassing the largest urban elderly population older than 60, whereas men over 60 are the largest population group in the rural areas of the region.

The population distribution by age and demographic structure has had significant changes owing to rural/urban migration (see table III). Migration accelerates urbanization; the formation of large peri-urban poverty belts; marginalization; total lack of services and infrastructure and fertility rates increase and maintain levels close to 3.1 per cent annually. The repercussion of this process is very varied, from the drop in food production, loss of values and traditional customs, environmental problems and, above all, family dismemberment, which provokes the loss of support mechanisms between generations. In turn, this has serious repercussions in the elderly rural population, although not exclusively. Chart 1 below reflects the life expectancy for women and men aged 60 and over between the years 1990-1995 and 1995-2025. Chart 2 below presents the population distribution and growth in the region.

Demographic analysis as part of an individual's life cycle requires that statistical concepts of measurement and valuation be expanded. In addition, it requires that: (*a*) definition of variables allow the inclusion of all the conditions of the elderly in population census; (*b*) definition of measurement and collection methodologies of demographic data include concrete and representative characteristics of an individual's life cycle; (*c*) the investigation be extensive regarding family and its evolution in time and space; (*d*) the methodology include variables that will measure the impact of economic, political and social phenomena at the micro and macro level; (*e*) systematic research and reliable statistics exist for the regular monitoring of the status and needs of the elderly, in particular, of elderly women.

Education

One of the most significant changes refers to the expansion of the education system. During the 1990s its coverage reached an average of 90 per cent of the children, with a strong growth in secondary and higher education. Change occurred as a result of specific political decisions and the application of several concrete socio-political projects between 1960 and 1970. State intervention was fundamental to the structuring of the formal education system and for the extension of the area covered. Nevertheless, there continue to be great differences based on gender and age in school enrolment. During the 1980s, illiteracy among the female population was around 21.2 per cent, whereas it was 18 per cent among men. During the 1990s the rate changes, 13.5 per cent in the first case and 12 per cent in the second. Nevertheless, illiteracy among women over 45 is close to 50 per cent in rural areas, which is an obvious disadvantage that can be corrected only with great difficulty.[30]

"For older women illiteracy is high in almost all developing countries, the long-term result of having no or very limited educational opportunity for older women will remain for the decades to come, constituting a disadvantage almost impossible to reverse. Illiteracy rates among women over 25 years of age are typically twice or more those of young women aged 15 to 24. Among women over 45 years of age, illiteracy rates in the late 1980s were close to 50 per cent and in some cases exceeded 70 per cent."[31]

When this female population grows old, its condition will be even more dramatic than that of previous generations. This is primarily due to access difficulties for adult literacy programmes and because education programmes available to these sectors correspond to the characteristic Latin American society of the late nineteenth century.

At present, it is imperative for the region to begin programmes structured on the basis of modern, twenty-first century concepts. This may include aspects such as quality and patterns of production and consumption; use and management of natural resources; application of the concept of sustainability and the precautionary approach of Agenda 21; incorporation of new methods and technologies, legal, political and legislative changes regarding the participation and performance of women; and the application of human rights and the eradication of violence against women. The

---

[30]*United Nations Trends and Statistics* 1995.
[31]Ibid.

Economic Commission for Latin America and the Caribbean considers that these and more changes require a great transformation of the education strategy based on high competitiveness and flexibility of permanent adaptation, autonomy and creativity. In addition, the education reform should reflect important changes in the level and forms of participation of the public and private sectors in structural and financial aspects in association with the beneficiaries.

Health

The constitution of the World Health Organization (WHO), signed on 22 July 1946, defined health as a state of complete physical, mental and social well-being and not merely the absence of disease or infirmity.[32]

In her publication, *Women's Health and Human Rights,* Dr. R.J. Cook, a lawyer specialist in human rights law, states that "many societies attribute low status to women and the social roles they are required to perform. This "devaluation" of women often leads to a denial of rights, such as the right to access to information, adequate nutrition and health services, to which they are entitled by the very fact that their Governments have signed international agreements. Some 500,000 women die each year from preventable causes..[..].. Many of the health disadvantages of women can be classified as injustices. Women's rights in the health care sector may be violated by the lack of certain health services, lack of information and appropriate technology to ease their burden inside and outside the home. The ranks of the poor are disproportionately filled with single women who are heads of households".

Women and men are living longer with continuing significant gains over the last two decades in life expectancy in every region. In most countries women live longer than men. There are different causes of death for women and men, different patterns of mortality and morbidity and different needs and uses of health services. But data collection and research to explore these differences are only beginning. Inadequate nutrition, anemia and early pregnancies threaten the health and lives of young girls and adolescents. Greater attention is therefore being given to the girl child's needs for health and nutrition from infancy up to adulthood. Women's life expectancies in Latin America and the Caribbean are nearly equal—between 72 and 74 years.[33]

Health is the product of a constant and dynamic interaction of a set of factors, including the physical, economic and social conditions of a person and those pertaining to the environment, and to psychological, emotional and cultural conditions. Gender differences in health and the surviving advantage attributed to women are not exclusively the result of scientific advances in medicine, in the pharmaceutical industry or the number of medical centres.

Mortality is an indicator that does not necessarily refer to variables pertaining to quality of a person's life or their survivors. It encompasses both genders with their specific levels of risk, but does not include other characteristics such as urban or rural condition of the population, the level of industrialization and/or mechanization of these sectors. Authors such as Rutzicka and López[34] have simplified two large groups of gender differentiated causes of mortality, with different forms of interaction in the different levels of development of the countries: the first is genetic, biological and environmental; the second is social, economic and cultural.

WHO attributes a decrease in the mortality rate of women in industrialized countries of the region to improvement in the quality of life due to access to physical, economic and social infrastructure. For example, in Caribbean countries where there is a mixed urban/rural condition in the 35-year-old age group, the rate of mortality for men exceeds that of women. After 40, there is a decreasing incidence of age-specific mortality rates for men and women, as they grow older.

Table IV below contains information on the five leading causes of death during the 1980s among women between the ages 45 and 64 in the Latin American countries where data is available. The countries are divided into three groups according to the predominant condition: urban, rural or both. Malignant tumours are the first cause of death. The second cause is cardiac illnesses, followed by cerebral vascular conditions, diabetes and accidents. Table V below refers to the first five causes of death among women over 65 in the same countries and decade. Nutritional deficiencies, intestinal and respiratory infections have the greatest incidence in rural areas. Tables VI and VII below present the two age groups in the Caribbean countries.

Morbidity is the other indicator of a specific nature whose risk is highly dependent on gender, age and collective circumstances. Women present a higher morbidity rate than men, as they are faces with a greater number of inconveniences and chronic diseases throughout their life. This biological difference, in the case of morbidity does not favour women—it becomes worse owing to their poor access to basic services (sanitation, nutrition, social security, medical and clinical

[32]World Health Organization, 1992.
[33]Ibid.

[34]Rutzicka and López, *Sex Differentials in Mortality,* in Sennot-Miller L., 1989.

care) according to social and ethnic conditions, place of residence and age (Gómez, 1997).

The analysis carried out by the Economic Commission for Latin America and the Caribbean and WHO as part of their contribution to the sixth Regional Conference on the Integration of Women into the Economic and Social Development of Latin America and the Caribbean, held in Mar del Plata, Argentina, in September 1994, divides women's life cycle in four periods: (a) childhood; (b) adolescence; (c) adulthood; and (d) middle age and old age. Most of the information available comes from demographic health surveys and census. According to the Economic Commission for Latin America and the Caribbean, the general limitations are great regarding availability, quality and reliability of the statistical data, which, in general, allow a cross-cutting result of the illustrative sample of the conditions of population groups.

The analysis and evaluation of middle-aged and older women's health and well-being in Latin America and the Caribbean should include the life cycle perspective. In this setting, interactions can consist of a set of personal character factors (genes, accidents, disease) with those of an individual character (education, nutrition, social security) and collective character (urban or rural population, access to housing, water, electricity and transportation) at a micro-economic level, with those pertaining to national infrastructure and decisions (laws) and global matters (external debt, globalization of investments) at the macro-economic level.

Individual and social concepts are needed in a longitudinal analysis that integrates the life cycle approach. This interaction requires a long term approach and a methodology that includes prospective and retrospective longitudinal elements at the same time. With manifestations that vary according to age, but present throughout life, four issues have been identified related to health that are very concretely gender specific: (a) nutrition; (b) mental health; (c) occupational health, and (d) sexual domestic violence. Malnutrition is probably the most important health hazard for women in the region, particularly of low income rural and peri-urban areas. There is information relative to the nutrition/malnutrition state of children and adolescence (life cycle 1 and 2). There is no reliable information regarding the nutritional level of elderly women in the region.

Health needs particular to the older population are slowly growing as its own proportion grows. As women are the main users of the medical care system, it could be assumed that, in this area, they would have a certain advantage. Nevertheless, due to the resulting readjustment processes of the external debt and the consequences of drastic government budget reductions of social services, in particular of those of the less favoured classes, privatization of public enterprises and consequent unemployment are factors that have a direct impact in the quality, frequency and options of health services for the older female population who cannot apply for pensions, or housing and care facilities.

Violence against women is one of the most persistent menaces during the life cycle in all regions worldwide. In reference to Latin America and the Caribbean, the Economic Commission for Latin America and the Carribean has carried out detailed and extensive studies and evaluations. The study of this issue is relatively recent within the context of health and quality of life, domestic violence, sexual abuse, and psychological and emotional abuse. To acknowledge it as a public health hazard and of global reach represents an important evolution in the understanding of grave prejudices and discrimination against women. Several countries have adopted specific legislation, as is the case of the Dominican Republic, whose Congress, in 1997, approved article 24-97 modifying several articles of the penal code to promote the reduction and elimination of domestic violence within the family.

Studies carried out in the United States of America have shown that approximately 17 per cent to 25 per cent of the total emergency cases correspond to wife beating, presenting 5 per cent of the lesions or sickness due to abuse. Generally, the aggressor does not allow his victim to seek medical assistance, making it very difficult to determine the real incidence. Since there are insufficient reports there is no methodology to identify the information. A survey carried out in 1994, showed that between 25 per cent and 50 per cent of the women surveyed testified that they had been victims of physical abuse. "The presence and persistence of violence against women is related to the power relation between the sexes and the subordinate position of women in societies where, by law or by custom, still allow and even encourage such behaviour" (Gómez 1997).

One of the cultural characteristics of the Latin American family regarding women's education, is that the family is the first priority and prevails above all else. Consequently, in the separation, dismemberment or abandonment that the family may experience, elderly women can experience a profound feeling of guilt and failure, two serious components of depression and anguish, which can become pathological health problems.

Studies regarding the mental health of women have identified the origins of discrimination in the concept of "machismo". This is a term used to describe a complex system of masculine domination which has prevailed in Latin America and the Caribbean in a way slightly different from its ethnic origins. Even though the origin of "machismo" goes back to Biblical times as a way of keeping power in the hands of the elite, through inheritance patterns and the control of women's sexual behaviour, the concept of "machismo" evolved towards a cultural pattern, not limited to the higher classes, applied to all aspects of the life of women and men in the new continent (Freire, 1983).

To conclude these brief reflections regarding the health of elderly women, one must point out situations relative to emotional depression, which, apart from physical (chronic disease) and social causes (poverty, illiteracy, migration, abandonment), is related to a combination of factors such as loneliness, insecurity, ostracism and insomnia. These factors can make women drug abusers, or dependant on alcohol, gambling and other addictive palliatives. The frequency, typology and incidence of these processes will necessarily depend on the standard of living and the particular circumstances of each individual. Addiction to gambling can be classified as representative of the middle and wealthy classes. Drug dependency on tranquillizers and analgesics probably affects all sectors of urban dwellers at all economic levels.

Studies carried out mainly by Moncarz, Velázquez, as well as by Braak and Mark show that: (a) the traditional medical model used to evaluate and define women's health is not sufficient or adequate; (b) there is not enough clinical and empirical evidence that analyses the concrete situation of women's health in general, and even less in the case of elderly women, according to the information provided by WHO; (c) including a gender perspective in the analysis of women's health as a complete state of physical, mental and social well-being could revolutionize the perception and understanding of the process of malaise/sickness/health/well being of women; (d) there is no general acceptance in the area of medical, pharmaceutical and technological investigation sector regarding the methods of applying the WHO's concept of health as an inalienable right of women; (e) in general, the health system now in place is still not sufficiently interested in the specific health problems of women; (f) the habitual consumption of drugs by women is a serious social problem; (g) there is no investigation or anecdotal references regarding the mental health of rural elderly women.

Environment and access to natural resources

There are no studies regarding the impact of geographic and environmental conditions on the standard of living of elderly women in particular, and of women in general. The diversity of geographic and environmental conditions is highly relevant to an understanding of the urban and rural characteristics of the population in Latin American and the Caribbean. Access to and control over natural resources are affected by numerous elements, including: the rural population; food security and subsistence regarding the quality of

the soil; erosion; lack or excess of water; irrigation systems; water supply and sanitation; electricity and fuelwood consumption as well as other energy resources; investment in agricultural mechanization; the growing urban voracity for physical space, water and energy. These elements have a direct on sustainability and the quality of development and on the standard of living of the rural and urban populations who are chiefly exposed to insufficiency, lack or abundance of resources.

Natural resources management, the deterioration of the environment and the individual and collective behaviour patterns have repercussions whose reach is not quantified or systematically measured. Nevertheless, rural elderly women are severely limited in their access to resources and opportunities to receive the benefits of development. These limitations are even greater when dealing with the understanding of practical advantages in the application of the principles of sustainable development, of the concept of "precautionary approach".

The resulting contradiction at the hemispheric level does not escape irony. For centuries, indigenous urban and rural populations of the continent, particularly in the Andean region, have practiced systems of communal social organization in farming and for food security, based on the respect and interaction with the ecosystem as one of the vital principles of their respective cultures. These principles were vanished by the processes of colonization, modernization and mechanization. At the end of the twentieth century, it is imperative for present and future that the management of natural resources be done in accordance with the levels of renovation and balance on which sustainability is based.

The rural population of industrialized countries in Latin America is around 14 per cent and is relatively stable, with the exception of Central America, which experiences an annual growth of 0.7 per cent.[35] It should be noted that this subregion has known two decades of intense civil wars that have decimated the rural population, in particular, the indigenous population.

It is estimated that more than 10 to 15 per cent of the rural populations of developing countries live in environmentally degraded or ecologically vulnerable areas. Men are not solely responsible for environmental degradation, nor are women natural protectors of the environment. Both women and men are involved in the environmental degradation, often associated with their struggle to survive, to exploit whatever natural resource they can.[36]

[35]*Las mujeres de edad mediana y avanzada en América Latina y el Caribe*, 1990, American Association of Retired Persons.

[36]United Nations, *The World's Women* 1995.

It can be said that women are in closer contact with their surroundings than men as they are the first to suffer when the environment is degraded. Poor rural women may be particularly vulnerable because of their already heavy workloads and worse health status. Conditions for older rural women are even worse. Women are not simply victims of environmental degradation; the relationship is much more complex. Most research on women and the environment has debated the effects of environmental degradation rather than the other way around.

Rural women in the region spend a lot of hours a day farming the family land, generally in eroded plots. They have to walk several kilometres a day to collect water and fuelwood for cooking. The greater the soil degradation, the greater the effort to obtain even an inferior product (quality and quantity). Forest degradation, and above all, the lack of electricity or gas, forces rural women to spend many hours a day collecting fuelwood and water. No doubt there is an environmental impact. There is also a grave impact of the quality of women's health, burdened with the weight on her shoulders, the pollution of carbon combustion and smoke and the low quality of the drinking water. This exponential impact will have negative impact on the health of rural women. Its repercussions will be clearly visible when they turn 50 or older and there is no medical attention.

According to estimates of the Food and Agriculture Organization,[37] 40 per cent of fuelwood is used daily by rural women in 14 countries of Latin America and the Caribbean. Table VIII below reproduces the 1990s estimated number of rural women affected by fuelwood scarcity in Latin America and the Caribbean. Table IX below refers to deforestation and the time women spend gathering fuelwood. Table X below refers to access to safe drinking water and sanitation services in 1990.

There is a need for investigation and specific studies in the area of health and life conditions of elderly rural and urban women. There is also a need, perhaps greater, regarding issues relative to: access and use of natural resources, food security, quality of water and sanitation services, quality of the soil, irrigation services, reforestation, access to energy services available to elderly women; and the development of a methodology to determine the standard of living of women in their different life stages to obtain a clear idea of all the problems confronted by the elderly population lacking resources.

Housing

Housing and human settlements require a specific focus on women. In the majority of countries, the need of women for shelter are still subsumed under those of the family, even though there is ample evidence that the specific needs of women and the contributions they can make are distinct from those of men.[38]

The Nairobi Forward-looking Strategies for the Advancement of Women placed women's issues prominently on the agenda initiating a process of promoting the role of women both as beneficiaries and as agents of change in the Global Strategy for Shelter up to the Year 2000. The shelter and infrastructure needs of women were to be assessed and specifically incorporated in housing, community development and slum and squatter projects. Concepts that have been discussed by the United Nations Commission on Human Settlements, giving particular attention to the role of women since the first United Nations Conference on Human Settlements in Vancouver, Canada, in 1976,[39] include: shelter policies and delivery systems; access to land and financial resources for housing; attending to the needs of vulnerable groups, among them the elderly; ensuring access to basic infrastructure and services.

When preparing this chapter, the available literature and documentation on Latin America and the Caribbean presents no reference to the housing condition, be it urban or rural, with or without services and infrastructure; with sufficient space or lacking it, very narrow, or inhabitable, or sumptuous. There is no reference regarding the physical or legal characteristics of housing, least of all a classification by activity or occupation. Neither is there information regarding conditions or housing facilities for the elderly. It is probable that specialized architectural, construction design literature has information in this field and that the reports of governmental housing agencies provide such material. Unfortunately, the available bibliographical resources and the lack of time do not allow the research.

In the extensive bibliography and surveys regarding the status of women as managers, organizers and home educators, there is no reference to the characteristics of the conditions of the house. Thus, the conceptual access to this fundamental element of well-being or survival must take into account the concepts and principles con-

---

[37]Forest Products, *World Outlook Projections*, Forestry paper No. 84, FAO Rome, 1988. *Forest Resources Assessment 1990*, Potential Vegetation Zones of the World, Forestry Paper No.124, FAO, Rome, 1990.

[38]*Towards a Strategy for the Full Participation of Women in all Phases of the United Nations Global Strategy for Shelter to the year 2000*, United Nations Centre for Human Settlements, Nairobi, 1990.

[39]*Compendium: Women and Habitat*, I.C. de Vries, S. Keuzenkamp, 1996.

tained in the HABITAT Agenda and the Istanbul Declaration.

Work, employment, access to credit

There is plenty of literature on the status of women in Latin America and the Caribbean, regarding mobilization in the labour market, services and social activities and limited participation in the political processes. The general tendency of these analyses is the quantitative categorization of women's participation—the number of women working in the textile industry, for example, or in the hotel industry, the number of parliamentary positions, or ministers, etc. The qualitative analysis of the condition and characteristics of employment has received a lot more attention as a phenomenon in itself, and least of all as an interactive factor that determines the standard of living of women throughout their life cycle.

The *Human Development Report 1993* presents a broader approach, encompassing two dimensions of women's participation, being qualitative and quantitative, expanding the framework for analysis, its conceptualization, and above all, facilitating an inter-sectorial and longitudinal approach more in accordance with the socio-economic reality of women's lives.

The reports states that the nature of economic participation can vary widely, from forms of drudgery to creative, productive and independent economic activity. Societies also vary greatly in the value they place on the form of employment ranging from the association of manual work with servitude to a respect for manual labour in more egalitarian societies. Closely related to this range of social attitudes is the nature of the work environment itself, which can be more or less participatory.[40]

There are important and significant changes, though they are not sufficient. According to the International Labour Organization (ILO)[41] women have far fewer job opportunities than men and are disproportionately found in lower paid and less prestigious occupations. They earn far less even when performing the same work as men. Women hold only a small proportion of management positions and are seldom in the leadership of trade unions. Women who work outside the home are still the only ones responsible for the domestic work of the household and thus bear a double work burden, which is an obstacle both to better employment opportunities and to social and political participation.

The *Human Development Report 1993* states that women are the world's largest excluded group. Even though they make up half the adult population and often contribute more than their share to society, inside and outside the home, they are frequently excluded from positions of power.

The World Bank, in its *Case Studies on Women's Employment and Pay in Latin America*,[42] employs an economic perspective and focuses on how women behave and are treated in the work force, taking into consideration the determinants of women's labour force participation and male-to-female earnings differentials. Female unemployment rates have been lower than male rates in the 1980s, although female underemployment is higher. Women are more heavily concentrated in the unpaid and family business, and are found primarily in commerce and service industries and the informal sector.

These and other important publications used in the preparation of this chapter have no indications or gender desegregated references by age group, location (urban or rural) or information sector regarding labour and employment conditions of women of the region. Neither is there any significant reference to the relationship between work, employment security and life conditions using a women's life cycle perspective. There are no valuable references of the application of the social security systems in the present elderly women population, or in their participation in the institutional and political processes of the region.

The ILOs publication, *The ILO and the Elderly*, refers in a general way to the labour, employment and economic security conditions of the elderly, their access to production goods, to social services and family support and the training and information needs of the elderly population. There is no evidence of its consumption patterns or information regarding the value of their contribution to the family's economic and social well-being, most of the time unpaid. Moreover, a large part of the adult and young population benefit from the economic resources of the retired persons, or from the domestic labour of farming products of elderly women farmers.

There is a great lack of quantitative and qualitative information regarding elderly women. From the analysis of their economic and social status, as well as from the level of institutional and political participation, several variables can be extrapolated that describe the condition of elderly women and their immediate possibilities. This method can be subtle at the diagnostic level, but it is insufficient as the basis of specific

---

[40]See Human Development Report 1993. United Nations Development Programme (UNDP), New York, 1993.

[41]*The ILO and the Elderly*, International Labour Office, ILO ,Geneva, 1992.

[42]*Case Studies on Women's Employment and Pay in Latin America*, World Bank Regional and Sectorial Studies, 1992, Washington, D. C. ISBN 0-8213-2308.

proposals and solutions to the acute problems that elderly women in Latin America and the Caribbean confront.

Any increase in knowledge and understanding of the elements that converge in the quality of life of the elderly will, undoubtedly, be a valuable mechanism with which to obtain equity for this important population group of the region. As such, the international Year of the Older Person is an important opportunity to promote a better analysis at the international and national level.

The transformation of the population structure, the economic and political changes, the social mobility and the challenges of the twenty-first century, present challenges of great magnitude for the elderly population, and more so, for elderly women. Thus, analysis and understanding with the aim of influencing policy and institutional changes require systematic and serious studies as well as reliable and timely statistical data for the regular monitoring of the status, needs and problems of the elderly and, in particular, of elderly women.

CONCLUSIONS AND RECOMMENDATIONS

1. It is important to address the process of ageing in a holistic and integrated manner, keeping in mind that the younger generations, in turn, will also become older in a not too distant future. The elderly, children and younger people have a very critical role to play in any given society, therefore the notion of "dependency" and "burden" should be deleted from the documents and analysis of this issue.

2. The analysis and recommendations emanating from the global United Nations conferences since 1992 are the fundamental wealth for the formulation of a conceptual framework interrelated and integrated to the status of the elderly, without losing sight of the peculiarities of a geographic, ethnic and cultural nature.

3. In the wake of changing family structures, the provision of social safety networks should be put in place, including public assistance programmes and innovative support mechanisms to render physical, psychological and emotional support to elderly.

4. It is vital to introduce flexible working arrangements to enable more older people and women to pro-

ductively utilize their wisdom and experience as a contribution to society.

5. The elderly population is an active element of human population and cannot be considered as a burden to assistance budgets, material for pharmaceutical of clinical experimentation or, least of all, a handicap to the actual production methods.

6. Support for the integration of the elderly into national development plans and programmes must generate research and production of reliable statistical information for the regular monitoring of the status and needs of the elderly, within the dynamic concept of the life span and the interaction between generations.

7. The diversity and heterogeneity of the elderly female population in Latin America and the Caribbean will necessarily require specialized studies by each country. International organizations should focus more concretely in the different areas in order to have enough significant data that will allow the adoption of institutional and political measures in favour of the elderly population.

8. Investigations regarding the economic, health, education, sanitation, transportation, housing and social situation of older women can be relatively easy to perform. Nevertheless, other issues should be prioritized, including: pension, remuneration, valuing and recognizing work (particularly in rural areas), environmental impact, impact of technology and the environmental processes, access to economic and financial instruments, and political and institutional participation.

9. The impact of migration, refuge and exile, civic, political and military violence and natural disasters should be included in studies of elderly women of the region.

10. Education programmes need to be structured in view of the requirements of the 21st century, without ignoring the needs of older populations that are reflected in the plans of action of the global conferences that have been ratified by Governments.

11. Involve Governments and civil society, including the business sector, with the aim of enhancing their knowledge and understanding of the challenges faced by the region in the next 20 years, in order that decisions may be made beforehand, using the principle that it's better to prevent than to cure.

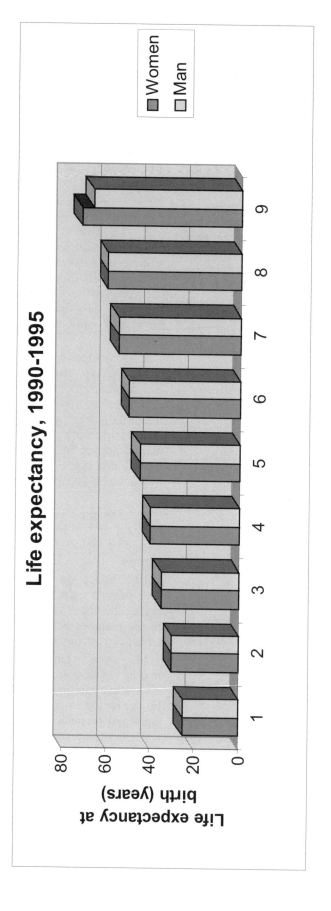

CHART 1

Life expectancy, 1990-1995

Women
Man

Life expectancy at birth (years)

86

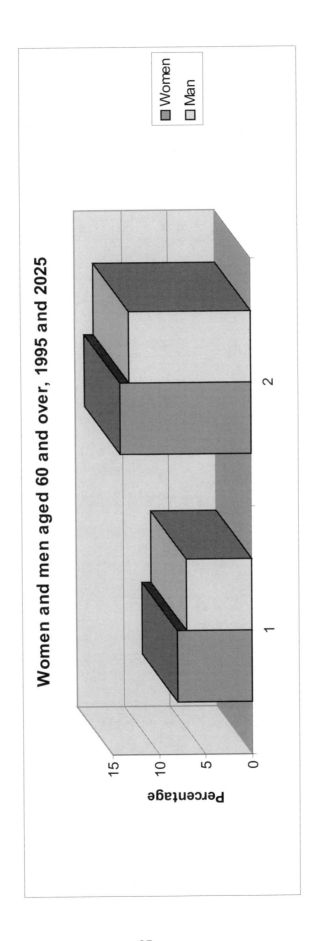

Women and men aged 60 and over, 1995 and 2025

TABLE III.   POPULATION, POPULATION DISTRIBUTION AND POPULATION GROWTH IN LATIN AMERICA AND THE CARIBBEAN

Country or area	Total population (thousands)			Population, 1995 (thousands)		Population distribution (%), 1995		Average annual change in population (%), 1990-95			Women per 100 men, 1995		% Women internal migrants 1995
	1970	1995	2010	Urban	Rural	Urban	Rural	Total	Urban	Rural	Urban	Rural	1995
Latin America and the Caribbean													
Antigua and Barbuda	66	68	76	23	44	35	65	0.71	2.24	-0.05			48
Argentina	23 962	34 264	10 193	29 965	4 300	87	13	1.17	1.48	-0.88	105	85	51
Bahamas	170	277	327	184	92	67	33	1.60	2.29	0.29			48
Barbados	239	261	284	125	137	48	52	0.33	1.62	-0.79	112	104	57
Belize	120	209	261	110	100	52	48	2.03	2.78	1.24			44
Bolivia	4 825	8 074	11 807	4 395	3 679	54	46	2.37	3.68	0.91	104	99	47
Brazil	95 847	161 382	194 002	127 043	34 339	79	21	1.59	2.50	-1.45	103	91	48
Chile	9 504	14 237	17 182	12 233	2 005	86	14	1.55	1.86	-0.24	106	83	50
Colombia	21 360	35 101	42 959	25 526	9 575	73	27	1.66	2.43	-0.25	108	87	52
Costa Rica	1 731	3 424	4 534	1 702	1 722	50	50	2.41	3.50	1.40	108	89	49
Cuba	8 520	11 091	12 155	8 427	2 664	76	24	0.89	1.52	-0.99	104	87	31
Dominica	70	71	73					-0.19					49
Dominican Republic	4 423	7 915	9 903	5 110	2 805	65	35	1.98	3.32	-0.25	103	86	35
Ecuador	6 051	11 822	15 510	7 166	4 656	61	39	2.28	3.76	0.2	103	93	50
El Salvador	3 588	5 768	7 772	2 692	3 076	47	53	2.18	3.18	1.35	114	97	50
French Guiana	49	114	162	87	27	76	24	3.04	3.55	1.47			44
Grenada	94	92	100					0.31					49
Guadeloupe	320	414	472	212	202	51	49	1.22	2.36	0.10			52
Guatemala	5 246	10 621	15 827	4 404	6 217	41	59	2.88	3.88	2.20	104	94	57
Guyana	709	834	986	295	540	35	65	0.94	2.40	0.19	109	98	45
Haiti	4 520	7 180	9 770	2 266	4 914	32	68	2.03	4.00	1.19	125	95	55
Honduras	2 627	5 968	8 668	2 844	3 124	48	52	3.00	4.74	1.53	106	92	48
Jamaica	1 869	2 547	3 012	1 410	1 137	55	45	1.02	2.16	-0.30	107	93	50
Martinique	326	377	415	294	83	78	22	0.92	1.78	-1.86			47
Mexico	50 328	93 670	118 455	70 532	23 138	75	25	2.06	2.80	-0.03	103	94	50
Netherlands Antilles	162	176	187					0.12					59
Nicaragua	2 063	4 433	6 728	2 787	1 646	63	37	3.74	4.76	2.13	116	92	50
Panama	1 531	2 659	3 324	1 459	1 200	55	45	1.90	2.64	1.04	105	88	47
Paraguay	2 351	4 893	6 928	2 480	2 413	51	49	2.69	4.01	1.43	104	91	47

88

TABLE III (*continued*)

Country or area	Total population (thousands)			Population, 1995 (thousands)		Population distribution (%), 1995		Average annual change in population (%), 1990-95			Women per 100 men, 1995		% Women internal migrants
	1970	1995	2010	Urban	Rural	Urban	Rural	Total	Urban	Rural	Urban	Rural	1995
Peru	13 193	23 854	31 047	17 228	6 626	72	28	2.03	2.71	0.36	99	98	49
Puerto Rico	2 718	3 691	4 202	2 828	863	77	23	0.89	1.60	-1.28	108	97	51
St. Kitts and Nevis	47	41	42	22	20	53	47	-0.30	1.19	-1.83			49
St. Lucia	101	142	171	66	77	46	54	1.35	2.28	0.59			51
St. Vicent/Grenadines	87	112	128	25	87	22	78	0.88	2.64	0.40			51
Suriname	372	463	566	233	230	50	50	1.86	3.02	0.75			48
Trinidad and Tobago	971	1 305	1 506	869	436	67	33	1.08	1.61	0.06	107	94	51
Uruguay	2 808	3 186	3 453	2 877	309	90	10	0.58	0.89	-2.11	110	71	53
US Virgin Islands	64	108	115	53	55	49	51	0.15	1.11	-0.74			53
Venezuela	10 604	21 483	27 609	19 953	1 530	93	7	2.12	2.65	-3.72	100	86	48

Source: The World's Women 1995, Trends and Statistics. U.N. 1995, Page 62-63.

89

TABLE IV. FIVE LEADING CAUSES OF DEATH AMONG WOMEN AGED 45 TO 65 IN LATIN AMERICA, 1980s

Type of country	Country	Cardiac disease	Cerebro-vascular Diseases	Malignant tumours	Diabetes mellitus	Accidents	Others
Highly urban	Argentina	2	3	1	5	4	
	Uruguay	2	3	1	4	5	
	Chile	2	3	1	-	-	Chronic liver diseases (4)
	Venezuela	2	3	1	4	5	
	Cuba	2	3	1	5	4	
	Puerto Rico	1	4	2	3	-	Cronic liver diseases (5)
Mixed	Brazil	1	3	2	4	-	
	Mexico	2	4	1	3	5	
	Colombia	2	3	1	5	4	
	Peru	2	5	1	-	-	Influenza and pneumonia (3); tuberculosis (4)
	Dominican Republic	1	3	2	5	-	Chronic liver diseases (4)
	Panama	2	3	1	4*	4*	Influenza and pneumonia (5)
	Costa Rica	2	3	1	4	-	Bronchitis. emphysema, asthma (5)
Higly rural	El Salvador	2	3	1	5	4	Intestinal infection (2): influenza and pneumonia (5); nutritional deficiencies (5)
	Ecuador	2	3	1	-	4	
	Paraguay	2	3	1	4	5	
	Guatemala	3	-	1	-	-	
	Honduras	1	3	2	-	4	intestinal infection (2); influenza and pneumonia

Ages 50-64
Ages 45-49
* Same
Source: Pan-American Health Organization, 1986.

TABLE V. FIVE LEADING CAUSES OF DEATH AMONG WOMEN 65 OR OLDER IN LATIN AMERICA, 1980s

Type of country	Country	Cardiac disease	Cerebro-vascular Diseases	Malignant tumors	Diabetes mellitus	Influenza/ pneumonia	Other
Highly urban	Argentina	1	2	3	4	5	
	Uruguay	1	3	2	4	5	
	Chile	1	2	3	5	4	
	Venezuela	1	2	3	5	4	
	Cuba	1	2	3	-	4	Accidents (5)
	Puerto Rico	1	2	3	4	5	
	Brazil	1	2	3	4	5	
	Mexico	1	2	3	4	5	
	Colombia	1	2	3	4	5	
Mixed	Peru	1	3	4	-	2	Tuberculosis (5)
	Dominican Republic	1	3	2	4	5	
	Panama	1	3	2	4	-	Accidents (5)
	Costa Rica	1	2	3	4	4	
	El Salvador	1	3	2	-	4	Accidents (5)
	Ecuador	1	2	3	-	4	Accidents (5)
Highly rural	Paraguay	1	3	2	5	4	Accidents (5)
	Guatemala	1	4	-	-	2	Intestinal infections (3); Nutritional deficiencies (5)
	Honduras	1	2	3	-	-	

Source: Pan-American Health Organization, 1986.

91

TABLE VI.   FIVE MAIN CAUSES OF DEATH AMONG WOMEN AGED 45 TO 65 OR OLDER IN THE CARIBBEAN, 1980s

Country	Cardiac disease	Cerebro-vascular Diseases	Malignant Tumours	Diabetes Mellitus	Accidents	Other
Bahamas	2	3	1	-	5	Chronic liver disease (4);
Barbados	2	3	1	-	5	Chronic liver disease (4);
Belize	1	2	3	4	-	Influenza (5); meningitis (5); tuberculosis (5)
Guyana	2	1	4	-	-	Non-malignant tumours, carcinima in situ (3); mental illiness (5);
Martinique	2	3	1	-	-	Chronic liver disease (4); mental illness (5);
Netherlands Antilles	1	2	1	3	5	Bronchitis, emphysema, asthma (4); Nephritis (5);
Saint Lucia	1	4	2	3	-	Nephritis (5);
Suriname	1	3	2	-	5	Chronic liver disease (4);
Trinidad and Tobago	1	4	2	3	-	Chronic liver disease (5);
Virgin Islands	3	2	-	-	3	Homicide (3), mental illness (3)

Source: Pan-American Health Organization, 1986.

TABLE VII. FIVE LEADING CAUSES OF DEATH AMONG WOMEN 65 OR OLDER IN THE CARIBBEAN, 1980s

Country	Cardiac disease	Cerebro-vascular diseases	Malignant tumours	Diabetes mellitus	Influenza	Other
Bahamas	1	2	3	-	4	Mental illiness (5);
Barbados	1	2	3	4	5	
Belice	1	3	2	5	4	
Guyana	1	2	4	-	-	Non-malignant tumours; carcinioma in situ (3); accidents (5)
Martinique	1	2	3	4	-	Mental illness (5);
Netherlands Antilles	1	3	2	5	4	
Saint Lucia	1	2	4	3	5	
Suriname	1	2	3	-	5	Bronchitis, emphysema, asthma (4)
Trinidad and Tobago	1	2	4	3	5	
Virgin Islands	1	2	3	-	-	Accidents (3)

Source: Pan-American Health Organization, 1986.

93

TABLE VIII. ESTIMATED NUMBER OF RURAL WOMEN AFFECTED BY FUELWOOD SCARCITY, 1990

	Forest as per cent of land area	Fuelwood status	Per cent of rural Population	Per cent of household energy fuelwood	Rural women aged 10-59	Estimated number of rural women affected by fuelwood scarcity
Latin America and Caribbean						
Argentina	16	PD: north	14	43	1 319	567
Bolivia	45	AS: west	49	81	1 088	881
Brazil	66	D: north-east and south-east; PD: central	25	32	11 345	3630
Colombia	52	D: central	30	60	2 949	1769
Cuba	15	D	25	25	930	233
Dominican Republic	22	D	40	55	851	468
Ecuador	46	D: central	44	65	1 405	913
El Salvador	6	AS	56	71	884	628
Guatemala	39	D: south	61	73	1 623	1185
Haiti	1	AS	72	72	1 433	1032
Jamaica	..	AS	48	61	360	220
Mexico	25	D: central, east, west	27	23	7 233	1664
Paraguay	32	D: east	53	68	657	447
Peru	53	AS: north,south, west, D: central	30	76	2 013	1530

Source: The World's Women, 1995 Trends and Statistics, United Nations publication, 91-1-161372-8.

94

TABLE IX. DEFORESTATION AND TIME WOMEN SPEND GATHERING FUELWOOD

Region, village and forest status		Time spent collecting fuelwood (hours/day)
Latin America		
Ecuador	1990	
North-east Amazon		
Napo and Sucumbios Province		
(a) < 50% private forests cleared		1
(b) > 50% private forest cleared		1.2
Mexico	1983	1.7-2.1
Peru	1981	
Highland Peru		
(a) Huancarama (access to private trees)		0.5
(b) Pinchos (restricted forests)		1.3
Puno in southern Andes	1985-1987	0.1

Source: The World's Women, 1995 Trends and Statistics, United Nations publication, 1995.

TABLE X. ACCESS TO SAFE DRINKING WATER AND SANITATION SERVICES, 1990

Country or area	Rural population without access to safe drinking water (%)	Percentage urban population without		Estimated number of urban women affected by lack of	
		safe drinking water	sanitation services	safe drinking water	sanitation services
Latin American and the Caribbean					
Argentina	83	27	[=<10]	3 8∠8	-
Bolivia	70	24	62	449	1 161
Brazil	39	[=<10]	16	-	9 125
Chile	79	[=<10]	[=<10]	-	-
Colombia	18	13	16	1 528	1 880
Dominican Republic	55	18	[=<10]	397	-
Ecuador	56	37	44	1 114	1 325
El Salvador	85	13	15	159	183
Guatemala	57	[=<10]	28	-	519
Haiti	65	44	56	456	580
Honduras	52	15	11	174	127
Jamaica	54	[=<10]	-	-	-
Mexico	51	[=<10]	15	-	4 659
Nicaragua	79	24	-	287	-
Paraguay	91	39	69	404	715
Peru	76	32	24	2 396	1 797
Uruguay	95	[=<10]	40	-	577
Venezuela	64	11	[=<10]	959	-

Source: *The World's Women, 1995 Trends and Statistics,* United Nations publication, 1995.

ABBREVIATIONS USED IN THE CHAPTER

AARP - American Association of Retired Persons

FAO - Food and Agriculture Organization of the United Nations

CSD - Commission for Sustainable Development

ILO - International Labour Organization

INSTRAW - International Research and Training Institute for the Advancement of Women

PAHO - Pan-American Health Organization

UNCED - United Nations Conference on Environment and Development

UNDP - United Nations Development Programme

UNEP - United Nations Environment Programme

UNFPA - United Nations Population Fund

UNSTAT - United Nations Statistical Division

UNU - United Nations University

WHO - World Health Organization

REFERENCES

Alatorre, Javier; et al. *Las mujeres en la pobreza* Centro de Estudios Sociológicos, El Colegio de México, 1994.

American Association for the Advancement of Science, Vol. 273, July 1996.

Bourdelais, Patrice, *L'Age de la Vieillesse*, Editions Odile Jacob, Paris, 1993.

Bold, Quarterly Journal of the International Institute on Ageing, United Nations, Malta, Vol.7, No.1, November 1996, Vol.7, No.2, February, 1997; Vol.7, No.3, May 1997.

Burin, M. Moncarz, E.. Velázquez, S, *El Malestar de las Mujeres, La Tranquilidad Recetada,* Editorial Paidos, Buenos Aires, 1991.

Caribbean Regional Newsletter, "Helpage International", Vol.2, No.1, 1994.

CEPAL, "Panorama Social de América Latina" 1994, Comisión Económica para América Latina y El Caribe, Santiago de Chile, Noviembre 1994.

"Formación de los Recursos Humanos Femeninos: Prioridad del Crecimiento y de la Equidad", por Nieves Rico, Serie Mujer y Desarrollo, Publicación de Naciones Unidas, Julio 1996. Santiago de Chile.

"La Salud y las Mujeres en América Latina y El Caribe: Viejos Problemas y Nuevos Enfoques" por Elsa Gómez Gómez, Abril 1997.

"Las Mujeres en América Latina y El Caribe en los años 90: Elemento de Diagnóstico y Propuestas", Unidad de la Mujer y Desarrollo de la Secretaría Ejecutiva de la CEPAL, Abril 1997.

ECLAC, (CEPAL) "Regional Programme of Action for the Women of Latin America and the Caribbean, 1995-2001", Economic Comission for Latin America and the Caribbean and United Nations Development Fund for Women, Santiago de Chile, 1995.

De Vries, I.C. and Keuzenkamp S. "Compendium: Women and Habitat", Department of Spatial Planning, Faculty of Policy Sciences, University of Nijmegen, the Netherlands,1996.

Dirección Nacional de la Mujer, "Plan de Igualdad de Oportunidades 1996 - 2000" , DINAMU, Quito, 1996.

Eisler, Riane et all, "Women, Men, the Global Quality of Life", The Center for Partnership Studies, July 1995.

Food and Agriculture Organization, "Forest Products, World Outlook Projection", Forestry Paper No.84, Rome 1988.

"Forest Resources Assessment 1990", Global Synthesis, Forestry Paper No.124, Food and Agriculture Organization, Rome 1995.

Garrett, James L., "Challenges to the 2020 Vision for Latin America: Food and Agriculture Since 1970". International Food Policy Research Institute Discussion Paper 21, Washington, D.C., June 1997.

ILO, "Underemployment: Concept and Measurement" Report I, Meeting of Experts on Labour Statistics, International Labour Office, Geneva, 14-23 October 1997.

"The ILO and the Elderly". International Labour Office, Geneva, 1992.

International Institute on Ageing, "Age Vault", by Saviour Formosa, International Institute on Ageing, United Nations Malta, 1995.

"Meeting the Challenges of Ageing Population in Developing Countries", Final Report, Malta, 23-25 October 1995.

INSTRAW/AARP: "Ageing: A Chronological Process in Life, Social and Economic Questions Arising from It", by Martha Dueñas, Santo Domingo, 1996, Report of the NGO Committee on Ageing, New York, 1996.

Report of the NGO Committee on Ageing, "Working for the Improvement of the Quality of Life for Older Persons in Human Settlements", Activities at HABITAT II: City Summit, June 3-14 1996, Istanbul, Turkey, New York, 1996.

INSTRAW/UNSTAT, "The Situation of Elderly Women, available statistics and indicators", United Nations publication, January 1993.

INSTRAW/UNESCO/CIPAF. " La Investigación sobre la Mujer en América Latina, Estudios de Género y Desafios de Sociedad". Coordinación Claudia Serrano, 1993.

INSTRAW, "Las Mujeres de Edad Madura en América Latina", monografia por María Soledad Parada, Agosto de 1988, Santo Domingo.

INSTRAW, "Improving Concepts and Methods for Statistics and Indicators on the Situation of Elderly Women", report of a consultative meeting, New York, 28-30 May 1991.

Karl, Marilee, "Women and Empowerment, Participation and Decision Making". Women and World Development Series, UN/NGO, Zed Books Ltd, 1995.

Levi, L.; Andersson, L., "Population, Environment and Quality of Life"., Swedish Royal Ministry for Foreign Affairs, 1978.

Listín Diario, "Todos Somos Envejecientes", Dra. Beatriz Z. Henríquez Portuondo, edición 10 de septiembre de 1997.

Marks, Dorrit, "Women and Grassroots Democracy in the Americas", North-South Center, University of Miami, 1992.

Masini E.; Stratigos, S., "Women, Households and Change", United Nations University Press, Tokyo, 1991.

National Geographic, "Ageing - New Answers to Old Questions" by Rick Weiss, National Geographic, Journal, Vol.192, No.5, Washington D.C., 1997.

Network News, "Newsletter of the Global Link for Midlife and Older Women" Vol.6, No.1, July 1991; Vol.7, No.1 July 1992 and Vol.7 No.2, December 1992.

New Scientist Supplement, "The Future - The New Human Condition", New Scientist Vol.15, October 1994.

New Scientist, "Life at 200: Will we always grow old?", New Scientist Journal, Vol.150 No.2035, June 1996.

OIT, "Género, Pobreza y Empleo: Guía para la Acción", International Labour Organization, Geneva, 1996.

OPS/AARP, "Las Mujeres de Edad Mediana y Avanzada en América Latina y El Caribe", Washington, D.C., 1990.

Sennott-Miller, Lee. "La Situación de Salud y Socioeconómica de Edad Mediana y Avanzada en América Latina y El Caribe", Pan American Health Organization, Washington, D.C., 1990.

Tapia, M., y Luciano L., "Condición Social de la Población Vieja". Memorias del II Seminario sobre Género y Vejez en República Dominicana, Centro de Apoyo Aquelarre, Santo Domingo, 1995.

UNICEF, "Children, Women and Poverty in Mountain *Ecosystems*" *by Dr. Jack D. Ives. UNICEF, January 1996.*

United Nations, *The Nairobi Forward-Looking Strategies for the Advancement of Women,* DPI/86-44198, April 1986. See also General Assembly resolution 40/108.

United Nations, *Report of the United Nations Conference on Environment and Development, Rio de Janeiro, 3-14 June 1992, Tokyo, 1991.* (United Nations publication, Sales No. E. 93. I..8).

United Nations Report of the World Conference on Human Rights, June 1993. United Nations, Vienna, New York, DPI/1394-48164-Octobre 1993.

United Nations, *International Conference on Population and Development, Cairo, 5-13 September 1994* (United Nations publication. Sales No. E. 95. XIII.18).

Report of the United Nations, *Global Conference on the Sustainable Development of Small Island Developing States, Bridgetown , Barbados, 25 April – May 1994* (United Nations publication, Sales No. E. 94. I.18 and corrigenda).

United Nations, *Report of the World Summit for Social Development, Copenhagen, 6-12 March 1999.*

United Nations, *Report of the Fourth World Conference on Women, Beijing, 4-15 September 1994 (*United Nations publication, Sales No. E. 96.IV.13).

United Nations, *Report of the United Nations Conference on Population and Development, Istanbul, 3-14 June 1996* (United Nations publication, Sales No. E.97.IV.6).

United Nations, "The World Food Summit", WSS/96/3, Rome, 13-17 November 1996.

United Nations Centre for Human Rights, "Human Rights Compilation of International Instruments", Vol. I (Part I) Universal Instruments, New York, 1993.

"Report on the World Social Situation, 1993", (ST/ESA/235 E/1993/50/Rev.1), Department of Economic and Social Development, United Nations, New York, 1993.

"Older Persons in Countries with Economies in Transition : Designing a Policy Response", Guidelines for Practical Strategies, (ST/ESA/248), Division for Social Policy and Development, United Nations, New York, 1997.

"Living Arrangements of Women and their Children in Developing Countries", (ST/ESA/SER.R/141), Demographic Profile, United Nations, New York, 1995.

"Women's Education and Fertility Behaviour, Recent Evidence from the Demographic and Health Surveys", (ST/ESA/SER.R/137), United Nations Population Division, New York 1995.

"The World's Women 1995, Trends and Statistics". (ST/ESA/STAT/SR.K/12), United Nations, New York, 1995.

"World Economics and Social Survey 1997: Trends and Policies in the World Economy" (ST/ESA/256), United Nations, New York, 1997.

"World Population Prospects", 1996 Revision, annexes II and III, Demographic indicators by major area, region and country. United Nations Population Division, New York, 1996.

"Humanitarian Report 1997", Department of Humanitarian Affairs, New York and Geneva 1997.

Wolfson, Elaine M., Ph.D, "Depresion and the Mature Woman: a multi-cultural perspective", Proceedings, 1997 Annual Spring Forum, the Global Alliance for Women's Health.

World Bank, "From Plan to Market", World Development Report 1996", Oxford University Press, Washington D.C., June 1996.

"Case Studies on Women's Employment and Pay in Latin America" by Psacharopoulos, G. and Tzannatos, Z. World Bank, Washington, D.C. 1992.

UNDP, "Human Development Report 1993", United Nations Development Programme 1993, Oxford University Press.

"Human Development Report 1995", United Nations Development Programme 1995, Oxford University Press.

"Human Development Report 1997", United Nations Development Programme 1997, Oxford University Press.

World Health Organizaton, "Women's Health and Human Rights" by R.J. Cook, World Health Organization, Geneva, 1994.

VI. GLOBAL AGEING AND THE INTERGENERATIONAL EQUITY ISSUE

*Steven K. Wisensale, Ph.D.**

Less than two decades ago the global population was viewed as "young" rather than "old." That is, 35 per cent of all persons in the world were 14 years of age or younger, compared to only 8.5 per cent who were 60 and over (Link Age 2000, 1998). It is not surprising, then, that most policy makers focused their attention on issues such as family planning, maternal and child health and education. Little attention, particularly in developing nations, was paid to a growing ageing population and the potential impact it could have on the economy, the social fabric and the political system of a given country.

But today, at the dawn of a new millennium, we are about to bear witness to a global society that is the oldest in the history of the world. The elderly population (aged 60 or over) is growing faster than all other age groups and will expand from 200 million elderly in 1950 to 1.2 billion in 2025, a six-fold increase over the past 75 years according to the United Nations statistics. Even more significant, perhaps, is the demographic picture that emerges when ageing populations in developed nations are compared to similar populations in developing countries.

In most western industrialized countries the speed of population growth for the aged moved fairly slowly, taking from 50-100 years for the percentage of the population over 65 years of age to double from 7 to 14 per cent. However, in most developing nations a comparable increase among the aged population will take place in fewer than 30 years (Link Age 2000, 1998). By 2025, one out of every four people (25 per cent) in the developed world is projected to be 60 years of age or older. In contrast, only 12 per cent of the developing world will be over 60. However, the latter percentage constitutes 860 million people, or 71 per cent of the world's elderly population! And, equally impressive, 84 per cent of the globe's population will be in the developing regions by 2025 (Chawla, 1993), with Africa's aged population projected to grow the fastest (United Nations, 1985).

Through a combination of declining fertility rates and a corresponding increase in life expectancy, both developed and developing nations are witnessing shifts in their respective population age structures that, ultimately, will affect their respective dependency/support ratios. This ratio represents the number of people under age 15 and over age 64 who are dependent on those who are usually participating in the work force (ages 15 to 64) and paying taxes to support the "too young" and the "too old." It is precisely at this juncture where questions concerning intergenerational equity are spawned. That is, how should resources be allocated across different age groups? And, who should pay, how much, and why?

Understandably, predictions of major demographic changes, combined with challenging policy questions such as those posed above, have produced much anxiety throughout the world. For clearly, "evidence is accumulating that the ageing of populations can have a strong influence on the course of development, both in economic and social terms" (United Nations, 1985). And, not to be overlooked, is the fact that the ageing of the world's population is occurring in the midst of an ongoing global economic transition (see Schulz, 1993). Therefore, to what extent the impact of population ageing depends or determines the outcome of the economic transition now in progress is a large, tantalizing and provocative "unknown" confronting policy makers throughout the world. Or, put another way, will older people be contributors to, or simply beneficiaries of, improved standards of living?

Concerned about such questions as early as the 1980s, the United Nations adopted the *International Plan of Action* on Ageing in 1982, the first internationally-negotiated action document that put forth specific recommendations to address the potential effects of global ageing. The Plan of Action was anchored to the basic principle that there is a symbiotic relationship between population ageing and economic development. "One basic objective of the Plan of Action, then, was to ensure that, as the population of the world ages, the elderly would themselves have opportunities to contribute to, as well as share in, the benefits of development" (Chawla, 1993).

Subsequent reports, including three quadrennial reviews of the implementation of the *International Plan*

*Steven K. Wisensale is an Associate Professor of Public Policy in the School of Family Studies at the University of Connecticut, United States of America

of Action on Ageing and a separate study, *The World Ageing Situation* (United Nations, 1991) have all drawn one common and troubling conclusion: "that the elderly have come to be viewed as dependent beneficiaries of development, rather than contributors to it" (Chawla, 1993). Under such circumstances the elderly may be perceived as not only obstacles to economic development, but also as societal burdens who divert needed resources away from other age groups. It is within this context, often referred to as the "intergenerational equity issue," that this chapter is structured.

The presentation that follows is divided into four major sections. First, there is a discussion of the general parameters that usually accompany any debate about intergenerational equity. What are the options for creating a framework for discussion and which sources, in particular, may prove most helpful in this process? Section two is devoted to an overview of the intergenerational equity debate in the developed world. Although the primary focus is on experiences in the United States of America, other post-industrial countries, such as Germany and Japan will also be discussed within this context. In section three the discussion concentrates on the policy implications of ageing in developing nations. Specific countries and regions will be identified and explored within the framework of the intergenerational equity issue. Presented in the fourth section of this chapter are selected recommendations and guidelines that nations may want to consult if, and when, the debate over intergenerational equity surfaces within their borders.

ESTABLISHING THE PARAMETERS OF THE
INTERGENERATIONAL EQUITY DEBATE

There are times when novels and folklore can serve as convenient vehicles for simplifying and diffusing complex and controversial issues. For example, in 1882 Anthony Trollope published *The Fixed Period*, a futuristic novel in which older citizens seemed to have outlived their usefulness and were viewed as burdens to society. The action takes place on Britannaula, a fictitious island. The younger citizens of the island had adopted a "fixed period" law under which all citizens 67 or older were "deposited" in a special honorary college known as a "necropolis". Here, members were expected to spend one year in deep thought and peaceful reflection before being chloroformed and cremated. This policy was intended to avoid the "imbecility and weakness of human life when protracted beyond its fitting limits" and to dignify death with "circumstances of honor and glory" (Trollope, 1882).

In philosopher Harry Moody's book, *Ethics in an Ageing Society*, the author begins a discussion about generational justice by referring to two stories from Eu-

ropean folklore. The first story is about a baby bird who rides on her mother's back while the mother searches for food. One day the mother asks the baby bird, "When I am old and frail will you carry me on your back just as I am doing now?" "Oh no mother," replies the baby bird. "I'll carry my little baby bird on my back just as you're doing now".

In the second story, a product of Simone de Beauvoir's novel *The Coming of Age*, a farmer decides he has no more room at the table for his old father who lives with the family. Sent to the barn, the frail old man must eat his meals out of a trough. When the father finds his own son in the barnyard playing with some wood he asks him what he is doing. "Oh father," replies the boy, "I am building a trough for you to eat from when you get old." That evening the frail old man was asked to rejoin the family at the dinner table.

All three stories offer lessons for today's policy makers to ponder as they address the issue of intergenerational equity. In Trollope's novel it was made clear that if the aged are viewed as burdens rather than resources, policies will be designed that favour the young over the old. In the first of Moody's folktales, the lesson concerns the limits of reciprocity. "No matter what the older generation has done for the younger, each generation's primary obligation is transitive. That is, we 'repay' the generosity of the preceding generation by giving in turn to our successors" (Moody, 1992). And, in the second of Moody's stories, the lesson comes in the form of a warning. That is, there may be a price to pay if the young act badly towards the old. After all, when we look at the aged and gear specific policies toward them, we are looking at our "future selves." Like the story about the farmer, "we need to take the whole life cycle into account in thinking about justice across generations" (Moody, 1992).

However, concepts such as reciprocity and equity, which have never been easy to master, become even more complicated when discussed within the parameters of public policy and intergenerational justice. But at least two things are certain: whoever participates in addressing the problem will most likely determine how it is framed; and two, how the problem is framed will ultimately determine the shape of its solution. Each is discussed below.

With respect to selecting the participants who will address the problem, Cohen (1993) reminds us that in thinking about "justice across generations" the traditional academic disciplines can only offer partial answers to the question. For example, historians may look at obligations that the old and young had towards each other in the past and how that has changed. Anthropologists may want to compare intergenerational relationships across different societies in search of a universal notion of justice. Philosophers might focus on whether the generosity and selfishness in one person's life can be compared with the generosity and selfishness in another person's life at different stages of their personal development. Economists may want to explore the allocation of public goods to persons of different ages and ask whether any given concept of justice can be achieved economically. And, while sociologists may focus on how families allocate the burdens of caring for their old and young, political scientists may examine how these burdens are addressed in formulating, implementing and evaluating public policy.

With respect to how the problem of intergenerational equity is framed, it is imperative that key words, such as "generation," "cohort," and "equity," be discussed and clarified. And, if possible, a consensus should be reached concerning their usage and meaning throughout the policy-making process. For example, "generation" can mean either a particular chronological age group, such as children under 14 or adults over age 65, or it can also be used in reference to a particular birth cohort, such as the "silent generation" of the fifties, baby boomers, or today's "Generation X."

When "equity" is added to the discussion the matter becomes even more complicated. Moon (1993), for example, reminds us that intergenerational issues tend to be discussed in an extremely broad context. For some, this means comparing different age groups at a particular point in time. Are elderly households today better off than younger households? Others see intergenerational equity as a comparison of cohorts at similar stages in their life cycles. How well off are we compared to our parents at our age? Or, put another way, how well off will our children be when they reach our age? Finally, and perhaps the most extreme view to be taken, is to compare the lifetimes of different generations. How well do generations fare when compared against the full range of experiences?

Two philosophers in particular who have devoted their careers to exploring issues associated with intergenerational justice may prove to be very helpful in assisting policy makers as they establish the parameters for debating the issue. Harry Moody (1992), who recognizes the difficulty in defining intergenerational equity, offers what some may refer to as a "back door approach" to the problem. That is, if we cannot agree on what generational equity is, can we at least agree on a set of guidelines to determine when it has been violated? Moody argues that, in order to prove unfairness in the distribution of benefits or burdens across generations or cohorts, we have to identify the following conditions.

(*a*)   A clear deviation from equal treatment, or from what was explicitly promised must occur. Has an "inter-generational compact" been violated? Would the privatization of a publicly-funded pension programme be an example of such a violation?

(*b*)   The deviation must be disproportionate and therefore unjustified. Is it unfair to raise the age for retirement in light of the fact that life expectancy has been increasing steadily over the years?

(*c*)   The inequity could reasonably have been foreseen or predicted—at least some part of the future is knowable. For example, if older people tend to get ill more than younger people, will not the former group use more health resources? Is this necessarily unfair? Or should there be health rationing based on age? (Callahan, 1987)

(*d*)   Someone is in a position to do something about it and therefore be held responsible. This would apply to legislators and others involved in the policy-making process.

Another philosopher, Norm Daniels, offers a different but not contradictory approach to Moody's. Building on the work of John Rawls, Daniels poses two questions that are directly relevant to this discussion First, what is a just or fair distribution of social resources among the different *age groups* competing for them? And second, what is equity between birth cohorts? That is, what is fair treatment of different cohorts as they age and pass through transfer and savings schemes that solve the age-group problem?

Daniels' (1988) solution is what he refers to as the "Prudential Lifespan Account." Instead of looking at birth cohorts or age cohorts being in conflict over resources at any given time, we should take each person's entire lifespan as the basic unit of consideration. Within this framework it would be reasonable to accept the proposition that the same person may gain differential access to differential resources over the course of his or her entire lifespan. "My account of justice between age groups builds on this basic point," writes Daniels. "Unequal treatment at different stages of life may be exactly what we want from institutions that operate over a lifetime. Since our needs vary at different stages of our lives, we want institutions to be responsive to these changes" (Daniels, 1993).

But clearly, problems associated with distributive justice across generations are not easy to resolve. In attempting to do so, however, it is important that the parameters of the debate be clearly established, that key words and concepts be carefully defined and clarified and that a variety of perspectives be brought to the table so that all viewpoints representing all age groups are heard. To what extent lessons learned from the intergenerational equity debate in one country can be transferred to other nations is of course an open question. However, such an effort is put forth in the next section with a discussion of the United States' experience with this issue.

THE INTERGENERATIONAL EQUITY DEBATE IN THE DEVELOPED WORLD: THE UNITED STATES, GERMANY AND JAPAN

The individual status of an aged person today and tomorrow depends to a great extent on the culture, customs, traditions and social policies of the particular country in which he or she resides. For example, distinct cultural differences in Sweden and Japan have produced different approaches to addressing the needs of their aged populations. In Sweden, a country with a long tradition of government activism, only 7 per cent of the elderly live with their adult children. Most live independently in their own apartments. This policy approach is in sharp contrast to Japan where greater emphasis on family care and less on government involvement results in 65 per cent of the elderly residing with their adult children (Link Age 2000, 1998).

But regardless of cultural diversity and differences in policy approaches among various countries, developed nations in particular have at least two characteristics in common. First, almost all are confronting the emergence of what is often referred to as the "inverse family pyramid". That is, where there was once a pyramid of many children, fewer adults and even fewer elderly within a family, we now see a different pyramid, consisting of only one or two children, two parents, four grandparents and possibly eight grandparents. The second characteristic that developed nations have in common is manifested in a public policy choice that they have before them. They can view older people as a distinct group in society and develop programmes that are designed to address their specific needs (age-based policy) or they can seek to adopt policies that support all individuals in society regardless of age (general redistributive policies) and then attempt to remove barriers that separate young from old.

How countries respond to such a choice may well determine how they choose to allocate their resources across generations and the extent to which a debate over intergenerational equity becomes deeply imbedded within the political landscape. What follows is a discussion of the intergenerational equity debate in the United States, followed by an overview of similar debates that are forming on the horizon in Germany and Japan.

The case of the United States

The debate over intergenerational equity in the United States began nearly two decades ago. In "The Graying of the Federal Budget," Hudson (1978) identified the tremendous growth pattern in the expenditure of funds on the aged (more than one quarter of the United States. annual budget) and sent forth a warning about the impending backlash that would afflict the growing ageing movement. Interestingly, one of the first indicators of an emerging backlash came in relation to defense spending, not in the form of an intergenerational equity question. In 1982 an economist in the Office of Management and Budget noticed the same "graying of the budget" as reported by Hudson and switched the commonly used metaphor of "guns vs. butter" to "guns vs. canes" (Binstock, 1992).

Reference to the intergenerational equity issue would emerge soon thereafter. In "The Aged as Scapegoat" (Binstock, 1983) and *Age or Need* (Neugarten, 1982), two internationally-recognized gerontologists echoed the alarm sounded by Hudson and, in doing so, identified the potential for intergenerational conflict. Later, others would introduce a new metaphor designed to simplify the problem: "kids vs. canes." As the debate unfolded, both the public and private sectors would become actively involved.

The United States debate in the private sector

Although American academics such as Hudson, Binstock and Neugarten had issued warnings about a potential generational conflict, the backlash had already begun in the private sector by the early 1970s. The target would be Social Security, the public pension programme for the retired elderly in the United States. Following a Social Security tax hike and the adoption of cost-of-living adjustments in 1972, the business community launched a major campaign to distort the public's image of Social Security as an insurance programme. "Reconstructing Social Security as an intergenerational tax rather than an insurance programme became the goal for opponents of the programme," states Jill Quadagno (1990), "and under the guise of intergenerational equity, a new attack was launched."

When the United States Federal Reserve Bank issued a special report on Social Security in 1972, the programme was described as a "huge Ponzi scheme" (*Fortune*, 1973). Writing in *Forbes* in 1980, Jerry Flint noted that the elderly are living well, not in poverty, as most believe. "The trouble is there are too many of them—God bless'em" (Flint, 1980). Bendix Corporation Chairman, William Agee, predicted that "young and old will be pitted against each other in a fearful battle over the remains of a shrinking economy" (Ehrbar, 1980). And by 1982, *Fortune* readers were being informed that "it is part of the sorrowful lot of the baby boom generation (those born between 1946 and 1964) that it will have to finance both its parents' retirement and a substantial portion of its own" (Ehrbar, 1980, p. 118). More significantly, however, the public debate over intergenerational equity in the United States was looming on the horizon.

The U.S. debate in the public sector

Although it is difficult to isolate the precise date and time when the public backlash began, Colorado Governor Richard Lamm's comments on national television can serve as an important reference point. Governor Lamm stated quite bluntly that he believed too many resources were devoted to the elderly, particularly in their last few years of life, in comparison to resources allocated for children. While the controversy surrounding the Governor's comment evaporated fairly quickly, it spawned a much broader question that demanded greater attention: in an era that is often depicted as one with limited resources, are the aged receiving a disproportional share of those resources in comparison to other groups? Abbreviated, it became the intergenerational equity question and soon numerous individuals and a variety of interest groups would participate in a very heated debate.

Beginning with his presidential address ("Children and the Elderly: Divergent Paths for America's Dependents") before the Population Association in 1984, and combined with his article in *Scientific American* shortly thereafter, Samuel Preston (1984) established the original parameters of the public debate. We simply cannot wish away, he argued, the possibility that there is direct competition between the young and the old for society's resources: "Whereas expenditures on the elderly can be thought of mainly as consumption, expenditures on the young are a combination of consumption and investment". Richman and Stagner (1986) put it another way, arguing that an ageing society poses two possible consequences for America's children: fewer in number, they may become either a treasured resource or a forgotten minority.

Others joined the debate as well. Daniel Callahan, in *Setting Limits* (1987), staked out the position that limited resources should prompt policy makers to consider a health care rationing programme based on age. Philip Longman, in *Born to Pay: The New Politics of Ageing in America* (1987), concluded that an unfair burden was placed on the baby boom generation to support a growing ageing population through Social Security and Medicare. Laurence Kotlikoff (1992), supported by Peter Peterson (1993), applied "generational accounting" in his analysis of the United States federal deficit. Created to measure lifetime tax rates (21.5 per cent for those born in 1900 compared to 33.5 per cent projected for those born in 1990), generational accounting in the United States means that the later people are born, the more they will work for everyone else and the less for themselves.

On the other side, Myles and Quadagno (1992), building on the works of Minkler and Robertson (1991), concluded that the intergenerational equity debate is merely a class war in disguise, designed to undermine the cross-class strengths of the old-age coalition and weaken the power of the elderly lobby in the United States. "The rhetoric of young versus old was promulgated by an elite group of policy makers, academicians and business leaders with a stake in remaking public images of the elderly in ways that would support decreased social spending" (Minkler and Robertson, 1991). Put another way by Binney and Estes (1988), the intergenerational equity debate is a carefully crafted diversion that frees up the State from responsibility for human needs and permits large budgetary reallocations to the military and major tax cuts for the wealthy.

Making sense of the debate in the United States: isolating the issues

The debate over intergenerational equity is often confusing, primarily because it revolves around the concept of "fairness" (Kingson, 1989)—never an easy topic for discussion - and also because intergenerational equity has come to serve a dual purpose in the United States: one, as an approach to framing policy questions, and two, as a provocative political slogan (Kingson and Williamson, 1993). Regardless of whether the debate occurs in legislative chambers, university seminar rooms, think tanks or board rooms of publishing houses, at least four major issues are regularly discussed within the context of intergenerational equity: (*a*) the allocation of resources between children and the elderly; (*b*) the concern over large national deficits; (*c*) the distribution of health care resources among groups with competing claims; and (*d*) the fairness of financing Social Security by younger generations. Each issued is discussed in some detail below.

First, with respect to the allocation of resources, the initial stage of the intergenerational equity debate in the early 1980s was confined to one of children versus elderly. Works by Palmer, Smeeding, and Torrey (1988), Preston (1984), Richman and Stagner (1986), Rodgers (1986) and Wolfe (1991) shoulder this theme. Simply put, while Social Security Cost of living adjustments and other increases in benefits helped to slice the elderly poverty rate from 30 per cent to 12 per cent in 20 years, the fact remains that 40 per cent of all those who are still poor in the United States are children.

The second issue concerns the growing national deficit. Sometime between the end of the Reagan administration (1988-1989) and the early years of the Bush presidency (1990-1991), the focus of the intergenerational equity debate began to shift, from "kids vs. canes" to one which focused on the growing federal deficit. According to this analysis, the primary reason for the expanding national debt in the United States was twofold. First, elderly entitlement benefits had increased from 27 per cent of the federal budget in 1960 to nearly 54 per cent in 1993 and second, Social Security, federal pensions, and health care benefits (Medicare and Medicaid) accounted for virtually all of the historical expansion in entitlements. Consequently, unless this pattern is checked, argue the critics, each family today will be leaving to its children the equivalent of a $140,000 mortgage in unfunded entitlement benefit liabilities (Peterson, 1993).

With such a diagnosis successfully inserted in the intergenerational equity debate, it is not surprising then that elderly entitlements have become a prime target of those seeking to reduce the national deficit. Subsequently, the rhetoric employed usually refers to an overburdened younger population that deserves relief—through a combination of means-testing elderly entitlements (some prefer the term "affluence test") and a move to privatize Social Security.

The third major component of the intergenerational equity debate is related to the distribution of health care resources among various age groups. More than coincidentally, the utilization of health care resources by an ever growing elderly population has been at the very heart of a national discussion over health policy. After all, more than one-third of the United States' national health care budget is devoted to older people. More significantly, projections are that it will increase drastically as the baby boomers retire over the next 20 years (Sonnefeld et al., 1991).

This issue climbed to a different level following the publication of Daniel Callahan's *Setting Limits: Medical Goals in an Ageing Society* (1987) and *What Kind of Life: The Limits of Medical Progress* (1990). For the first time on a large scale aged-based health rationing was given a public forum. However, to date, not only has age-based health rationing, as in the United Kingdom, not been adopted in the United States, it has yet to be placed on the national legislative agenda.

The fourth issue in the intergenerational equity debate concerns the financing mechanism that is employed to support Social Security. Begun as a pure transfer payment and classified as an "insurance programme," Social Security has relied on what is commonly referred to as a "healthy dependency ratio". That is, through an income transfer, in the form of a wage tax matched by employers, workers support retirees. When Ida Fuller, the first beneficiary in the history of Social Security, left her job for permanent retirement, there were 42 workers for every retiree. Today, however, the ratio is less than 4 to 1, and by 2030, when all of the baby boomers will be in retirement, the ratio is expected to fall to 2 to 1 or even lower!

In order to address the looming problem, young Americans today are being taxed at a higher rate than would be required under the original transfer ("pay as you go") model, in an effort to build up the surplus needed to support retired baby boomers. This policy, once it made its way into the popular media, provided a wedge for those who wanted to demythologize Social Security's insurance metaphor. For example, *Forbes* magazine informed its readers in 1982 that "taxes deducted from your pay are not insurance premiums; they are taxes"(p. 242). *The New Republic* followed suit when it reminded its readers in 1987 that "Social Security is primarily a redistribution scheme, rather than an insurance programme." In short, by the 1990s, what once was a model of intergenerational trust had been transformed into a debate over fairness among age groups.

The evidence is clear. Beginning in the early 1970s, and particularly from the 1980s, the backlashing (Hudson, 1978) and scapegoating (Binstock, 1983) directed toward the elderly in the United States have been relentless. This history, brief as it is, stands in sharp contrast to ageing policy in other industrialized countries where an intergenerational debate has never emerged on as large a scale. Broad-based universal health and social welfare policies, some with a major family focus, have served as inoculants against such divisive politics. However, this peace may soon be threatened in other developed countries such as Germany and Japan, although it remains to be seen whether or not these and other countries will produce the generational warfare rhetoric that has become so commonplace in the United States. Each of these nations is discussed below.

Germany's concern

Since the end of the Second World War, Germany has been upheld as one of the successful models of the social welfare state. With a system that provides universal health insurance regardless of age, grants parents at least $1,000 a month per child, and offers unemployment benefits that exceed two-thirds of a worker's take-home pay, Germany has been admired for decades by conservatives and liberals alike. Recently, however, due in part to the absorption of 18 million citizens of the former East Germany, the Government announced it was retrenching. Its generous social safety net and comprehensive job-training programmes were to be reduced substantially. While some observers are quick to point to the unification of the two Germanise as the cause of the country's economic ills, others view the situation from a different perspective and offer a rapidly changing demographic profile as a possible explanation (Newsweek, 1993).

Not unlike the United States, a major lightning rod for policy debates in Germany has been the Social Security system. Simply put, with the number of elderly citizens increasing at a rate relative to the number of working-age people who can support them, the Government is presented with a choice that is politically unpopular: either cut benefits to the aged or raise taxes on the young. It is this dilemma that places Germany at the same intersection of the intergenerational equity debate where the United States found itself more than a decade ago. However, there are at least four reasons why the growing concern over intergenerational equity in Germany is potentially far more explosive than it has been in the United States.

First, due to an alarmingly low birth rate and a relatively high life-expectancy rate, Germany already has proportionately more elderly to support than the United States. Only Italy has a lower birth rate among western industrialized nations (Newsweek, 1991). Second, the social security system is far more generous in Germany than in the United States, not only in the amount of individual retirement stipends, but in the application of full benefits at age 61. Third, compared to American workers, Germans leave the labour force at a much earlier age, thus greatly increasing the ratio of retirees to the working population. And fourth, because fewer German women enter the labour force than in the United States, the German tax base is smaller. Thus, those who do work, primarily young people, must shoulder the burden of taxation in order to support the elderly (The American Institute for Contemporary German Studies, 1997).

Although Germany appears ripe to engage in a major debate over resource allocation across generations, it has managed to avoid doing so thus far. This may be at least partially explained by the fact that its social welfare system has such a long history of universal coverage. Therefore, its citizens may have very few reasons for being dissatisfied with the system, unlike the United States which has adopted more of an age-based approach. However, like the United States and other western industrialized nations, Germany is beginning to feel the impact of major demographic changes, particularly with respect to the number of young versus old. But this phenomenon is not confined to Europe and North America. Japan may be facing an even greater challenge.

Japan's challenge

Like Germany, Japan is bearing witness to major demographic changes as we approach the new millennium. It has the world's longest average life span (for girls born in 1996 it is 86 years, for boys it is 80 years) and one of the globe's lowest birth rates (only 1.4 babies per woman when 2 per woman are need to maintain a population at a steady rate). With such numbers, Japan is expected to replace Sweden by 2005 as the country with the oldest population in the world. Those 65 and older already constitute 15 per cent of the population, with some predictions taking that particular age cohort as high as 20 per cent of the Japanese population by 2005 and up to 33 per cent by 2050. But most surprising, perhaps, are government projections that suggest the population will decline by more than half over the next century, from 125 million today to 55 million by 2100, provided birth rates and life expectancy statistics remain the same (Coleman, 1997; Kristof, 1996).

Recent works by Hashimoto (1996); Bass, Morris, and Oka (1996); and Kumagai (1996) have all addressed the "ageing of Japan" and its potential impact on the future of that nation's social policy. How, they ask, will the demographic transitions that will make Japan one of the societies with the largest proportion of elderly within the next 25 years affect the overall health and general well-being of younger generations? How, they ask can this large group of elderly be assured necessary medical care and financial security without sacrificing the future of the nation's children?

Although generational conflict has not surfaced in Japan as it has in the United States, the potential for its emergence, as is the case in Germany, should not be ignored. However, a very important factor present in Japan that distinguishes it from the other two countries is its unique culture and the role it plays in influencing policy. More specifically, the role of the family in providing care to the elderly is rooted deeply in Japanese history. Thus, government policy has not moved toward institutionalizing the frail aged. Consequently, in a country with very few nursing homes, about 60 per cent of the elderly live with their middle-aged children or other relatives who provide needed services and personal care.

To some policy analysts, the government is making a mistake in assuming that families will continue to carry the burden of caring for Japan's old and frail. "The Government still thinks that co-residence is Japan's latent asset, but it's not true," said Naohiro Ogawa, an expert on ageing at Nihon University. "Family structure sets Japan apart from the West, but.....the value shifts, the generational gaps in terms of values, are quite serious" (Coleman, 1997). That is, presently, the conflict between generations in Japan may be more of a debate over cultural values than a battle over the allocation of resources based on age.

That said, at the very heart of the "values debate" is Japan's large corps of primary caregivers: women. Typically, wives are expected to stay home and raise their children with little, if any, assistance from anyone else, particularly the Government, and then to devote much of their middle age years caring for their husband's parents as well. However, as reported previously, more women are seeking careers a fact which has contributed to a decrease in the fertility rate and an increase in the graying of Japan. If this trend continues, it is unlikely that families will continue to serve as caregivers and the burden of responsibility will shift to the Government. This, in turn, will result in a government demand for greater tax revenues to fund more social service programmes. Consequently, the younger generations will be called upon to support the old. And, therefore, as has been learned in the United States, it is at this juncture where the soil is most fertile for intergenerational conflict to take root.

AGEING IN DEVELOPING COUNTRIES

While the interest in global ageing has grown in recent years, most researchers have focused their attention on developed nations rather than on developing countries. But today, of the approximately 580 million elderly people, that is, those 60 years of age or older, in the world, about 355 million live in developing nations. And, if predictions hold, by 2020 more than 1 billion people 60 years of age older will be living in the world, with more than 700 million of them residing in developing countries. More specifically, the rate of increase of older people in developing countries, such as Colombia, Malaysia, Kenya, Thailand and Ghana, is expected to be 7 to 8 times higher than the rate in Sweden and the United Kingdom, for example (World Health Organization, 1998).

This trend may be problematic for at least three reasons. First, as populations age in poor countries, the addition of more older dependents to a family may have a negative impact on the subsistence level of other members of the family. So in one sense, at least, there may be intergenerational conflict emerging within poor societies at the most basic level: the family.

Second, the graying of populations in poor countries, in particular when there is significant migration of younger people from rural to urban areas, as tends to occur with industrialization, may force Governments to assume greater responsibility for providing services to the elderly. Consequently, not only will migration deplete the elderly of many potential personal caregivers, younger workers will have to be taxed in order to meet the needs of the aged. So, on one hand we may witness the social division of families and the isolation of certain age groups as has occurred in developed nations. On the other hand, the potential for conflict between generations because of economic issues, such as tax policies that are perceived to be unfair by the young, may grow.

It should be emphasized here that the place of residence of both young and old, whether it is in urban or rural areas, may affect the willingness or resistance of individuals and Governments to allocate various resources across generations. For example, in some countries elderly people currently living in urban areas ranges from 25 to 30 per cent, a percentage that is expected to increase to 40 per cent by 2000. This fact alone raises yet another challenging question for policy makers to ponder: if this trend towards urbanization continues, will it create conflicts among generations both in rural and urban areas? (United Nations Department of International and Economic Affairs, 1995).

And third, important decisions must be made with respect to the type of pension programme that may work best for a given economy. Today, there are three different pension programmes from which nations choose to address the financial needs of their retirees. They include (a) public "pay-as-you-go" programmes, (b) employer-sponsored plans, and (c) personal savings and annuity plans. The most popular plan of the three is the public "pay-as-you-go" model. It is particularly popular in high income countries where coverage is universal and only somewhat widespread in middle income countries. Under this model, the government mandates, finances, manages and insures public pensions. Its benefits are pre-determined, not necessarily linked to the contributions made by retirees, and are financed by a payroll tax on active workers. Such a scheme, which can be a rich breeding ground for intergenerational conflict, is rare in developing countries. Instead, nations such as India, Indonesia, Mexico, South Africa, and Zimbawe have opted for employer-sponsored plans, also known as "employer-sponsored" systems. Voluntary personal saving is surfacing in more countries each year and may be managed either by Governments (for example Malaysia, Singapore and several African countries) or by several private companies on a competitive basis (currently in Chile and soon to be adopted in Argentina, Colombia and Peru). However, whatever model is selected, there is substantial risk involved (World Bank Policy Research Report, 1997; Link Age 2000, 1998).

Even if Governments choose to pay a small pension to each older retiree, the number of elderly is so large that the total budget becomes huge and individual pensions will be extremely low. For example, if India decided to pay 100 Indian rupees each month to each older person, by the year 2000 the monthly budget would be 7,600 million rupees, an overwhelming sum for any poor nation. Yet, the 100 rupee pension is insufficient to cover even one meal a day. And, to make matters even more complicated, developing countries tend not to have any organized collection system that transfers pension funds from younger generations to old—the so-called "pay-as-you-go" schemes. Such models have gone bankrupt in almost all developing countries. Thus, policy makers in the developing world would be better served if they thought of alternate forms of funding pensions, such as "fully-paid" schemes (Link Age 2000, 1998). Examples of two countries that wrestled with this issue in recent years are Chile and Brazil. Each issue is discussed below.

Chile's approach

Nearly 100 years after Otto Von Bismarck created the world's first state-run social security system in Germany in 1883, General Augusto Pinochet of Chile introduced the world's first state-endorsed privatized pension system. Convinced by free-market advocates from the outside that the combination of an ageing population and a dropping birth rate would make a traditional "pay-as-you-go" social security system impossible to sustain, the Pinochet Government adopted privately managed, individually owned retirement accounts. It was believed that such accounts, if properly diversified, would respond to the rise and fall of the Chilean stock market. However, although intergenerational conflict has been averted for the last two decades, indications are that privatization does not guarantee financial security at retirement.

Under the Chilean model, those who entered the work force after 1981 were required to automatically put 10 per cent or more of their wages into an individual retirement account (IRA), which is not taxed until withdrawal. Older workers who entered the labour force prior to 1981 had the option of remaining in the traditional social security system; more than 90 per cent accepted it. Upon retirement, a retiree's pension depends on the amount a worker accumulates, along with the investment returns earned by whichever one of 14 private pension fund companies the worker selects to manage the account. All portfolios are regulated and monitored by the Chilean Government (Krauss, 1998).

By 1997 the funds totalled more than $30 billion, having delivered an impressive 12 per cent average annual return in the first 15 years. Not surprisingly, other countries, including Argentina, Bolivia, Colombia, El Salvador, Mexico, Peru and Uruguay adopted some form of Chile's model. It also gained the praise of key officials in the United States who are concerned about the current "pay-as-you-go" system that is contributing to intergenerational conflict. But, Chile has not been on a smooth ride so far. The average returns for the pension funds fell from an 18 per cent gain in 1994 to a 2.5 per cent loss in 1995, followed by gains of 3.5 percent in 1996 and 4.7 per cent in 1997. Within the first eight months of 1998, Chile's stock market lost more than 25 per cent in dollar terms (Krauss, 1998).

As can be seen from the above, although privatization may be a viable option for replacing a traditional "pay-as-you-go" social security system, and it may prove helpful in either pre-empting or diffusing intergenerational conflict, such an approach is very

risky. If fluctuating stock markets result in long-term negative returns and retirees find themselves either in poverty or on the edge, the Government will be forced to make some very controversial decisions regarding the allocation of resources across generations. In short, has Chile actually prevented intergenerational conflict from occurring or merely postponed the confrontation until a later date?

Brazil's problem

While Chile clearly has seen its share of problems in attempting to address the needs of its ageing population, Brazil is confronted with a far more serious problem, particularly with respect to its national pension system. According to a recent article in the *Wall Street Journal*, the nation's state-run pension system is in deep trouble. For example, with no minimum retirement age in place, the majority of those who retired with social security benefits in 1997 were in their forties. In the same year, about 15,000 Brazilians still in their thirties also retired. Not only do civil servants receive full pay when they retire, but they may get as much as a 20 per cent raise when they leave work. And, further, all retirees are guaranteed any additional raises awarded to those who are still employed.

Not only does Brazil find itself in the midst of growing intergenerational conflict, the situation is complicated by two other factors. One, those who worked for the Government are awarded special treatment upon retirement when compared to those who worked in the private sector. And two, there is also a growing conflict between two distinct economic classes: the rich and the poor. For example, public-sector workers qualify for full pensions after only 25 years of service, compared with 35 years for those employed in the private sector. In 1997 half of the $85 billion paid out in pensions went to 2.7 million former career civil servants at an average of about $16,000 per year. This is in sharp contrast to the other half of the $85 billion that went to 17.7 million private sector workers who received an average of only $2,500 a year each. Even more disturbing to some, is the fact that because public servants did not begin paying into the national pension system until 1992 their benefits are primarily subsidized by relatively poor workers employed in the private sector (Fritsch, 1998).

Owing in part, to a mismanaged pension programme and a series of major economic recessions in its recent past, the Brazilian economy finds itself in a very vulnerable position. Clearly, a default in Brazil, the world's ninth-largest economy and home to more than half of South America's 300 million people, could set off repercussions around Latin America (Schemo, 1998). Equally troubling for some is the fact that a watered-down pension-reform bill failed to pass recently because political leaders were unable to establish a legislative quorum. Under such circumstances, the elderly, in particular, may find themselves in a very treacherous financial situation.

However financial concerns should not be the only worry of the aged and those who support them, regardless if they live in a developed or a developing country. There is at least one other component of the intergenerational equity debate that needs to be identified and addressed: health care and its associated costs.

With more people living longer, chronic and long-term debilitating diseases will become more prevalent and, therefore, health care costs will increase substantially.

It is estimated that, by 2020, three-quarters of all deaths in developing countries could be age-related, with the greatest share of these deaths expected to be caused by non-communicable diseases, such as cancers, diabetes and circulatory diseases . In some Latin American countries circulatory diseases and certain cancers are responsible for 60 per cent of all deaths. In African countries hypertension is on the rise, particularly in Seychelles, South Africa and Mauritius. And in parts of Asia, circulatory diseases and cancers are now the two leading causes of death, with hypertension having been found to affect up to 15 per cent of the adult population in India, Indonesia, and Thailand (World Health Organization, 1998).

Non-communicable diseases, in particular, can have a very negative impact on the health economics of a nation. In the United States, for example, the American Heart Association reports that cardiovascular diseases cost $151.3 billion annually. This includes both medical treatment and lost productivity due to disability. Similarly, diabetes, which affects about 143 million people worldwide, consumes about 8 per cent of the total annual health budgets of industrialized nations. And cataracts, which are often related to the ageing process, are expensive to correct. In the United States alone, 1.35 million cataract surgeries are performed each year at an annual cost of about $3.4 billion. (World Health Organization, 1998).

Identifying specific diseases and deciding on their respective treatments is one thing but, determining how much it will cost and who should pay for the treatment is quite another matter.

It is not surprising then that those who are young and employed are expected to assume some financial responsibility in this regard. And clearly, as more young people (the employed non-elderly) in developed and developing countries are expected to carry the burden of supporting the old through financial assistance and health care coverage, the seeds for intergenerational conflict are being planted daily.

It remains to be seen if other countries will follow in the footsteps of the United States and engage in open verbal combat over intergenerational accountability, but it does appear that, as the world ages in both the developed and the developing world, new challenges will surface that will require creative solutions. Presented here has been a discussion of one challenge in particular, intergenerational conflict, that has already surfaced in some countries and will most likely emerge in other countries as we pass into a new century. In the end, how countries respond to this issue may be determined by how they pose the question and frame the debate. What follows is a discussion of some guidelines and recommendations that may prove helpful in discussing this problem and in shaping its solution.

PARTICIPATING IN THE DEBATE: GUIDELINES AND RECOMMENDATIONS

The intergenerational equity question is steadily making its way onto political agendas throughout the world. Because of historical, political and cultural differences, and depending where nations may be on the continuum of economic development, the equity issue, if it emerges at all within a given nation, may take on a variety of forms. Therefore, it is difficult to design and apply a set formula to address it. However, in response to generational conflict in the United States, Generations United (1992), an intergenerational organization formed to diffuse the divisiveness of the equity debate, has put forth seven guidelines and recommendations that other nations may find helpful. Each is presented and discussed briefly below.

1. *Avoid misunderstandings about the implications of population ageing.* An ageing society can create much anxiety. This anxiety, sometimes referred to as "apocalyptic demographics", often revolves around the "dependency ratio", the number in the labour force compared to those under age 18 and those over 64. However, two points should be emphasized. One, this ratio is questionable because it fails to take into account the constantly changing labour force participation of women, the potential for the elderly to postpone retirement and work longer and the possibility of economic growth. And two, this ratio also tends to ignore the fact that policy makers can make a difference. Adjustments in monetary and fiscal policies, a shift in education policy that can affect worker productivity and a different focus on research can all help shape a different future than that projected. Demography need not be destiny.

2. *Recognize the diversity of the elderly population.* The elderly population in any nation is heterogeneous. They are rich and poor, strong and week, "young old" and "old old," conservative and liberal, and at times burdens and contributors. Failure to recognize the

heterogeneity among the elderly may lead to how social problems are defined and, therefore, ultimately determine how they are addressed. Stereotyping, particularly that which furthers certain political ends, such as a reduction of social programmes, should be challenged.

3. *Be prepared to correct any misunderstandings about relations between generations*. Although examples of conflict between age groups can be found on occasion, even in the United States, which is in its second decade of debating intergenerational equity, such conflict is more the exception than the rule. In short, while there will always be some tension between various groups in society, the bonds between generations remain strong. For in the end, people understand that successive birth cohorts and generations (particularly within families) are interdependent. If the young generation chooses to dismantle social programmes for the old, it is also dismantling social programmes for itself.

4. *Avoid using narrow and misleading definitions of fairness*. Although it may be desirable to achieve equity between generations, such an outcome would be fairly narrow in that it would not necessarily address other questions of social justice within a given society. For example, the idea that per capita public expenditures on children and the elderly ought to be equal sounds good, but it is probably not realistic. As Norm Daniels (1988) has argued, we all have different needs at different stages of our lives. Thus, to pit one age group against the other is not only unfair but it diverts attention away from other inequities that may exist. In the words of Robert Binstock (1985), the current preoccupation with equity between generations "blinds us to inequities within age groups and throughout our society".

5. *Do not rely on limited measures to draw broad conclusions*. According to Generations United (1992), those who attempt to measure the various flows of resources between generations to determine the fairness to particular cohorts have set an impossible task for themselves. Since each generation receives transfers from those that precede it and also gives transfers to those that follow it, to reach accurate conclusions about equity between generations would require finding answers to some very difficult questions. For example, how should the economic and social investments made by previous generations be valued? Should part of what is spent on the elderly be counted as a return on their investments in younger generations? Should part of what is spent on children be considered an investment in the future productivity of that society? And, even if one forgets about the elderly, how should investments made in research, conservation, environmental protection and defense be allocated across age groups? Unless adequate answers can be provided for these questions, no major conclusions should be drawn about equity between generations.

6. *Avoid any misunderstanding about the common stake in social policies*. In the United States certain policy issues have been framed in terms of competition and conflict between generations. This way of framing the issue implies that public benefits directed toward the elderly represent only a one-way flow from young to old and that reciprocity between generations does not exist. Such an approach only fuels misunderstandings about the costs and benefits of programmes directed towards the older population. Recently, however, more efforts have been made to design and enact intergenerational policies such as the Family and Medical Leave Act of 1993. Under this law, an employee may take time off from work to care for a sick child or a frail parent in need. For a nation to ignore the potential social and political benefits gained from carefully crafted intergenerational public policies is risky to say the least (Wisensale, 1988, 1991, 1993).

7. *Avoid participating in a zero sum game*. If the framework that pits young against old over scarce resources is accepted, it is assumed then that there exists a "fixed pie" from which only one slice can be cut - for either the elderly or the young. Such a zero sum game assumes wrongly that the limited pie cannot be expanded by economic growth or that slices devoted to military spending cannot be reserved for social needs, whether they be for the young or the old. Today, limited resources are a fundamental reality of all societies. However, it is important to remember that both economic growth and various trade-offs are still possible. "An approach to public policy that assumes that whatever resources are directed towards one age group diminishes the quality of life for another just does not square with reality" (Generations United, 1992).

CONCLUSION

The United Nations has a proud history in addressing ageing issues. Since 1982 when it adopted the International Plan of Action on Ageing, which was the world's first international document on ageing, the United Nations has issued numerous proclamations and held various conferences on age-related matters. Each proclamation issued or conference convened was a reflection of the specific ageing concerns that were being raised at a given point in time. Such is the case with the United Nations declaration of the International Year of Older Persons in 1999.

Most appropriately, the theme for the United Nations International Year of Older Persons is "Towards a Society for All Ages". Recognizing that the globe is graying rapidly, that this process is not confined to just the wealthier western industrialized societies and that there is great potential for conflict between generations over limited resources, the United Nations has adopted a plan of action that is designed to initiate and maintain a dialogue on this very important issue.

Meanwhile, the intergenerational equity question is gradually making its way onto the political agendas of nations throughout the world. Whether or not the discussion concerning this issue is always anchored in accurate information is, of course, another question. However, as nations attempt to shape their social welfare policies for the future, there are at least two fundamental questions that should be addressed. First, is intergenerational equity morally justified? And second, is intergenerational equity something towards which any society should strive?

It can certainly be argued that intergenerational equity is always morally justified. The real question, however, is whether or not it can be achieved politically at a reasonable price. Obviously, as has been discussed here in some detail, the fair allocation of resources between and among various birth cohorts and age groups is not an easy task. Nevertheless, theoretical models do exist and should be explored further. For example, Norm Daniels (1983) has developed a framework from the work of philosopher John Rawls (1971) that could, in principle, justify age-based allocation or denial of resources according to an equitable distribution procedure over an entire lifespan.

With respect to the second question, intergenerational equity is definitely a goal towards which any society should strive. But equally important, the goal can also serve as a compass throughout the debate. To paraphrase Harry Moody (1982) in his discourse on ethics and long-term care, intergenerational equity should not be viewed as simply a code word for "smart politics" or "sound public policy" or become the latest buzzword of "politically-correct language." Instead, it should become a means to keep the debate going, to keep the dialogue responsible and, whenever possible, to guide us towards a better understanding of our societal principles and toward wiser decisions in our personal lives.

REFERENCES

Bass, S, Morris, R., and Oka, M., *Public Policy and the Old Age Revolution in Japan*, New York, Haworth Press,1996.

Binney, E. and Estes, C., " The retreat of the state and its transfer of responsibility: the intergenerational war", *International Journal of Health Services*, vol.18,1988.

Binstock, R., " The aged as scapegoat", *The Gerontologist*, vol. 23, 1983.

Binstock, R., "The oldest old: a fresh perspective on compassionate ageing revisited", *Millbank Memorial Fund Quarterly/Health and Society*, vol. 63, 1986.

Binstock, R., " Policies on ageing in the post-cold war era", in W. Crotty (Ed .), *Post-Cold War Policy, Volume I: Domestic and Social*, Chicago, Nelson-Hall, 1992.

Callahan, D. , *Setting Limits: Medical Goals in an Aging Society*, New York, Simon and Schuster, 1987.

Callahan, D., *What Kind of Life: The Limits of Medical Progress*, New York, Simon and Schuster, 1990.

Chawla, S., Demographic ageing and development, *Generations*, Vol.17, No. 4, 1993.

Cohen, L., *Justice Across Generations: What Does it Mean?* Washington, D. C., Public Policy Institute, American Association of Retired Persons, 1993.

Coleman, J., "Ageing of Japan seen as bringing opportunities and problems", *The Seattle Times*, December 11, 1997.

Daniels, N. , "Justice between age groups: Am I my parents keeper?", *Millbank Memorial Fund Quarterly*, Summer, 1983.

Daniels, N., *Am I My Parents' Keeper? An Essay on Justice Between the Young and Old*, New York, Oxford University Press, 1988.

Daniels, N., " The prudential lifespan account of justice across generations", L. Cohen (ed.) *Justice Across generations: What Does it Mean?*, Washington, D.C., Public Policy Institute, American Association of Retired Persons, 1993.

De Beauvoir, S., *The Coming of Age*, New York, Putnam, 1972.

Ehrbar, A., "The wrong solution", *Fortune*, 17 August, 1980.

Flint, J., " The old folks", *Forbes*, 18 February, 1980.

Forbes, "The truth about Social Security", *Forbes*, 6 December, 1982.

Fortune, "Social Security, the real costs of those rising benefits", *Fortune*, 20 December 1973.

Fritsch, P., "Brazil's pension system is a potential time bomb", *Wall Street Journal*, 9 July, 1998.

Generations United, *The Common Stake: the Interdependence of Generations: a Policy Framework for an Ageing Society,* Washington, D.C., Generations United, 1992.

Hashimoto, A., *The Gift of Generations: Japanese and American Perspectives on Ageing and the Social Contract*, New York, Cambridge University Press, 1996.

Hudson, R., "The graying of the federal budget and the consequences for old age-policy", *The Gerontologist*, vol. 18, 1978.

Kingson, E., "Understanding and learning from the generational equity debate", *The Aging Connection*,vol. 9, October/November, 1989.

Kingson, E. and Williamson, J., " The generational equity debate: A progressive framing of a conservative issue", *Journal of Aging and Social Policy*, vol. 5, No. 3, 1993.

Kotlikoff, L., *Generational Accounting: Knowing Who Pays, and When, and for What We Spend*, New York, The Free Press, 1992.

Krauss, C., " Social security, Chilean style: Pensioners quiver as markets fall", *The New York Times*, 16 August, 1998.

Kristof, N., "Baby makes three, but in Japan that's not enough", *New York Times International*, 6 October, 1996.

Kumagai, F., *Unmasking Japan Today: the Impact of Traditional Values on Modern Japanese Society*, Westport, Connecticut, Greenwood Press, 1996.

Lane, C. , " Is Europe's social welfare state headed for the deathbed?", *Newsweek*, 23 August, 1993.

Link Age 2000, Policy implications of global ageing, 1998: http://library.advanced.org/10120/cyber/extended/polity.html.

Longman, P., *Born to Pay: the New Politics of Aging in America*, Boston, Houghton-Mifflin, 1987.

Minkler, M. and Robertson, A.., *Ageing and Society*, 11, 1-22, 1991.

Moody, H., Ethical dilemmas in long-term care. *Journal of gerontological Social Work,vol. 5, 1982.*

Moody, H., *Ethics in an Aging Society*, Baltimore, Johns Hopkins University Press, 1992.

Moon, M., "Measuring intergenerational equity" in L. Cohen (ed.), *Justice Across Nations: What Does it Mean?* Washington, D.C. Public Policy Institute, American Association of Retired Persons, 1998.

Meyer, M., "Be kinder to your kinder: Trying to change the child unfriendly Germans", *Newsweek*, 16 December, 1991.

Myles, J. and Quadagno, J. (Eds.), *States Labour Markets, and the Future of Old Age Policy*, Philadelphia, Temple University Press, 1993.

Neugarten, B., *Age or need: Public policies for older people*, Thousand Oaks, California, Sage, 1982.

Palmer, J., Smeeding, T., and Torrey, B., *The Vulnerable*. Washington, D.C., The Urban Institute Press, 1988.

Peterson, P., *Facing Up: How to Rescue the Economy from Crushing Debt and Restore the American Dream*, New York, Simon and Schuster, 1993.

Preston, S., "Children and the elderly in the United States", *Scientific American*,1984.

Quadagno, J., " Generational equity and the politics of the welfare state", *International Journal of Health Services*, Vol. 20, 4, 1990.

Rawls, J., *A Theory of Justice*, Cambridge, Massachusetts, Harvard University Press, 1971.

Richman H. and Stagner, M., "Children in an ageing society: Treasured resource or forgotten minority?", *Daedalus*, vol. 115, 1985.

Rodgers, H., *Poor Women, Poor Families: The Economic Plight of America's Female Headed Households*, Armonk, New York, M.E. Sharpe, Inc, 1986.

Schemo, D., "Brazilians scale back pledges to cut budget", *The New York Times*, 12 November, 1998.

Schulz, J., " And then chicken little cried, 'the sky is falling' ", *Generations,* vol. 17, 1993.

Sonnefeld, S., Waldo, R.; Lemieux, J.; and McKusick, D., "Projections of national health expenditures through the year 2000", in *Health Care Financing Review*, Vol. 13, 1991.

The American Institute for Contemporary German Studies. " Germany's social insecurity: The twin challenges of unemployment and the future of the German public pension system", Baltimore, Maryland, Johns Hopkins University, 1997: http://jhuniverse.hcf.edu/-aicgsdoc/aicgs/events/pass.htm

The New Republic , "An exchange on Social Security" *The New Republic*, 18 May 1987.

Trollope, A. (1882), *The Fixed Period,* reprinted in N.J. Hall (Ed.), *Selected Works by Anthony Trollope*, 2 vols. Salem, New Hampshire: Ayer, 1981.

United Nations, *International Plan of Action on Ageing*, Vienna and New York, United Nations, 1982.

United Nations, *The World Ageing Situation: strategies and Policies*, New York, United Nations, 1985.

United Nations,. *First Review and Appraisal of the Implementation of the International Plan of Action on Ageing,* Report of the Secretary-General, New York, United Nations, 1985.

United Nations, *Second Review and Appraisal of the Implementation of the International Plan of Action on Ageing,* Report of the Secretary-General, New York, United Nations, 1989.

United Nations, *World Population Prospects, 1990,* New York, United Nations.

United Nations, *The Sex and Age Distribution of Population, 1990 Revision*, New York, United Nations, 1990.

United Nations, *The World Ageing Situation*, New York, United Nations, 1991.

United Nations, *Third Review and Appraisal of the Implementation of the International Plan of Action on Ageing*, New York, United Nations, 1993.

United Nations, The ageing of the world's population. The United Nations Population Division, New York, United Nations, 1994: www.un.org/esa/socdev/agewpop.html.

United Nations, Multi-generational relationships. Division for Social Policy and Development. New York: 1990: www.un.org/esa/socdev/iyop/iyopcf3.html.

Wisensale, S., "Generational equity and intergenerational policies", *The Gerontologist*, vol. 28, No. 6, 1988.

Wisensale, S., "An intergenerational policy proposal for the 1990s: applying the Temporary Disability Insurance model to family caregiving", *Journal of Aging and Social Policy,* vol. 3, 1991.

Wisensale, S., Generational equity, in R. Kastenbaum (Ed.), *Encyclopedia of Adult Development*, Phoenix, Oryx Press, 1998.

Wolfe, B., Treating children fairly, *Society*, September/October, 1991.

World Bank Policy Research Report, Averting the old age crisis: policies to protect the old and promote growth, World Bank, 1997: http://library.advanced.org/10120/cyber/extended/alt_Financing.html.

World Health Organization, "Population ageing - a public health challenge", Fact Sheet No. 135, World Health Organization, Geneva, 1998: www.who.int/inf-fs/en/fact135.html.

VII. REWRITING LIFEMAPS: TOWARDS FLOURISHING LIVES

*Brigid Donelan**

INTRODUCTION

Two themes have dominated the public discourse on ageing in recent decades: the immediate *cost* of old age dependency in terms of health care and income security and future-oriented dramatic demographic projections couched in such terms as "apocalyptic demographics" and the hidden "age bomb".

Immediate needs and future forecasts must be examined, but will not be dealt with here. Instead, this paper explores the meaning of late-life in our times. And it takes the view that we would not live to be 80 or so if it didn't have a "meaning for the species".

Section I, *Towards a high age*, examines approaches to late-life down through the years, showing varied and contradictory constructions. It considers how today's age-advanced societies have tended to perceive late-life narrowly in terms of "patients and pensioners". This perception is derived from a preoccupation with props or supports in late life rather than with investing in its potential. If we rewrite the scripts for living in late life in more expansive terms, encompassing "doing, becoming and being", we will expand elder's choices and redefine the meaning of life's end-stage for humanity. For, as Gilligan (1982) remarked: "a change in the definition of maturity does not simply alter the description of the highest stage, but recasts the understanding of development, changing the entire account".

Section II, *Middlescence*, underscores the transitional nature of mid-life and makes the point that for latelife potential to flourish, investments must be made in mid-life, as investments are now made in youth for adulthood. Mid-life education could encompass the four areas advocated for lifelong learning by a Commission of the Untied Nations Educational, Scientific and Cultural Organization (UNESCO), learning "to know, to do, to be and to live together".

Section III, *Adult years*, argues for a better distribution of time between work, home, education and "leisure", so as to enable individuals accumulate stores of

economic, social and human capital which enriches adult years and provides the necessary securities for well being in later years. The current concentration of adult years on work is a legacy of industrialization which segregated education, work and leisure horizontally by age-set: education in youth, work in adult years, leisure in late life. A vertical distribution of these opportunities over the entire lifecourse, as is more common in pre-industrial societies, would give workers more time for continuing education (necessary to avoid social and skills obsolescence in a fast changing world); more time for family and community life (necessary as women worldwide join men in the paid workforce), and gradual and phased retirement (necessary as longevity extends this phase of life from a few years, when retirement was first introduced, to a few decades as is more often the case now).

A graphic portrayal of the horizontal industrial distribution of opportunities and the emerging vertical distribution could be shown as follows:

	Industrial pattern	Pre- and post-industrial patterns		
Old age	leisure	e d u c a t i o n	w o r k	l e i s u r e
Adult years	work			
Youth	education			

Section IV, *Youth and childhood*, notes some implications of longevity for the early phases of life. Young people inherit a world in transition and except for a few things, cannot know what their end-stage will be. Abused or lost opportunities for education, work and health are likely to be paid for in later years in unemployment, poverty and poor health. And age prejudice or "ageism" on their part creates a mental ghetto they themselves are likely to live long enough to enter. Youth should be encouraged to greater self-reliance and forethought, and to think of life as a marathon which requires a special kind of preparation and pacing.

Childhood has been termed the "cradle of longevity". The wide implications are not explored here except to note the importance of the emotional imprints acquired

---

*Brigid Donelan is Social Affairs Officer in the Division for Social Policy and Development, Department of Economic and Social Affairs

112

for dependence, counter-dependence, independence and interdependence. Each imprint can infuse the lifepath with capabilities for trusting, seeking innovation, taking initiatives and collaborating.

The paper quotes from many fields: anthropology, psychology, sociology, economics, development studies, fine literature and the popular press. It explores concepts in the belief that these shape perceptions and attitudes which, in turn, fuel actions and policies. As noted by the Secretary-General of the United Nations, when addressing the media (1996):

> "Ideas can often be more important than actions. Events dominate our lives, but trends of thought may be far more significant in shaping the future".

I. OLD AGE OR HIGH AGE?

Old age today is a new frontier. Longevity and cultural change are expanding its duration and redefining its scope. Our maps for it are out-of-date, often saying more about its limitations than its possibilities, notably in age-advanced industrialized countries.

In something of a linguistic somersault, industrialization created an age ghetto at the high end of life:

> "The word 'old' was, until very recently, associated with the impairment of certain physical capacities such as eyesight, teeth and so on. (Despite this), manifestly relative terms like the 'ageing' or the 'elderly' have now come to denote a precise chronological category: the 60 or 65 plus age group. It is something of a linguistic somersault.
> (Chawla, 1988)

As years were being added to life, they were, ironically, being stripped of meaning. By the mid-twentieth century, older people in industrialized countries were being moved to society's margins and defined primarily as "patients or pensioners" (Cole and Winkler, 1994). Furthermore:

> "Old age was removed from its place as a way station along life's spiritual journey and redefined as a problem to be solved by science and medicine" and

> "ageing as a mysterious part of the eternal order of things gradually gave way to the secular, scientific, and individualistic tendencies of modernity" (ibid).

Compassion as much as chauvinism came to belittle older persons, prompting Binstock (1983) to coin the term "compassionate ageism". Compassionate ageism is the tendency to focus excessively on support to the neglect of innate potential and meaning. To use a metaphor from the theather: it accords priority to the stage props rather than to the actors scripts.

Ageism, like sexism and racism, discounts people's own worlds, their subjective experiences, their inner landscapes. This makes it easy to set people apart, turning them into "other".

Older persons are becoming "other" at a time, ironically, when their numbers and proportions are increasing. As developing countries age in the coming decades, at rates considerably faster than those of developed countries, their traditional respect for elders may be shaken. "It is the scarce resource which achieves the status of the sacred or valued" and in as far as ageing is associated with diminished economic and social functions, it is increasingly likely "to be viewed as both a societal and familial burden" (Grieko and Apt, 1996).

A. *The many faces of late life*

There is a rich and contradictory legacy of material on which to rewrite late-life scripts encompassing paradox, dichotomies, honours and exclusions. Its essential paradox has been captured by artists—by Picasso, when he remarked that "It takes a long time to grow young" or Oscar Wilde who, in *The Picture of Dorian Grey*, remarked that:

> "The tragedy of ageing is not based on the fact that one is old but rather that one is young."

Dichotomies abound. Late life is seen as a time of forgetfulness, but also wisdom, of exclusion, yet of status, of decline, yet continuing development. It can be termed old age, but also high age.

Societies have expected older persons to be engaged, disengaged or to follow an age-specific script, as in ancient India. During the Vedic period three and a half thousand years ago (1500 BC) active old age was encouraged, including sexual activity. A thousand years later, disengagement from society was fostered in the Buddhist canonical writings (500-200 BC). Later, Brahmanic writings (200-100 BC) set forth age-appropriate behaviour for the different stages of life (Tilak, 1989).

Older persons have been honoured, often inspired by religious or cultural values. For example, writing many centuries ago, Confucius remarked:

> "Nowadays filial piety seems to mean that a man just supports his parents, he does the same for his horses and dogs. Reverence of a parent is what distinguishes filial piety."

Elders have also been abandoned, killed or sacrificed, particularly in times of scarcity or in harsh environments. Herodotus, reported that, among the fifth century *Massagetae* of the northern Caucasus, elder sacrifice was an envied experience:

> "when a man is very old, all his relatives give a party and include him in a general sacrifice of cattle: then they boil the flesh and eat it. This they consider to be the best sort of death. Those who die of disease are

not eaten, but buried, and it is held a misfortune not to have lived long enough to be sacrificed".
Philibert (1984)

In more recent times, ageing in stages is a part of the Kenyan Samburu man's life script. Having spent his youth as warrior, more associated with bush and cattle than with camps and kin, the Samburu man then returns to the community where he may progress through four stages of elder-status: probationary, patron, judicial-ritual, and retired or declining elder. Among the Samburu:

"elders are associated with settlements and social order. They are expected to instruct their juniors in proper behaviour and to resolve conflicts and disputes through discussion and the moral power of blessing and curse. Thus, the Samburu age-set system establishes an opposition between *moran* (warrior) and elders. *Moran* have physical ascendancy, elders moral ascendancy. However, elders also have economic power through their control of most livestock and the labour of their wives and children. The Samburu age-set system thus creates a form of gerontocracy that enhances (but does not guarantee) the chances for a successful old age.
(Albert and Cattell, 1994).

Older women's scripts seem to have been *less* expansive than older men's but, in many places, have been *more* expansive than the cultural scripts written for younger women of reproductive years. Late life has often been a time when women are:

"much less subject to male authority and may engage in a variety of activities not permitted to younger women. Nor do they need to exhibit the same degree of deference to males or hold to the same rules of modesty in dress and action. They may ignore some language taboos and begin to speak freely and with authority. ... They may also travel from home much more freely than younger women. All this means that older women potentially have more possibility to challenge men in the councils, engage in commerce and trade beyond the boundaries of their villages and collaborate in organizational activities" (as quoted by Chaney, 1990)

A less happy picture has been painted by another author, when referring to widowhood:

"In Bengal, where I come from, many believe ... that there are four kinds of dead: the dead, the widowed, the childless and the leper. ...Widowed women are one kind of the dead. They are not allowed to eat meat or fish or eggs or onion or garlic. They may only eat once a day. They may not eat after the sun goes down, and they may not drink anything... In some societies, even the number of mouthfuls that may be eaten are circumscribed." (Mukerji, 1997)

The author goes on to note the similarity between symptoms of depression and prescribed female (and sometimes elder) behaviour that is, inactivity, lack of initiative and lethargy. A study has shown that getting patients "to act as if they were depressed or manic led to the biochemical changes associated with depression or mania" (Post and Goodwin, 1973).

The current status of older women bears special mention, as noted by the Secretary-General (on the occasion of the International Day of Older Persons on 1 October 1997):

"Women are also more likely than men to be poorer in old age, for various reasons: their involvement in home-making and child-bearing; the interruption of their careers because of family responsibilities; lower investments in women's training and education; labour-force discrimination and lower-paying jobs."

Material poverty limits choices for women and men, affecting an estimated fifth of the world's population. A cultural poverty can also limit choices, clouding vision and aspirations. Poor or negative cultural perceptions of late-life can inhibit older persons actions and dampen younger persons aspirations for their later years. According to anthropological, cross-cultural studies, old age is the least desired stage of life in all societies, yet:

"the proportion of people holding strongly negative views of old age drops with increasing age, a finding suggesting that upon reaching old age one discovers that it is not so bad as expected. (Swane, 1996, lecture abstract)

As often remarked: "Old age is always about 15 years older than I am".

Diversity increases with the years. The longer people live, the more different they become:

"Eight year olds are more alike than eighty-year olds" (Hagestad, 1996).

"Lives fan out with time as people develop their own patterns of interests and commitments, their own sequences of life choices, their own psychological turning points, and their own patterns of relations." (Neugarten, 1979)

Explorations and expressions of late-life diversity can help to put health care needs in perspective. While some elders require assistance in daily living, many do not, including a remarkable cadre of the "oldest old". There appears to be an age bump on life's road "after which, having passed through the perilous years when the age-related diseases weed out the majority, one can expect a relatively smooth ride for a decade or more. The longer people live, the longer they live. For men, the bump seems to come in the late 80's; for women, in the early or mid-90s" (*The New York Times*, 20 June 1996).

Upon becoming a fellow in geriatrics, Perls (1995) remarked that he was "surprised to find that the oldest old were often the most healthy and agile of the senior people" and, with few exceptions, the centenarians he met "reported that their 90s were essentially problem free. As nonagenarians, many were employed, sexually active and enjoyed the outdoors and the arts. They basically carried on as if age were not an issue."

It is estimated that about 95 per cent of those over age 60, and 75 per cent over age 80 are active and self-reliant, some assisted by technical aids or care personnel for a variety of minor needs. The remaining 5 per cent over age 60 and 25 per cent over age 80 are in need of full-time and/or longterm-care.

The needs of this minority of older persons for full-time care can be intense, stretching over 24-hours-a-day, 7-days a week and 365-days a year. It can make great demands on families and be particularly hard on primary cares (women but increasingly also men) who may simultaneously be caring for children and whose caring role precludes the possibility of paid work and pensions options.

Elder care is most frequently needed in the last few years of life, whenever these fall.

"Old age, the period of sharp decline followed by death, remains what it always was, a relatively short time in the life course of the individual. This is underscored by American Medicare statistics, which indicate that the last two years of life, whenever they fall, are the ones that contain the major use of this social insurance. Old age, the period of increasing frailty that ends in death, is still what it was in the past, a relatively short and catastrophic time for most".
Greenberg (1990)

A recognition and celebration of late-life diversity would encompass, as one of its many elements, the "patient" category. Similarly, the "pensioner" category could be embraced without it having to dominate the definition of late-life, particularly in view of the fact that the majority of the world's elders living in developing countries do not have pensions nor can the younger cohorts following them hope to have universal pensions and income security in their later years.

Affordable and sustainable pensions and health-care systems are needed, but so too is a sense of the essential meaning of late life together with socio-economic structures that foster the release of its varied potentials. Later life still, however, "remains a season in search of its purpose" (Cole, 1995).

B. *Re-writing latelife scripts*

From the above short exploration of the rich and sometimes contradictory faces of old age we can find many elements and inspirations for rewriting the scripts. Three essential ingredients of such scripts are: active ageing, self-actualization and transcendence. Or put more simply: doing, becoming and being.

An exploration of doing, becoming and being in latelife could help trigger a *conceptual* somersault in places where old age has been equated with dependency and decline. It could trigger a *linguistic* somersault also, as new terms emerge to fit new roles and relationships in late life including, for example, the use of the term high age, with its implication of continuing psycho-social development, in tandem with the term old age, implying physical decline.

Doing

The term "active ageing" has gained currency in industrialized countries in recent years but has been, and continues to be, a natural and customary characteristic of life in the pre-industrial world. It secured its place in industrialized countries when, at the Denver Summit in 1997, the leaders of the Group of Eight industrial countries indicated in their communiqué that they had discussed the idea of active ageing, which they described as the desire and ability of many older people to continue work or other socially productive activities well into their later years. They stressed that old stereotypes of seniors as dependent would be abandoned and, with due regard to individual choices and circumstances, they said they would promote active ageing, including by removing disincentives to labor force participation and lowering barriers to flexible and part-time employment.

While moving towards greater scope and flexibility for older persons to continue working, opportunities for retirement should not be abandoned. As one scholar noted:

"When people work(ed) 70 hours a week, in mines, factories or on the land, for slave wages, expecting an early death, and in execrable environmental conditions, it made (makes) sense to offer respite by pensioning at 60 or 65 years of age. Now with the growth of service, leisure and light industrial work opportunities, career changes, part-time or shared posts, and computer links into the home, retirement as we have known it may itself become redundant (Tout, 1997).

Active ageing could, if promoted indiscriminately, result in exaggerated demands on older persons to be in perpetual activity just as earlier definitions of passivity tended to brand all older persons as non-contributing.

One example of an active ageing initiative is Japan's "Silver" human resource centres. The centres, located in municipalities and supported by the national Government, employ persons over age 64 in community service. Public and private parties, including families, can request the services of older persons for temporary but not permanent or regular work. Services vary and typically include office, craft, guard, delivery and light manual work (Schulz, 1991). Both older persons and communities' benefit.

The resource centres operate according to the twin principles of independence and interdependence, according to Prime Minister Hashimoto. These principles are expressions of a sense of mutual concern and respect among self-reliant people. They form the twin pillars of society with self-reliance and self-help efforts of an individual as a vertical pillar and the spirit of social solidarity as a horizontal beam. (Speaking at the East Asian Ministerial Meeting on Caring Societies, 5 December 1996).

Society benefits from active ageing. Through paid and unpaid work, older persons are "generative". Generativity, the driving force and central purpose of mature adulthood, according to Erik Erikson (1968), is the desire to nurture the next generation and to create and leave a heritage or legacy. Stagnation occurs, Erikson surmised, when an older adult fails to be generative. Four kinds of generativity have been identified:

- Biological (begetting, bearing and nursing offspring);
- Nurturing (cultivating and supporting);
- Technical (passing on knowledge and know-how);
- Cultural (the site of most generative ingenuity) (Kotre, 1984)

Older persons, freed from biological generativity, can turn their attention to nurturing. In Uruguay, for example, a programme entitled "Grandparents by choice" trains older volunteers to nurture self-esteem as well as social and technical skills among distressed children from unstable families, preempting thereby behavioural patterns that frequently lead to crime and conflict (Pelaez, 1997). With the projected rise of orphans as a result of the AIDs epidemic, five million as of 2000, new demands are being made on grandparent nurturing.

As well, elders have much to contribute to cultural life, blending tradition and innovation, particularly if we accept the definition of culture forwarded by the United Nations Educational, Scientific and Cultural Organization (UNESCO):

"the whole complex of distinctive, spiritual, material, intellectual and emotional features that charac-terize a society or social group. It includes not only arts and letters, but also modes of life, the fundamental rights of the human being, value systems, traditions and beliefs"
(UNESCO, 1994).

A generative impulse may be innate but it also needs to be fostered by society. It requires, inter alia:

- A cultural demand that adults take responsibility,
- An inner desire for symbolic immortality,
- A conscious concern for the next generation (McAdams and de St.Aubin, 1992)

The generative mind-set was cultivated by certain Native American nations through the maxim that decisions be made with seven future generations in mind. Conversely, it was a sense of continuity with earlier generations that preserved forests intact in areas of Africa which would otherwise have been deforested, the locations in question being revered as a living continuity with ancestors (Lash, 1997).

Becoming

"Becoming" in the sense of continuing self-actualization is only possible when life's basic needs have been met, including security and physiological needs (the focus of national and international measures and strategies). Basic needs are not so much ends in themselves as prerequisites (and catalysts) of self-actualization, which, in the view of Carl Gustav Jung, was a defining purpose of the second half of life. Maslow (1970) placed self-actualization at the apex of his ladder of needs, following loosely on having secured, in turn (though not necessarily age-graded) measures of esteem, belonging, security and physiological needs.

Manheimer (1989) discussed ageing in terms of adaptation and transformation. The former implying adjustment to age-appropriate behaviour and expectations. The latter, transformation, implying continuing development in an age-irrelevant society.

Jung's self-actualization or Manheimer's transformation can be of two kinds: monotypic, meaning continuing development of the same sort or heterotypic, being something different as in the case of the butterfly emerging from the caterpillar (i.e. transformations).

Literature can foster and express awareness of continuing development. A "narrative quest" allows an individual to achieve a "secular redemption" or triumph over adversity and past events (religious redemption, in contrast, generally seeks triumph over sin) (Manheimer, 1989). An increasing number of "winding-up" stories are being written, complementing the "growing-up" stories that have dominated literature and legends worldwide: *Vollendungsroman* for late life; *Bildungsroman* for early life (Rooke, 1992) .

One author believes that if we accept "wholeness" as a potential of the later years, we will need to depart from "accustomed behaviours", accepting a "multiplicity of selves" and recognizing that the "ego may be an impediment to growth" (ibid). In short, achieving wholeness can require some deconstruction of our earlier selves, a process often made easier by a measure of disengagement.

While scholars have wide-ranging hypotheses about cognitive and other changes in later years, they commonly agree that:

"... with maturity comes increasing ability to live with lack of clarity and closure, an increasing readiness to think in relative terms, a readiness to live without clear answers, and an ability to see the search for understanding as a never-ending, reflexive process"
(Hagestad, 1996).

Hagestad goes on to note that a group of researchers (Featherman, Smith and Peterson, 1990) argue that in modern society, developmental tasks in the first part of life often take the form of puzzles, clearly defined tasks with identifiable solutions. In the second half of life, which is less structured, tasks more often take the form of open-ended dilemmas. Rational problem-solving is suitable for puzzles (predictable with clearly specified conditions), reflective thinking is required for dilemmas, which generally have fuzzy boundaries and unspecified conditions.

Reflective thinking is central to theories of modernity and to living with constant change, which:

"requires us to treat all knowledge as hypotheses, constantly open to revision (Hagestad, 1996).

The ubiquitousness of change also calls for reskilling, of both technical skills and life skills.

Reskilled and reflective ageing cohorts would be a powerful force, capable of fulfilling the promise inherent in the United Nations Proclamation on Ageing of 1992, which, when declaring 1999 as the International Year of Older Persons, did so in:

"recognition of humanity's demographic coming of age and the promise it holds for maturing attitudes and capabilities in social, economic, cultural and spiritual undertakings, not least for global peace and development in the next century" (General Assembly resolution 47/5)

Reflective thinking, or "reflexivity" as it is sometimes called, is a mind-set suitable for negotiating the rapid changes of post-industrialization. It is also a quality akin to wisdom that has guided human affairs in the pre-industrial world up to the present. We may think of reflexivity as a modern manifestation of wisdom, and a counterweight to the relentless drive of the contemporary world towards:

"higher and higher, faster and faster, further and further, more and more complex, more and more perfect, more intense, more and more excessive, louder and louder, more and more informed, (while remaining) ethically, existentially, and meaningfully, nothing more than a system designed to quantify" (Rentsch, 1997).

Being

The experience of being, which has been cultivated by ancient civilizations, is generally informed by an awareness of life's fragility and insubstantiality. With advancing age, encounters with fragility and finitude increase. Loss is a frequent feature of late life.

Individual reactions to loss vary and, in the view of some researchers (Neugarten et al. 1961 and 1968), fall into four categories:

- Integrative (adjusting to change);
- Armoured-defensive (in denial of change);
- Passive-dependent (in "collapse");
- Disorganized (could be early stage of dementia);

The "integrative" response reorganizes to accommodate loss, sometimes limiting activities to a small set of feasible and highly rewarding ones. The so-called "armoured-defensive" response denies decline by intensifying activities or by dwelling excessively on what has been lost because of age. The "passive-dependent" response to decline and loss is one that relies excessively on others for help or withdraws excessively from human intercourse becoming apathetic. The fourth and final kind of response identified by the researchers has been termed "disorganized" as, for example, in the early stages of dementia.

Viewed from another perspective, however, loss can lead to gain. Initially, the experience of transience and "the ease with which some forms of happiness slip away" can lead to disillusionment, but may ultimately bring about "a calm view, without deception", which is not "a pitiful renunciation, but is rather the highest form of existential sovereignty and human self-assertion" (Rentsch).

Even for those living with severe frailty or disability or in adverse circumstances "the personal management of meaning" may compensate for some of the inevitable losses of old age (Ruth, 1996). A dissociation between the ageing body and the inner 'ageless self' can add to feelings of vitality.

This vitality derives from within. As we progress from the world of simple external facts into the more "intimate functioning of the unconscious psyche, we find ourselves reaching domains in which our logical understanding no longer suffices; it can help us no further" (Whitmont 1991). The realization of the existence of one's inner world as an entity of its own "comes to consciousness relatively late" (Ibid).

For William James (1961) rational consciousness is "but one special type of consciousness, whilst all about it, parted from it by the flimsiest of screens, there lie potential forms of consciousness entirely different. No account of the universe in its totality can be final which leaves these other forms of consciousness quite disregarded".

Varied forms of consciousness are being validated by the emergent field of "noetic science" (from the Greek world *nous* meaning all-encompassing ways of knowing), encompassing scientific study of the mind and human potential as well as knowledge that is received intuitively, instinctively and spiritually.

For some, death serves as a doorway into other forms of consciousness. Ancient cultures had a "remarkably sharp awareness of the spiritual and philosophical importance of death", which they expressed in their 'books of the dead', including: the Egyptian Book of the Dead (the oldest); the Tibetan Book of the Dead (the most renowned), the Mayan Book of the Dead in Mesoamerica; and the *Ars moriendi* (Art of Dying) of Europe (Grof, 1994).

First viewed by scholars as fictitious accounts of the posthumous journey of the soul and, as such, wishful fabrications of people unable to accept the grim reality of death, the ancient books of the dead are now seen by scholars as "maps of the inner territories of the psyche encountered in profound non-ordinary states of consciousness...." (ibid).

The experience of the non-ordinary state of consciousness is something akin to 'dying before dying', Grof says, and it has two important consequences. It liberates the individual from the fear of death and changes his or her attitude towards dying. By eliminating the fear of death, it transforms the individual's way of being in the world.

Among the Marshall Islanders, to cite one contemporary example, it is customary for the living to believe that the deceased continue to interact with them. Death is not an end. Among them, when the body is dead, the "spirit continues to exist, to communicate with the living through dreams, apparitions or other means. Some living people seek advice from spirits and spirits continue to play a part in the lives of their families." (Albert and Cattell, 1994).

As we move into the twenty-first century, "it is the work of all human beings to attend to the health of both our 'inner' and 'outer' houses: the inner house of ourselves, the limitless world within, and the outer house of the world in which we live our daily lives" (Arrien, 1993). Many people in contemporary society feel little or no connection between these two worlds, "a state that the indigenous, land-based peoples of the earth, whose cultures reach back thousands of years, would find not only sad but incomprehensible".

An exploration of the world of being can be enriched through a dialogue of pre and post industrial cultures, and through channels of communication between old and young.

Doing, becoming and being, are overlapping conditions, but each has a distinctive character and a multiplicity of expressions according to age, temperament and culture. "Doing" in late life can create a unique legacy for the next generations. "Becoming" through self-actualization may open up to us the true potential of late life and "being", as experienced in the later years, may give access to a transcendent reality beyond ego consciousness.

Doing may decline in late life, but becoming and being should, as a result of inner growth, tend to expand and become enriched. All three processes lend themselves to rich explorations in the growing body of *Vollendungsroman* or winding-up stories now being written by an increasing number of individuals of the high age.

The gift of longevity challenges individuals and societies to conceptualize anew the construction of late life scripts, using, in the process, both science and belief, fact and imagination. And elaborating along the way a new vocabulary and a pantheon of new images.

II. "MIDDLESCENCE"

Falling roughly between ages 40 and 60 years, mid-life is a time of transition in family life, work and personal identity. The nature and extent of the transition is shaped by innate individual potential interacting with external conditions. Where poverty, violence and sickness dominate an individual's life, there will not be much time for considering internal or external transitions.

In the normal course of events, mid-life is a pivotal time for life-review and preview. It is more "developmentally flexible than childhood or old age", according to Orville Gilbert Brim (1996) of the MacArthur Foundation's Research Network on Successful Midlife Development:

"The early and late stages of life are ruled in part by a biological clock, success in middle age is more shaped by personal and social factors."

Mid-life is a potential rebirth that offers exhilarating new possibilities, but only for those who are aware and who prepare. It is the pivotal point between a 'first adulthood', which just happens to you and a 'second adulthood', which can be custom designed according to Gael Sheehy, who has explored this newest of life transitions in a series of books: *Passages* (1976); *The Silent Passsage* (1993); *New Passages* (1995) and, most recently, *Understanding Men's Passages* (1998). Men, Sheehy notes, can succeed in second adulthood only if they move from competing to connecting and aim for redirection rather than retirement.

Mid-life's pivotal nature has been captured by the term "middlescence" (coined by Dychtwald), reminding us of adolescence, that period of transformation between childhood and adulthood.

Looking ahead is important in mid-life, but also looking back. A mid-life review is a:

"naturally occurring, universal mental process characterized by the progressive return to consciousness of past experiences, and, in particular, the resurgence of unresolved conflicts; simultaneously, and normally, these revived experiences and conflicts can be surveyed and reintegrated" (Butler, 1963).

Mid-life traits have been identified by Neugarten (1968), as summarized below:

- A change in time perspective, from counting up to counting down;
- Body-monitoring, as physical changes affect self-concept;
- Parenting-sponsoring trait, or the "creation of social heirs";
- Heightened self-understanding, from knowing those ahead/behind;
- "Self-utilization", replacing youthful "self-consciousness";
- A heightened sense of expertise.

Sheehy sees two predominant traits:

- Executive processes of the personality, including self awareness, selectivity, manipulation and control of environment, mastery, competence, and a wide array of cognitive strategies;
- Reflection, encompassing stocktaking, heightened introspection, integration of experiences that is, turning them towards achievement. Midlife reflection is different from the "reminiscence" of later years, but may be its precursor.

The maturation of the mind is not a preordained, genetically driven process, but one that requires inputs of knowledge, experience and the passage of time. It requires a learning environment, as set out in the UNESCO medium-term strategy, 1996-2001:

"Advancing towards lifelong education for all implies moving towards a 'learning society', in which each person is a 'learner' and at the same time a 'source of learning', and in which each individual will have the opportunity to learn what he or she wants when he or she wants."

The International Commission on Education for the Twenty-first Century of UNESCO saw the need for lifelong education in four dimensions:

Learning to know - combining broad general knowledge with in depth attention to a few subjects. Also, learning to learn, so as to benefit from the opportunities education provides throughout life;

Learning to do - developing occupational skills, team-skills and the ability to adjust to new work ;

Learning to live together - developing an understanding of other peoples and cultures, an appreciation of the dynamics of interdependence, and the skills to live peacefully in a pluralist society;

Learning to be - developing one's own personality for ever greater autonomy, judgement and personal responsibility, employing potentialities, including memory, reasoning, aesthetic sense and communication skills.

This broad kind of education would go beyond improving work skills and maintaining "employability" to encompass life skills, such as maintaining relationships in ever more complex environments and formulating individual aspirations, which may then become self-fulfilling prophecies—elements of internalized lifescripts that enable individuals to see and create opportunities in their environment.

The structures for lifelong education, and education in mid-life, are underdeveloped today, as were those for primary education a hundred years ago. At that time, universal primary education would have seemed an impossible dream. Today, primary school enrolment is well over 80 per cent worldwide, and secondary enrolment is at about 40 per cent (United Nations Development Programme 1993).

III. ADULT YEARS RESTRUCTURED

The industrial lifemap that ascribed education to youth, work to adults and retirement to elders, upon reaching age 60 or so, was the backbone of a system of factories, bureaucracies and armies that generated wealth, prestige and power. It is being adopted worldwide. For men, and increasingly for women too, paid work occupies the core of the day, the major portion of the week, and all but a few weeks of the year.

Challenging this dominance of work are new realities: the need for continuing adult education in a changing world; the need for leisure time to maintain family and social networks and the need for the increasing numbers of older persons to have opportunities for

119

work in order "to add life to the years added to life" (a time-work trade-off between adult years and late life).

Thus, the horizontal distribution of education, work and leisure in youth, adulthood and old age needs to give way to a vertical distribution of simultaneous life-long opportunities for education, work and leisure. According to Best (1995), the changing nature of work now allows for this flexibility. He notes that work is :

- Increasingly flexible, project-oriented and non-hierarchical;

- Progressively decentralized, and moving away from the need to group workers and equipment in fixed locations;

- More tailored to the individual consumer, moving from "mass production" of standardized goods and services;

- More based on what might be called "personal capitalization", in which the tools and information needed for economic activity are increasingly accessible to the average worker.

Another author notes, however, that:

"There is a tendency to view employment as an all-or-nothing proposition. While there are many part-time and seasonal jobs, full-time, full-year jobs typically dominate the employment market, especially in industrialized countries." (Schulz, 1991)

When work is organized as "all or nothing", those in the "all" category suffer time-poverty (with time being the most non-renewable resource of anyone's life) and those falling into the "nothing" side of the equation experience material poverty, with its attendant social exclusions and powerlessness.

For all of these reasons, it is urgent that adult years be restructured allowing men and women alike the opportunities to accumulate stores of economic capital through work, human capital through continuing education and social capital through cultivating family and social networks. A store of all three kinds of capital is made increasingly necessary by longevity, so as to help individuals to take (in a manner of speaking) the high road to the high age. A store of emotional, social and financial goods helps to counteract the losses that occur in old age, the loss of friends and relatives, the loss of earning power and the loss of physical strength.

Continuing education. Despite work's dominance of adult time, adult education has been expanding. Its global expansion was noted at the fifth International Conference on Adult Education (organized by UNESCO and the International Council for Adult Education in Hamburg, Germany, in 1997:

- In India, a vast adult literacy programme is reaching out to some 30 million people;

- In Canada, more than one adult in three is pursuing an educational programme, compared to one in fourteen in 1969;

- In Japan, over half the adult population is engaged in adult learning;

- In Ecuador, over 70 per cent of adults with incomplete education have participated in the literacy campaign.

In addition to general programmes of adult education, universities of the third age have been established throughout Europe, many in conjunction with formal universities and with support of local governments. In Italy, some of these institutions are being expanded into "universities of the three ages".

The European Year of Lifelong Learning in 1996, generated initiatives throughout the region, including a proposal within the then Parliament of Norway for a "sabbatical" for workers every tenth year, to enable them to hone their work skills, to be paid for by employers and the State (*The New York Times*, 13 December 1996). A decision on the proposal has been delayed owing to a change of Government.

Continuing education can improve work skills, a technical endeavour, as well as life skills, a more subtle task encompassing the ability to know oneself and relate to others in increasingly complex clusters of family, work and community. Improving work and living skills generates human capital, which, when a critical mass is achieved, creates the "learning society" (a core dynamic of social as well as economic capital).

Family leave. The all or nothing work structure was established at a time when men worked and women stayed at home. Today, women's participation in the paid workforce, according to the Human Development Report 1997, is nearly on a par with men's. In developing countries, women's share of earned income is currently approximately at 32 per cent and their share of professional and technical workers is 40 per cent. In industrial countries it is 38 per cent and 48 per cent respectively.

Women's entry into the formal workforce has improved their autonomy and status in innumerable ways while, simultaneously, enabling them to save and acquire pensions for their own old age. It has left them bereft of time, however, as they endeavour to juggle new work opportunities with traditional multiple roles, including household management, kin-keeping, child-bearing and -rearing and, in ageing populations, elder care.

Time-poverty afflicts many fully employed women and men with family responsibilities. Flexi-time and flexi-place work arrangements can enable adults to better balance the needs of work and home and may include such measures as:

"home-working or tele-working; career break schemes;... compassionate leave allowances; and job-sharing" (Pearson, 1996).

Family leave, for example, has been shown to benefit individuals and families, and also to improve work productivity (Goldsmith, 1993):

".... in a Johnson and Johnson study, it was found that absenteeism among employees who used flex-time and family leave was on average 50 per cent less than for the workforce as a whole, that 58 per cent of the employees surveyed said that such policies were 'very important' in their decision to stay with the company and the number of the employees using the benefits increased to 71 per cent."

Goldsmith goes on to ask why, since family leave is such an obvious societal good, policies for it are not more widespread and comes to the conclusion that national histories and prevailing expectations of the role of employer, family and government are the cause. In early industrial Europe, socialist parties and labour unions succeeded in having social welfare policies adopted, including maternity leave. The feminist movement in Europe focused on securing pregnancy and paternity leave and on national child-care policies. By contrast, in the United States, feminists might have feared that making an issue out of biological differences between men and women could lead to women being labeled as marginal or temporary workers, thus making it more difficult to achieve total equality in the work and political spheres.

Job redistribution

While many of the fully employed experience time-poverty, the unemployed suffer material poverty, affecting their present and future well being. One billion people or 30 per cent of the workforce is estimated to be under or unemployed, most of them living in developing economies (ILO, 1996).

A more equitable distribution of work could relieve unemployment, as pointed out by Bosch (1997): "persistent mass unemployment" was avoided during the past 120 years in industrialized countries by cutting work time almost in half. And as work time was being halved, incomes saw a "9 to 10 fold increase", stimulated in part by the impetus time-cuts gave to finding new, more intensive forms of work-organization and utilization of capital stock.

Further cuts in working time could be made today, Bosch claims, but need certain pre-conditions including: (a) flexible work scheduling, encompassing new forms of work organization better suited to shorter working times; (b) social security contributions made proportional to hours worked (so that two or three part-time workers would not cost an employer twice or three times the social security contributions of one full time worker on overtime); (c) a skilled population, without which work cannot be redistributed; and (d) some measure of trade-off between wages earned and hours worked (such as an increase in hourly pay but an initial reduction in overall take-home pay).

In short, cuts in working time and more flexibility in work-scheduling could lead to job sharing and this, in turn, could help reduce unemployment in a global market.

Gradual retirement. Early retirement has been used as a labour market tool in developed economies in recent decades, siphoning off older employees from the workplace when jobs are scarce in order to, in theory, allow younger workers access to jobs, usually at lower pay. The short-term macro-economic advantages create longer-term disadvantages, including an unsustainable expectation and sense of entitlement to early retirement, which is difficult to reverse when the worker-retiree ratio declines (though this decline can be offset through other measures: expanding employment of women or immigrants, for example, or by increasing worker productivity).

Some individuals want early retirement; others regard it as exclusion. Some need to continue working for psychological or financial reasons. Since individuals and their circumstances vary, choice is important. But insofar as a new model of retirement is needed, it could be based on the age-old custom of gradual retirement. This could be instituted by systematizing part-time work, not only for late life, but throughout the lifecourse for those who needed it (two working parents, for example; workers caring for frail elder parents; individuals returning to school part-time, etc.). One scholar stresses that:

"We must develop regular part-time work, not only as a transition from full employment to full retirement, but also as a means of redefining full employment.... National governments can make an enormous contribution by supporting employers willing to develop gradual retirement options" (Reday-Mulvey, 1996).

The expansion of part-time opportunities, however, "is widely condemned by many people as a threat to full-time jobs, as a precarious form of employment and as a source of unequal treatment of women workers" (Schulz, 1991).

An increase in "project-oriented, non-hierarchical and decentralized work", as pointed out by Best, as well as increasing opportunities for 'personal capitalization' and access to credit and training, are creating the foundations for all kinds of work in late life, relying more on individual skills and market demands than on a secure slot in a largescale enterprise.

The post-industrial future, therefore, may be leading us back to pre-industrial informalities and flexibilities of family and community enterprises for workers of all ages.

IV. YOUTH EXPANSION: CHILDHOOD IMPRINTS

A paradox confronting many young people was noted in the World Programme of Action for Youth to the Year 2000 and Beyond (UN, 1995), namely that youth must decide whether to seek integrating into an existing order or to serve as a force to transform that order.

While youth are seeking their way in a new world order, they are additionally being challenged to anticipate their own unknown extended future—being required to stretch their consciousness horizontally, taking in what is currently out there, while also stretching it vertically, anticipating the vicissitudes of their own high age.

To youth, the high age may seem to lie a long way off. As Schopenhauer (1966) remarked, "to youth, life is an infinitely long future" but from the point of view of old age, it is "a very short past". One must become old, that is, to have lived a long time, in order to recognize how short life is.

Though it may seem a long way off, youth soon come to occupy the cultural space defined as "old age", which some have likened to an "age-ghetto" characterized by "ageisms" in language, attitudes, behaviours, laws and exclusions. During the European Year of the Elderly and Intergenerational Solidarity, in 1993, Irish schools explored the many dimensions of ageism, assisted by interactive booklets for primary and secondary schools. Ageism may include, for example:

- Ageist language (labeling older persons as patients/ pensioners, burdens/victims, wrinklies/ wobblies, 'the old and the lonely');

- Ageist attitudes (assuming that elders are physically or intellectually deficient, and that only youth is beautiful);

- Ageist behaviour (dismissing/ridiculing old people; discounting their health and social needs);

- Ageist laws (compulsory early retirement);

- Ageist exclusions (customary absence of elders from public debates and images in advertising, films, theatre).

Ageism, first coined to fit prejudices against elders, could also apply to youth or other age groups customarily dismissed by the dominant culture. The age-fragmentation of modern societies may be fostering ageism by clustering peer groups into separate institutions such as kindergartens, schools, workplaces and retirement settlements, trends discernible in developing countries, even as they are abhorred.

Improved channels of communications between these age-fragmented institutions and the creation of more age-integrated institutions and communities would bring the age groups into daily contact in varied settings, which would help younger generations to "preview" and older generations to "review" their lives. The experience would impart a sense of the essential unity of the lifecourse, and an awareness that "the end is in the beginning, and the beginning in the end". For example, smoking is estimated to have caused 30 million premature deaths in the 1990s, more than half while in middle age, notably among the 800 million (and rising) smokers in developing countries.

Diet too is taking its toll. The diet which fuelled human evolution, fruits, vegetables, legumes and low saturated fat, is being replaced, particularly among the urban poor, by a so-called affluent diet of processed and junk foods that slowly fuels chronic diseases. More easily prevented than cured, chronic diseases tend to have a slow gradual onset leading to a slow debilitating decline in later years by contrast with infectious diseases where onset and demise both tend to be sudden. Chronic diseases kill about 24 million people a year and are on the rise in developing countries as these continue to battle infectious diseases (which kill about 17 million a year out of a total 52 million deaths yearly) (World Health Organization, 1997).

With information and empowerment, youth can better steer a way through complex choices knowing which will strengthen or poison the body, expand or close the mind, enrich or constrict the emotions.

A Swaziland AIDS programme (Friedman, 1996) provides an example of a good habit with potential life-long empowering effects. It aims to put youth in the driving seat of their own lives, alerting them to the fact that everything you do after waking up in the morning is a decision and involves a choice. Youth are facilitated in developing life, communication and leadership skills and in building self-esteem. They form clubs, write their own constitutions, elect officers and determine their own activities. In sex education classes, they get information about choices and their consequences and they learn about parenting.

As with any phase of life, the boundaries are fluid but, for statistical purposes, various institutions define life stages by years. For the United Nations youth programme, youth extends from age 15 through 24. For UNICEF, childhood stretches from infancy to age 18.

Childhood, the cradle of longevity. The material needs of children worldwide have occupied the world community for decades, to ensure that childhood is not a cradle of death but a cradle of life and of longevity. The World Summit for Children set concrete objectives for 2000 including (among others) the eradication or reduction among children of polio, neonatal tetanus, guinea worm disease, measles, diarrhea and respiratory infections.

Creating a benign physical environment is important for ensuring physical life, and a benign emotional environment is needed for emotional life. Recent research points to four psychosocial stages through which individuals develop living skills: namely, dependency, counter-dependency, independence and interdependence (Weinhold, 1993).

The experience of dependency, rooted in infancy, is thought to shape an individual's lifelong capacity for trust. Trust will be needed throughout life at all times but especially during times of illness, unemployment or other experiences of powerlessness.

Counter-dependency occurs at about age two when the child separates from the mother or carer, recognizing him or her as a somewhat separate entity. If supported during this phase, an individual develops a sense of autonomy, which can guide subsequent life transitions in youth, midlife and so on, and may help in steering a steady course through our world of perpetual change.

Independence is thought to be the third major developmental step, occurring roughly between age three and six. If initiatives are discouraged or punished, independence can be undermined with clear lifelong disadvantages for living in an age of rapid transformation and enterprise. The resourcefulness with which individuals "manage meaning" and live with their "inner ageless self" while external powers decline in later years may originate in these early years.

Next, between the ages of six to 18, interdependence is the developmental challenge. It is acquired as an individual finds his or her place in family, school and neighbourhood. The essential tools of interdependence, cooperation and negotiation are best acquired when an individual has already developed, from the earlier years, a sense of trust, autonomy and independence.

Cultures foster different capabilities. The closeness of mother and child in Kenya and Uganda have been observed to cultivate trust and confidence in young children who:

"...were born at home and were never separated from the mother, who carried them unsaddled in a sling next to her breasts. Mothers massaged, caressed, sung to and fondled their children continually. They slept with the child and allowed it to breast-feed on demand. The mother knew instinctively when the child had to urinate and defecate and would take the child to the bushes when necessary" (ibid).

Researchers found that the Kenyan and Ugandan children, compared with European or American children, "were months ahead on all scales of development. These gains held steady as the children crawled, walked, talked and advanced continuously far beyond Western children until the age of four" (ibid).

By contrast, many of the developed countries are less child centered, and attempt to move the child out of the bonding stage as quickly as possible, often before the child is ready. According to experts this causes the child to act separate or independent before the child is ready:

"This attempt to end the bonding stage prematurely can give rise to forms of addictive behaviour in adults as they seek substitutes to fill the psychological hole left by incomplete bonding. Addictions to substances such as food, alcohol or drugs are seen in this context as adaptive attempts to meet bonding deficits" (ibid.).

The emotional landscape of early life can leave long-lasting imprints that pre-condition, to varying degrees, capacities for trusting, negotiating change, taking initiative and collaborating with others. These fundamental life skills are components of "emotional intelligence".

V. SUMMING UP: TOWARDS FLOURISHING LIVES

To draw a sensible map, we must begin with our destination. Most world citizens can now hope to reach age 60, or 80 or even 100. Older persons of the future will be living in radically altered cultural, social and economic environments. Today's elders can attest to the rapidity of change. To live latelife meaningfully, its many potentials need to be continually explored or invented within the new contexts, and then examined critically and debated widely. Some latelife potentials have been examined here in terms of doing, becoming and being.

Lives won't suddenly flourish upon reaching age 60. They will manifest the kinds of investments made earlier. Mid-life investments are critical, for individuals to have a second chance, correcting earlier mistakes or develop neglected talents. Mid-life, in turn, depends on the vitality of adult years—the extent to which adults have had time enough for cultivating work, social, family and personal life (permitting the accumulation of economic, social, and personal capital as insurance for the later years).

Youth like to explore and experiment. Just as they are enthusiastic about investigating life's current possibilities, they may be eager to envision its future potentialities, and their own place in that future. Their effectiveness in forging a personal path and shaping the collective one will be conditioned in no small way by earlier childhood experiences. Many of the emotional imprints of childhood last a lifetime. Psychology validates the wisdom of the Sufi dictum that "the end is in the beginning, and the beginning in the end."

REFERENCES

Albert, Steven M., Cattell, Maria G. , *Old Age in a Global Perspective*, G.K.Hall and Co, New York, 1994.

Alma Ata 1978, *Primary Health Care*, report of the International Conference on Primary Health Care, 6-12 September 1978, jointly sponsored by the World Health Organization and the United Nations Children's Fund.

Beattie, R.A. and Warren McGillivray, "A risky strategy: reflections on the World Bank report 'Averting the Old Age Crisis'", in the International Social Security Review, Vol 48, 1995.

Best, Fred J., "Does Flexible Life Scheduling Have a Future?", *in Rethinking Worklife Options for Older Persons*, edited by Jack Habib and Charlotte Nusberg, Brookdale Institute of Gerontology and Adult Human Development in Israel and the International Federation on Ageing, 1990.

Best, Fred J., *Conditions of work in the future* (for *Encyclopedia of the Future*), MacMillan Publishing Co., New York, 1995.

Binstock, R. , "The aged as scapegoat", The Gerontologist, Vol. 23, 1983.

Bosch, Gerhard, "The reduction of working time, pay and employment", World Conference on Working Time, Tokyo, 1997.

Brim, Gilbert, "Research Network on Successful Midlife Development", the MacArthur Foundation (as quoted by Beth Azar in the *American Psychological Association's Monitor*, November 1996. (see http://midmac.med.harvard.edu)

Butler, Robert N., "The life review: an interpretation of reminiscence in the aged". *Psychiatry* Vol. 26 (February 1963).

Cassel C. and B.L. Neugarten, "The goals of medicine in an ageing society", in R. Binstock and S. Post (editors), *Too old for health care*? Baltimore, Johns Hopkins University, Press, 1991.

Chaney, Elisa M., as quoted in "Empowerment of older women: evidence from historical contemporary sources", in *Empowering Older Women: Cross-Cultural Views*, American Association of Retired Persons and International Federation on Ageing, Washington D.C., 1990.

Chawla, Sandeep, "The Participation of the Elderly in Development", unpublished background paper for the International Seminar on the Participation of the Elderly in Development at Valetta, Malta, United Nations, 1988.

Cole, Thomas R. and Mary G. Winkler (editors), *Oxford Book of Aging*, Oxford University Press, New York, 1994.

Cole, Thomas R., "What have we "made" of Ageing?", *Journal of Gerontology: Social Sciences.*, Vol.50B, No.6. 1995.

Dychtwald, Ken, "AgeWave Speaks", newsletter of Agewave Communications Corporation, California, 1994.

Erikson, Erik, *Identity: Youth and Crisis,* W.W. Norton, New York, 1968.

Friedman, Sara Ann, "Tackling tradition and change in Swaziland", in *First call for children*, a UNICEF quarterly, December 1996, No. 4.

Gilligan, Carol, *In a different voice,* Harvard University Press, 1982.

Goldsmith, Beard Elizabeth, "Family Leave: Changing Needs of the World's Workers", Occasional Papers Series, No. 7, 1993.

Greenberg, Filker Estelle, "Ripeness is all", *Gerontology and Geriatrics Education,* Vol.11, 1/2., Haworth Press, 1990.

Grieco, Margaret and Apt, Araba Nana, *Bulletin on Ageing,* United Nations, No.2/3, 1996.

Grof, Stanislav, *Books of the Dead*: *manuals for living and dying,* Thames and Hudson, New York, 1994.

Hagestad, Gunhild O., "Cultural and Personal Constructions of Healthy Ageing in a Changing Societal Context", in *Culture and Health*, report from international UNESCO conference, Oslo, 1996.

Herodotus, The Histories, translated by Aubrey de Selincourt, Harmondsworth, 1954.

James, William, *The Varieties of Religious Experience*, Colier, New York, 1961.

Kinsella, Kevin and Tauber, Cynthia, *An Aging World II,* Bureau of the Census, Economics and Statistics Administration, United States Department of Commerce, 1995.

Kinsella, Kevin and Gist, Yvonne J., *Older Workers, Retirement, and Pensions: A comparative international chartbook*, Bureau of the Census, Economics and Statistics Administration, United States Department of Commerce, 1995.

Kotre, J. , *Outliving the self,* Baltimore, Johns Hopkins University Press, 1984.

Manheimer, Ronald J., "The narrative quest in qualitative gerontology", *Journal of Ageing Studies,*. Vol. 3 (3), 1989.

Manheimer, Ronald J., Snodgrass, Denis D. and Moskow-McKenzie, Kiana, *Older Adult Education*, Greenwood Press and University of North Carolina, 1995.

Maslow, A., *Motivation and Personality,* Harper and Row, New York, 1970.

McAdams, D. and de St. Aubin, E., "A theory of generativity and its assessment through self-report, behavioural acts, and narrative themes in autobiography", *Journal of Personality and Social Psychology,* 62, 1992.

Minos, Georges, *History of old age,* translated by Sarah Hanbury Tenison, University of Chicago press, 1989.

Mukerji, Runi, "A South Asian Perspective: Depression and the mature woman", Global Alliance for Women's Health, 1997 annual spring forum, edited by Elaine M. Wolfson.

National Council for the Elderly, Ireland, *In Due Season* (publication no. 31), published with the assistance of the Commission of the European Communities and the Irish Coordinating Committee of the European Year of Older People and Solidarity between Generations, 1993.

Neugarten, B.L., R.J. Havighurst and S.S. Tobin, "The measurement of life satisfactions", *Journal of Gerontology*, Vol. 16, 1961.

Neugarten, B.L., R.J. Havighurst and S.S. Tobin, "Personality and pattern of ageing" in B.L. Neugarten (ed) *Middle Age and Ageing*, Chicago University Press, 1968.

Neugarten, Bernice, in "A study of auxiliary personnel in education", conducted by Bank Street College of Education, New York, for the Office of Economic Opportunity, Washington D.C., 1968.

Neugarten, Bernice, essay entitled "The Young-old and the age-irrelevant", 1979.

O'Leary, Eleanor, *Counselling Older Adults*, Chapman and Hall, 1996.

O'Sullivan, Anne, Aging and meaning: a literature review (unpublished), 1998.

Pearson, Maggie, *Experience, Skill and Competitiveness: Implications of an Ageing Population for the Workplace*, European Foundation for the Improvement of Living and Working Conditions, European Communities, Luxembourg, 1996.

Pelaez, Martha, "Grandparents by choice (Uruguay)", *Bulletin on Ageing, No. 2-3*, 1997.

Perls, Thomas T., "The Oldest Old", *Scientific American,* January 1995.

Post, R.M. and F.K. Goodwin, "Simulated behaviour states", British Journal of Psychiatry, vol. 7, 1973.

Reday-Mulvey, Genevieve, "Part-time work - an important step to full retirement", *Global Ageing Report,* Vol. 1, No.3, American Association of Retired Persons, Washington, D.C., 1996.

Rentsch, Thomas, "Ageing as becoming oneself: a philosophical ethics of late life", University of Florida, *Journal of Aging Studies*, Vol. 11, No. 4, 1997.

Rooke, C. , "Old age in contemporary fiction: a new paradigm of hope" *Handbook of the Humanities and Ageing,* T.R. Cole and D.D.van Tassel and R. Kastenbaum eds., Springer, New York, 1992.

Ruth, Jan-Erik, "Coping and Management of the Self in Later Life: some future perspectives", from Human Ageing: Adding Life to Years, UNESCO sponsored international conference, Paris, 17-20 June 1996.

Schopenhauer, A., *The world as will and representation*, Dover, New York, 1966.

Schulz, James H. and John Myles, "Old age Pensions: A Comparative Perspective" in *Handbook of Aging and the Social Sciences*, Academic Press, Inc., 1990.

Schulz, James H., *The World Ageing Situation 1991*, United Nations publication, V. 91. 31447.

Sheehy, Gail, 1995, *New Passages: Mapping Your Life Across Time*, Random House, 1991.

Smith, Jeanne E., "The Impact of Longevity on the American Higher Education System" unpublished manuscript, 1998.

Swane, Christine E., "Cultural construction—attitudes and images of ageing" (abstract), from Human Ageing: Adding Life to Years, UNESCO sponsored international conference, Paris, 17-20 June 1996.

Tilak, Shrinivas, *Religion and ageing in the Indian tradition,* State University of New York Press, Albany, New York, 1989.

Tout, Ken, "Ageing in the twenty-first century", paper presented at the Intergovernmental Conference on Ageing Populations in the Mediterranean Region, International Institute on Ageing, Malta, 4-6 December 1997.

United Nations, *International Plan of Action on Ageing, Report of the World Assembly on Ageing, Vienna, 26 July-6 August 1982* United Nations publication, Sales No. E.82. I. 16), chap.VI.

United Nations Development Programme, *Human Development Report 1990*, Oxford University Press, 1990.

United Nations, *Proclamation on Ageing*, General Assembly resolution 47/5, annex.

United Nations Development Programme, *Human Development Report 1993,* Oxford University Press, 1993.

United Nations, "Older Persons in the Family: Facets of Empowerment", Occasional Paper No. 4,. International Year of the Family, 1993.

United Nations, *Copenhagen Declaration and the Programme of Action* of the World Summit for Social Development, *Report of the World Summit for Social Development, Copenhagen, 6-12 March 1995* (United Nations publication, Sales No.E.96.IV.8), Chap. I, resolution 1, annexes I and II.

United Nations, *Conceptual framework of a programme for the promotion and observance of the International Year of Older Persons in 1999*, (General Assembly document A/50/114).

United Nations, World Programme of Action for Youth to the Year 2000 and Beyond, General Assembly resolution 50/81, annex.

United Nations, Beijing Declaration and the Platform for Action of the Fourth World Conference on Women, *Report of the Fourth World Conference on Women, Beijing, 4-15 September 1995* (United Nations publication, Sales No. E.96. IV.13), Chap. I, resolution 1, annexes I and II..

United Nations, Habitat Agenda and Istanbul Declaration, *Report of the United Nations Conference on Human Settlements, (Habitat II)*, Istanbul, 3-14 June 1996 (United Nations publications, Sales No. E.97.IV.6), Chap. I, resolution1, annexes I and II.

United Nations Economic and Social Commission for Asia and the Pacific, *Lifelong preparation for old age in Asia and the Pacific, 1996.*

United Nations, Message of the Secretary-General for the International Day of Older Persons, 1 October 1997, Press Release SG/SM/6339.

United Nations Development Programme, *Human Development Report 1997,* Oxford University Press.

UNESCO , *Culture Plus,* No.12-13, 1994, an information bulletin on the World Decade for Cultural Development (1988-1997).

UNESCO, *Medium-term strategy for 1996-2001*, 1996.

UNESCO, *Learning: the treasure within*, report of an international commission, 1996.

United States Administration on Ageing, "Ageing America: Priority Initiatives of the Administration on Ageing" fact sheet. Department of Health and Human Services, 1994.

Weinhold, Janae B. and Barry K. Weinhold, *Partnership families*, United Nations, Vienna, 1998.

Whitmont, Edward C., *The Symbolic Quest: Basic concepts of analytic psychology*, Princeton University Press, Princeton, 1969 and 1991.

Woodman, Marion and Elinor Dickson, *Dancing in the Flames*, Shambhala, Boston and London, 1996.

World Bank, *Averting the Old Age Crisis: Policies to protect the old and promote growth*, a World Bank policy research report (prepared by a team led by Estelle James), Oxford University Press, 1994.

Litho in United Nations, New York
27777—February 2001—4,630
ISBN 92-1-130205-6

United Nations publication
Sales No. E.00.IV.4
ST/ESA/271